See page 20

"Here are deep matters, not easily to be dismissed by crying blasphemy."

the Magic Island

William Seabrook

Illustrations by Alexander King

Foreword by Joe Ollmann

Introduction by George A. Romero

Afterword by Wade Davis

DOVER PUBLICATIONS, INC.
MINEOLA, NEW YORK

Bibliographical Note

This Dover edition, first published in 2016, is an unabridged republication of the work originally published by Harcourt, Brace and Company, Inc., New York, in 1929. The present edition adds a new Foreword by Joe Ollmann, a new Introduction by George A. Romero, and a new Afterword by Wade Davis.

Library of Congress Cataloging-in-Publication Data

Names: Seabrook, William, 1884–1945, author.
Title: The magic island / William Seabrook ; illustrations by Alexander King; foreword by Joe Ollmann ; introduction by George A. Romero.
Description: Mineola, New York : Dover Publications, [2016] | "Originally published: New York : Harcourt, Brace and Company, Inc., 1929."
Identifiers: LCCN 2015039447| ISBN 9780486799629 | ISBN 048679962X
Subjects: LCSH: Haiti—Social life and customs—20th century. | Vodou—Haiti. | Witchcraft—Haiti. | Blacks—Haiti.
Classification: LCC F1926 .S43 2016 | DDC 972.94/06—dc23
LC record available at http://lccn.loc.gov/2015039447

Manufactured in the United States by RR Donnelley
79962X01 2016
www.doverpublications.com

To

MAMAN CÉLIE

for reasons which

appear hereafter

Contents

Foreword by Joe Ollmann xi

Introduction by George A. Romero xv

Foreword to the 1929 Edition 3

Part One
The Voodoo Rites

I. Secret Fires 7

II. The Way Is Opened and Closed 16

III. The Petro Sacrifice 28

IV. The "Ouanga" Charm 45

V. Goat-Cry Girl-Cry 54

VI. The God Incarnate 70

Part Two
Black Sorcery

I. The Altar of Skulls 81

II. ". . . Dead Men Working in the Cane Fields" 92

III. Toussel's Pale Bride 104

IV. Célestine with a Silver Dish 115

Part Three
The Tragic Comedy

I. A Blind Man Walking on Eggs 127

II. A Nymph in Bronze 134

III. "The Truth Is a Beautiful Thing" 142

IV. "Ladies and Gentlemen, the President!" 150
V. But the Truth Becomes Somewhat Tangled 162

Part Four
Trails Winding

I. The White King of La Gonave 171
II. The Black Queen's Court 185
III. A Torn Scrap of Paper 194
IV. Portrait of a "Gros Nègre" 203
V. "Polynice and His White" 207
VI. The "Danse Congo" 219
VII. "No White Man Could Be As Dumb As That" 227
VIII. Portrait of a Scientist 239
IX. Morne la Selle Adventure 247
X. The Soul of Haiti 270

From the Author's Notebook 283

Afterword by Wade Davis 337

List of Drawings by Alexander King

Here are deep matters, not easily to be dismissed by crying blasphemy *Frontispiece*

Louis' face glowed with a light that was not always heavenly 8

Dort Dessiles, who was a *papaloi* 20

Maman Célie, high priestess of the mysteries 26

The *mamaloi* in a scarlet robe 34

Blood-maddened, sex-maddened, god-maddened . . . danced their dark saturnalia 42

But marked for death by the Voodoo curse, they died 50

At the left of the altar were the *Rada* drums 58

And as she sang, she was a daughter doomed to die 67

They were staring fixedly as entranced mediums stare into crystal globes 74

Croyance, leading the nine dead men and women 82

Strange tales are told of Voodoo in the boudoir and salon 92

No one dared to stop them, for they were corpses walking in the sunlight 98

Antoine Simone, president of the republic, was active in black sorcery 112

Face mat gold like a Byzantine polychrome 154

He had to whip her once or twice a year 190

Polynice was smarter than anybody 206

When the combat begins, the two owners remain in the ring 214

She began a dance in rhythm with his 246

Dark mother of mysteries 276

The photographs are inserted at page 310.

FOREWORD BY JOE OLLMANN

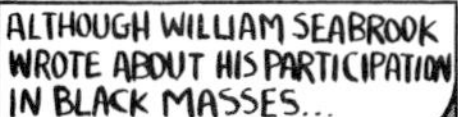

PROBABLY MORE IMPORTANT THAN HIS "INTRODUCTION" OF THE ZOMBIE WAS HIS THEORY THAT THE ZOMBIE WAS MORE A PHARMACOLOGICAL PHENOMENON THAN A SUPERNATURAL ONE.
DATURA
+ PUFFER FISH
+ SEA SNAKE
=

DECADES BEFORE HARVARD ETHNO-BOTANIST WADE DAVIS POSITED THE SAME CONJECTURE.
W.D.
the Serpent and the Rainbow
WADE DAVIS

THE WIDELY-ANTHOLOGIZED CHAPTER FROM THIS BOOK, DEAD MEN WORKING IN THE CANE FIELDS, IS OFTEN PEOPLE'S GATEWAY DRUG TO THE WORK OF WILLIAM SEABROOK.

THE MAGIC ISLAND COULD BE SAID TO HAVE STARTED THE ZOMBIE PHENOMENON, WHICH HAS FOR DECADES BEEN SOLIDLY RESPONSIBLE FOR A LARGE PORTION OF THE G.N.P. OF THE ENTIRE ENTERTAINMENT INDUSTRY.
UUUUH...
1950 1990 2000 2015
ZOMBIE PROFITS

THIS BOOK IS THE SOURCE OF THE 1932 BELA LUGOSI FILM, WHITE ZOMBIE. THOUGH SEABROOK'S NAME DOESN'T APPEAR IN THE CREDITS.
WHITE ZOMBIE

I SUSPECT THE 1943 JACQUES TOURNEUR FILM, I WALKED WITH A ZOMBIE ALSO OWES A DEBT TO THE MAGIC ISLAND. (IT'S ALSO A FAR BETTER FILM.)
I WALKED WITH A ZOMBIE

SEABROOK'S EDITOR WARNED HIM:
"NO WHITE MAN CAN WRITE A BOOK THAT'S ANY GOOD ABOUT VOODOO."

IMPLYING THAT THE HAITIANS, STILL UNDER THE OCCUPYING FOOT OF THE U.S. MILITARY...

...WOULDN'T LIKELY BE OPEN TO SHARING THE SECRETS OF THEIR VOODOO FAITH WITH SOME WHITE WRITER.

IT'S A TRAVELOGUE, A CULTURAL AND POLITICAL HISTORY OF THE ISLAND, IT DOCUMENTS A MOUNTAIN CLIMBING EXPEDITION...

AND, IN *THE MAGIC ISLAND*, HE DOES TEND TO ACCENTUATE THE:

"blood-maddened, sex-maddened...saturnalia..."

...ASPECTS OF VOODOO.

ALEXANDER KING'S CONTROVERSIAL ILLUSTRATIONS, INCLUDED IN THIS EDITION, WERE PART OF THE SENSATION AND CONTENTION SURROUNDING *THE MAGIC ISLAND*.

KING'S ILLUSTRATIONS HAVE BEEN MUCH-DEBATED. DISMISSED OUT OF CONTEXT AS RACIST CARICATURES OR POSITIVELY COMPARED TO THE WORK OF HARLEM RENAISSANCE PAINTER AARON DOUGLAS.

SEABROOK HIMSELF IS LARGELY RESPECTFUL OF THE CULTURE AND TAKES A - FOR THE TIME - NON-ANTHROPOLOGICAL, FULL-IMMERSION APPROACH TO HIS STUDY OF VOODOO.

HE WAS SERIOUS ENOUGH ABOUT A TRUE, RESPECTFUL PRESENTATION OF VOODOO THAT HE TURNED DOWN A $15,000 ($200,000 IN TODAY'S CURRENCY!) MAGAZINE SERIALIZATION OFFER...

...WHEN THEY REQUESTED CHANGES WHERE, "EVERYTHING BETWEEN THE LINES CHANGED COLOR OR EVAPORATED."

SEABROOK REPRODUCED THE PRAYER HE SPOKE DURING HIS INITIATION IN THE OUANGA CHARM CEREMONY:

"PROTECT ME FROM MISREPRESENTING THESE PEOPLE, AND GIVE ME THE POWER TO WRITE HONESTLY OF THEIR MYSTERIOUS RELIGION, FOR ALL LIVING FAITHS ARE SACRED."

IT MAY HAVE BEEN THIS PROMISE THAT KEPT SEABROOK HONEST AND RESPECTFUL IN HIS ACCOUNT OF HAITI AND ITS PEOPLE AND THEIR FAITH.

INTRODUCTION

I've been asked to write an introduction for this newly reprinted edition of a travelogue, originally published by Harcourt, Brace and Company in 1929, called *The Magic Island.* Written by W.B. Seabrook, with illustrations by Alexander King and photographs by the author, the book claims to be a journalistic study of the island nation of Haiti. Seabrook's "journalism" has come into question over the years, and indeed in this book he seems drawn to sensationalism and to subjects which satisfy his own personal interest in the occult.

In the book, originally published at 336 pages, Seabrook devotes 224 of those pages to physical descriptions of the island and its people seasoned with abundant accounts of Voodoo rites, practices, and superstitions, remarking on how parallels might be drawn "not only with those of negroes in Georgia and the Carolinas, but with the mediaeval folk lore of white Europe." Ghosts, vampires, werewolves, and sorcerers freely inhabit this book and while Seabrook professes a certain distance he is obviously intrigued more by the *"Magic"* than by the *"Island"* of the title.

In only twelve pages, a single chapter titled "...Dead Men Working in the Cane Fields," does the author speak about a creature which he considers to be "...exclusively local—the 'zombie.'" The word had appeared in print earlier, but Seabrook's book is credited as being the first important reference to the creature, which he describes as "...a soulless human corpse, still dead, but taken from the grave and endowed by sorcery with a mechanical semblance of life—it is a dead body which is made to walk and act and move as if it were alive." He uses the word exactly thirty-two times in that single twelve-page chapter, but that was enough to elevate the "zombie" into the ranks of pop-culture stardom. Three years later, a Broadway play called *Zombie* appeared, followed in the same year by the film *White Zombie.* Ever since, the "zombie" has appeared in print and on-screen, joining such venerable monsters as Frankenstein, Dracula, and the Wolfman. Today, "zombies" are running...or should I say shambling...way ahead of their partners in mayhem. Brad Pitt's filmed version of Max Brooks's brilliant novel *World War Z* and hit television shows like *The Walking Dead* are breaking viewership and box office records.

But today's "zombies" are not brought to life by sorcery. They are variously spawned by a virus run amok, a bio-weapon spill, or a returning space probe. The curse afflicts not just those targeted by a *bocor* (a Voodoo witch doctor), but entire populations, even threatening mankind's very existence. Everyone in the world is a potential victim. Today's "zombies" are...the neighbors.

I have been credited by some as being the one who brought these "modern zombies" into being. It's appropriate, I think, to offer some back-story here. In 1967 my friend John Russo and I wrote the screenplay for a horror film which we called *Night of the Flesheaters.* We were young and foolish enough to believe we could actually produce the film. With a few other friends, most important among them being Russ Streiner, a partner in the company that we owned called The Latent Image, we set about the task of trying to raise money to finance production.

We weren't completely mad. The Latent Image was a film services company surviving on the production of television commercials, industrial shorts, and political campaign films. We had our own equipment, cameras, grip and gaffing gear, and lights, while two of our frequent associates, Marilyn Eastman and Karl Hardman, who were in the business of producing radio commercials, had microphones and recorders. We persuaded five other close friends who had also been bitten by the movie bug to come in with us and we each kicked in $600, ending with a total of $6,000.

The story was set almost entirely in and around an old farmhouse in Western Pennsylvania, near Pittsburgh, where we all lived at the time. We found a perfect location, an abandoned house isolated in the middle of an enormous field, with nothing visible around it. The owner was planning on tearing the place down so we were able to rent it very inexpensively. We filled it with borrowed and contributed furniture, and boldly began to shoot our script.

We were shooting on film. Back in '67, there was no such thing as videotape, at least not available to the public. Cities the size of Pittsburgh all had film labs that processed and printed 8mm, 16mm, and 35mm. Even news reports were on film back then. Journeymen editors, like crusty old-fashioned newspaper hacks, were on-call twenty-four-seven to glue together celluloid stories about local fires, bank robberies, and social or political events. There were three such labs in Pittsburgh at the time. We all learned our craft from those journeymen.

Robert Rodriguez famously produced *El Mariachi* for a total of $8,000. He was shooting Hi-8 video. We were shooting on 35mm film. It cost big bucks, even way back then, to process and print a 400-foot roll of 35, which, at a speed of 90 feet per minute, represents just over four minutes of running time. And, of course, you don't use every foot that you shoot. We wound up using one foot out of every six that ran through the camera. Clearly we were going to need more than the $6,000 we had in hand...much more. Russ set about the task of raising money from outside investors. We were receiving a lot of unpaid-for publicity from a local radio and television personality named Bill Cardille, who hosted a Saturday night fright-fest called Chiller Theater. Enamored of the idea that some crazy guys were actually trying to shoot a feature film in Pittsburgh, he talked about us every Saturday and had us on his show several times. He even agreed to come out and do a cameo in our movie, playing a news reporter who interviews a local sheriff. Word got around pretty quickly that *Night of the Flesheaters* was a "happening thing."

Miraculously, Russ was able to raise $60,000. We still had to defer payment to labs and other suppliers who provided services. Once the film was in the can and edited, we needed to mix the soundtrack. Russ actually played a game of chess with Jack Napor, whose WRS Film Laboratories had audio facilities...and Russ won our mix. This was really guerrilla filmmaking. The production ended up costing $114,000, all in, leaving us owing $44,000 in deferments. But we had, against all odds, actually finished a real, honest-to-God MOVIE!

Russ and I drove the first answer print to New York to show it to distributors. The Walter Reade Company eventually picked it up, but they found that there was already a film in distribution called *The Flesheaters,* so Reade came up with a new title...*Night of the Living Dead*...and put it into release. Our little film from Pittsburgh has since gone on to become somewhat of a cult classic. It was invited into the permanent collection at MOMA and on most lists it's among the top ten horror films ever made, with some lists placing it first. The film was born out of our love for the medium and out of the tireless dedication of all who worked on it. But I believe its success was, in at least two particular ways, accidental.

First, a copyright dispute which remains ongoing allowed theaters to play the film, and later for fly-by-night video labels to reproduce it without paying royalties. As a result, millions of people saw it on their home screens or at special midnight showings at venues like the Waverly Theater in New York, where it rivaled *The Rocky Horror Picture Show* in popularity and played for over a year. Second, and most important, I think, is the fact that our leading actor, Duane Jones, who plays Ben, is an African American. In our screenplay, Ben is described only as "large and crude, in coveralls and tattered work shirt." The character is called simply "Truckdriver" until page 66, when other characters appear and we learn that truckdriver's name is Ben. When we were writing the screenplay, both John and I thought of Ben as a white man. When Duane agreed to play the role, he didn't want to be "crude," so we corrected the grammar in some of his speeches. He wanted to look "respectable" so we 86'd the "coveralls" and gave him an Arrow shirt, khaki-green slacks, and a cardigan sweater. Otherwise we made no script changes and were quite pleased with ourselves, reasoning...hoping...that Duane would be accepted, without prejudice, as any other actor might be. It was enough, we thought, that we were expressing our own predilections by casting a black man in a role that would probably, in most cases, have been played by a white, in a film where race was in no way a central theme.

Our story was about people in a crisis situation who find it impossible to communicate, much less cooperate with one another. They board themselves up inside a farmhouse and while the whole world outside is being turned upside down, they are arguing among themselves about their petty differences. They argue until it results, tragically, in their own downfall. There's never a mention of any racial issue, even when Harry Cooper, the principal antagonist who is white (played by the aforementioned Karl Hardman) and Ben come to blows.

The night when Russ and I were driving that first answer print to New York, somewhere along the Pennsylvania Turnpike, we heard on the car radio that Martin Luther King, Jr. had been assassinated. From that moment on, it became impossible to view *Night of the Living Dead* as anything but a racial "statement." When observers began to write about the film, calling it "important," it was almost uniformly regarded as such because a black man gets gunned down in the end by a posse of white, redneck, good-ole-boys. It would have been just as ironic an ending if, as John and I had originally envisioned, Ben, the stalwart hero, was white, and after fighting his way through a night of terror, was gunned down by the people he hoped might save him. But when Ben is a black man, even I am forced to see the racial overtones. Unfortunately, the world hasn't changed much. Back then there was rioting in Watts; today there's rioting in St. Louis.

I should note here that we never used the word "zombie" in our screenplay. We called the creatures that were outside banging on the boards "ghouls." Something...we didn't really care what, God or the Devil...had changed the rules and the dead were coming back to life. The *recently* dead, that is. They weren't coming up out of their graves. They wouldn't have had the strength to dig themselves out. They were coming out of hospitals and morgues, or off the street where people were being attacked by those recently dead and brutally murdered. And to make matters worse, the ghouls were eating the flesh of their victims. That's what was turning the outside world upside down while our protagonists were arguing over matters important only to them.

We never thought of the creatures in our film as "zombies" because, like everyone else at the time, we believed "zombies" to be those bug-eyed, soulless beings that wandered the fields in Haiti. Our monsters were flesh-eating corpses acting on their own, not commanded by a sorcerer, and they were ordinary people, the butcher, the baker, the candlestick maker. In that sense, I guess we *did* create the modern "zombie." But we never used the word. In my second film, *Dawn of the Dead,* after much had been written about *Night,* I did use the word, eagerly and gratefully. And I gave a little nod to the Voodoo side of things by having the main character, Peter (played by Ken Foree, also an African American), quote an old island proverb which says, "When there's no more room in hell, the dead will walk the Earth."

So I believe the success of *Night of the Living Dead* came, at least in part, by accident. In a curiously similar way, *The Magic Island* became a success by accident, or at least Seabrook's "zombies," to whom he only devoted twelve pages, became more popular in the eyes of the public than any other subject in his book. Though he tells amazing stories of...

> "...fire-hags who left their skins at home and set the cane fields blazing; of the vampire, a woman sometimes living, sometimes dead, who sucked the blood of children and could be distinguished because her hair always turned an ugly red; of the werewolf—*chauche*—a man or woman who took the form of some animal, usually a dog, and went killing lambs, young goats, sometimes babies."

...though he even goes so far as to provide Voodoo remedies...

> "For toothache. Get hold of a new nail and threaten the tooth three times with a stone, saying, 'Abracadabra' three times. Go to a mango tree and make a cross on it, saying, 'Abracadabra' twice. Cut off the cross and boil the bark and wet the sick tooth. The ache will certainly be relieved."

...though he outlines instructions...

> "To call up spirits."
> "To call up the dead."
> "To put a woman to sleep that you may know her guiles."

There's a "Prayer against bullets." There's a way to "Avoid persecution," to "...be released from prison," even "To insure the success of a new undertaking."

Seabrook even provides processional chants, both lyrics and actual music charts:

> *"Dam-ba-la Oue-do He! Ke-le-man-yan*
> *Oh! Da-me-ci Oue-do oh! Ke-le-man-yan*
> *Oh! nan point jou ma son-ge loi moin Ay-bo-bo!"*

Yet despite all this, the "zombie" came out the winner. The walking dead man captured the public's imagination and is still creating nightmares today.

In 1985 Wade Davis published a book called *The Serpent and the Rainbow*. It, too, claimed to be a nonfictional account of the author's visit to Haiti. He purports to have discovered how the so-called sorcerers are able to bring the dead back to life. The secret is...they're not dead at all. Davis reports that a secret potion is mixed containing a nearly deadly substance derived from a certain blowfish. The cocktail, when served to a human victim, puts him or her into a state of suspended animation so deep that even a doctor will pronounce the victim dead. The victim is subsequently buried and after the crowd goes home, the sorcerer can return in the night and retrieve the "corpse." Afterwards, when the victim is seen alive again, though glassy-eyed and sluggish with a blowfish hangover, folks believe that the sorcerer is powerful enough to create "zombies."

I've heard tell of high-priced sushi restaurants where this same fish is served raw. If someone dies from it, the chef is obliged to kill himself. I say I've heard tell of such places. I'm not sure they really exist. Seabrook often presents characters in his book that recount tales not of what they have seen, but what they have heard about. Or characters speak of things that *must* be true, otherwise why would this *other* thing exist. For example, in the chapter titled "...Dead Men Working in the Cane Fields," a man whom Seabrook describes as "his rational friend Polynice" assures the author that what is sometimes labeled as "superstition" is often some "evil practice connected with the dead." "Why do you suppose," asks Polynice, "that even the poorest peasants, when they can, bury their dead beneath solid tombs of masonry. Why do they bury them so often in their own yards, close to the doorway. Why, so often, do you see a tomb or grave set close beside a busy road or footpath where people are always passing. It is to assure the poor unhappy dead such protection as we can."

Polynice later claims to have seen "zombies" himself. He tells the author that once he has seen them, "with their faces and their eyes in which there is no life," he will believe in the magic. He actually brings Seabrook to a place where three supposed "zombies" are laboring near a cotton field under the supervision of a "big-boned, hard-faced black girl." Seabrook looks into the face of one of the workers and reports that "...the eyes were the worst. It was not my imagination. They were in truth like the eyes of a dead man, not blind, but staring, unfocused, unseeing. The whole face, for that matter, was bad enough. It was vacant, as if there was nothing behind it. It seemed not only expressionless, but incapable of expression."

The black girl pushes Seabrook away, saying *"Z'affai' neg pas z'affai' blanc"* (Negroes' affairs are not for whites). It springs to Seabrook's mind that the girl is a "keeper" and that the "zombies" that he saw were nothing but "poor, ordinary demented human beings, idiots, forced to toil in the fields." Seabrook comes away from the encounter a skeptic, but we can sense in his narrative that he has been seduced by the idea...by the hope, it seems...that there is some supernatural phenomenon that he is always just inches away from uncovering.

The popularity of *The Magic Island* may have come as the result of a different sort of accident, as well. One of timing. The book first reached the public at nearly the same time that Hollywood was finding success with its early *"Famous Monsters of Filmland,"* so the collective ear was to the tracks, so to speak, primed and ready for some new demon to come steaming along...and steam the "zombie" did. It's hard to remember a year since *White Zombie* hit the screen that some being from among the living dead hasn't appeared, in print, on film, or in comic books.

In the past several years, Zombie Walks have become major events in cities all around the world. My wife, Suz, and I live in Toronto, Canada, where a Zombie Walk draws thousands of participants annually. Cities compete. We were in Dallas recently, where a promoter proudly approached us, saying, "We had five-thousand this year, bet that's more'n Toronto had!" People of all ages, all colors, all professions, come out in full make-ups, some of them truly as good as the ones my professional staffers deliver, and they shamble from Point A to Point B, designated by city ordinances and monitored by the police. In Toronto the Zombie Walk is almost as important an event as The Santa Claus Parade or the parade on Gay Pride Day. Oh, what have we wrought, Seabrook and I.

W.B. Seabrook is said to have been somewhat of an unsavory sort. A member of *"The Lost Generation,"* indeed the man did seem lost. Jay A. Graybeal writes: "Big, lusty, restless, red-haired William Buehler Seabrook spent more than 20 years seeking fantastic adventure, then putting what he found into books which thrilled some, shocked many. But he will never write the story of his greatest adventure. Secretly and alone he embarked upon it not long ago by way of an overdose of sedative. The coroner says Bill Seabrook committed suicide. But his friends have a different explanation for what happened. They say he only was making another more drastic attempt to accomplish what he had tried, vainly, all his life to do—to get away from himself."

Aleister Crowley was an acquaintance of Seabrook's. He wrote an entry in his diary that said, "The swine-dog W.B. Seabrook has killed himself at last."

Throughout *The Magic Island,* the author presents to the reader a teeter-totter, the ends of its board alternately rising and falling, with belief on one end, skepticism on the other, while he sits atop the fulcrum, never fully deciding which end he favors. He ends his "zombie" chapter with a note of skepticism. He pays a visit to Dr. Antoine Villiers, of whom he says, "...there is no clearer scientifically trained mind, no sounder pragmatic rationalist...." Seabrook asks if the "zombie" phenomenon could be somehow connected to suspended animation. (Remember, this was written fifty-six years before Davis wrote *The Serpent and the Rainbow.)*

Villiers shows him the current *Code Penal* (Penal Code) of the Republic of Haiti, specifically Article 249:

> "Also shall be qualified as attempted murder the employment which may be made against any person of substances which, without causing actual death, produce a lethargic coma more or less prolonged. If after the administering of such substances, the person has been buried, the act shall be considered murder no matter what result follows."

It would seem, unless the author invented this Article of Law, that such "substances" have been in use on *The Magic Island* for quite some time—since long before W.B. Seabrook first brought the word "zombie" into public awareness. My copy of the Collins Dictionary defines the word first as "a person who appears lifeless, apathetic, or totally lacking in independent judgement." It's only the second definition that describes a "zombie" as "a corpse brought to life by witchcraft." Ah, well, I suppose one who devotes one's life to compiling dictionaries must, by nature, be a pragmatist. The adventurous among us must, by nature, leave the door open to all possibilities.

George A. Romero
Toronto, Canada
April 2015

the Magic Island

FOREWORD TO THE 1929 EDITION

OUR West Indian mail boat lay at anchor in a tropical green gulf.

From the palm-fringed shore a great mass of mountains rose, fantastic and mysterious. Dark jungle covered their near slopes, but high beyond the jungle, blue-black, bare ranges piled up, towering.

At the water's edge, lit by the sunset, sprawled the town of Cap Haïtien. Our boat lay so close that in the bright, fading light it was easy to distinguish landmarks.

Here amid more modern structures were the wrecked mansions of the sixteenth-century French colonials who had imported slaves from Africa and made Haiti the richest colony in the western hemisphere.

Here was the paved pleasance on the waterfront, scene of white massacres when the blacks rose with fire and sword.

Here in ruins was the palace built for Pauline Bonaparte when Napoleon sent his brother-in-law with an imperial army to do battle with slaves who had won their freedom.

On a peak behind the Cape loomed the gigantic fortress which the self-crowned black king Christophe had built after every soldier of that white imperial army was dead or had sailed back to France.

And now above the present-day government headquarters in the town floated the red-blue flag made by ripping the white from the French tricolor. Thus it has floated for more than a hundred years as the symbolic emblem of black freedom.

All this was panoramic as we lay at anchor in the sunset, but as night fell it faded to vagueness and disappeared.

Only the jungle mountains remained, dark, mysterious; and from their slopes came presently far out across the water the steady boom of Voodoo drums.

WILLIAM SEABROOK
New York
September, 1928

Part One:
THE VOODOO RITES

Chapter I

SECRET FIRES

LOUIS, son of Catherine Ozias of Orblanche, paternity unknown—and thus without a surname was he inscribed in the Haitian civil register—reminded me always of that proverb out of hell in which Blake said, "He whose face gives no light shall never become a star."

It was not because Louis' black face, frequently perspiring, shone like patent leather; it glowed also with a mystic light that was not always heavenly.

For Louis belonged to the chimeric company of saints, monsters, poets, and divine idiots. He used to get besotted drunk in a corner, and then would hold long converse with seraphim and demons, also from time to time with his dead grandmother who had been a sorceress.

In addition to these qualities, Louis was our devoted yard boy. He served us, in the intervals of his sobriety, with a passionate and all-consuming zeal.

We had not chosen Louis for our yard boy. He had chosen us. He had also chosen the house we lived in. These two things had happened while we were still at the Hotel Montagne. And they had seemed to us slightly miraculous, though the grapevine telegraph of servants in Port-au-Prince might adequately have explained both. Katie and I had been house-hunting. We had been shown unlivably ostentatious plaster palaces with magnificent gardens, and livable wooden villas with inadequate gardens or no gardens at all, until we had begun to despair. One afternoon as we left the hotel gate, strolling down the hill to Ash Pay Davis's, a black boy, barefooted and so ragged that we thought he was a beggar, stopped us and said in creole with affectionate assurance, as if he had known us all our lives, "I have found the house for you." Not *a* house, mind you. Nor was there any emphasis on the *the;* there couldn't be in creole. He said literally, "*M' té joiend' caille ou*" (I have found your house).[1]

What we did may sound absurd. We returned to the hotel, got out our car, took Louis inside—he had wanted to ride the running-board—and submitted to his guidance. He directed us into the fashionable Rue Turgeau toward the American club and colony, but before reaching that exclusive quarter, we turned unfamiliarly left and then up a lane that ran into the jungle valley toward Pétionville, and there where city and jungle joined was a dilapidated but beautiful garden of several acres and in its midst a low, rambling, faded pink one-story house with enormous verandas on a level with the ground.

Some of the doors were locked; the rest were nailed up. Behind the house were stone-built servants' quarters and a kitchen, also locked. There was a *bassin* (swimming-pool) choked with débris and leaves.

Who owned this little dilapidated paradise, whether it was for rent, how much the rent might be—these were matters outside the scope of Louis' genius. He had not inquired before coming to find us, and he made no offers or suggestions now.

We thanked Louis, dropped him at Sacré Cœur, told him to come see us at the hotel next morning, then drove to Ash Pay's and discovered after considerable telephoning that the place belonged to Maître Morel and might be rented for thirty dollars a month. Toussaint, black interpreter for the brigade who dabbled helpfully in everything, would get us the keys on Wednesday afternoon when Maître Morel returned from Saint Marc.

Louis did not come to the hotel next morning, nor the morning after, but when we went with Toussaint three days

[1] See Appendix, page 285.

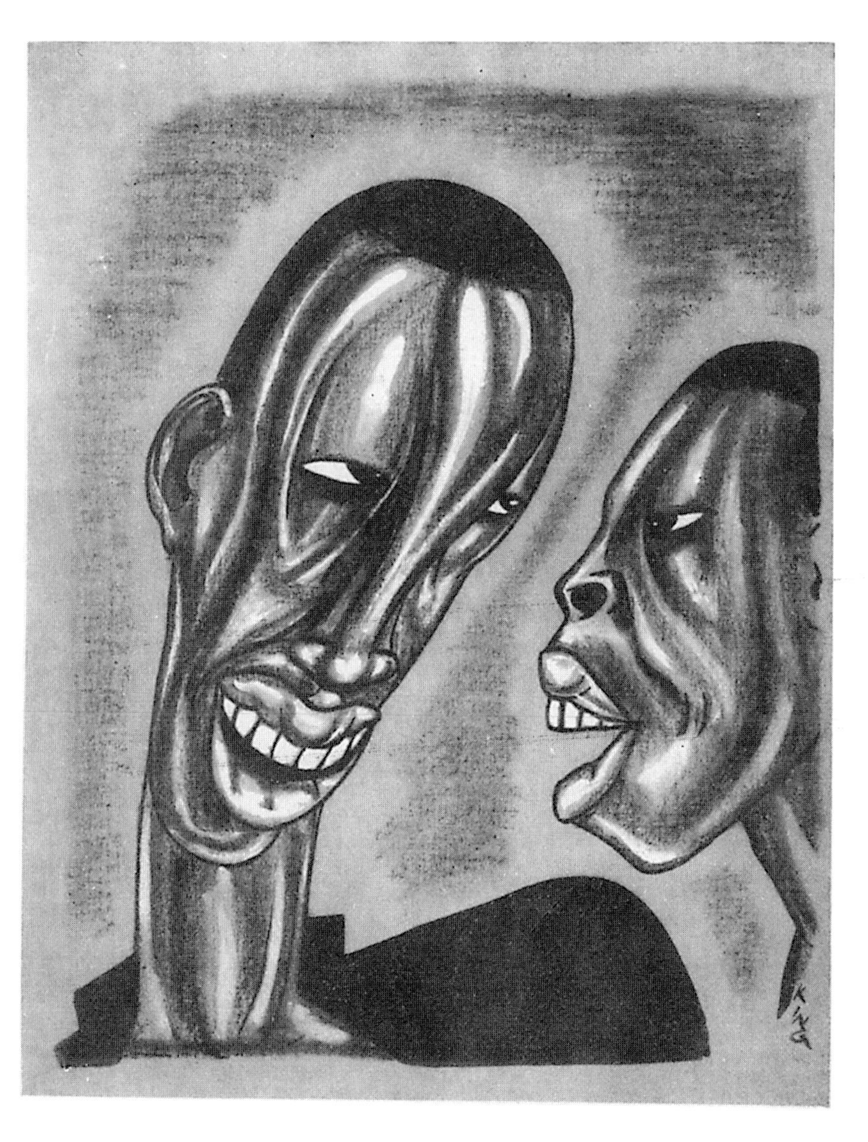

"Louis' face glowed with a light
that was not always heavenly."

later to open the house, we were received blandly by Louis, who was already at home in a corner of the brick-paved veranda to which he had in the interval transported all his earthly possessions, consisting of a pallet, an old blanket, an iron cooking-pot, a candle-stub, and a small wooden box containing doubtless his more intimate treasures. In the pot were the remains of some boiled plantain, apparently his sole sustenance.

Neither he nor we ever mentioned the matter of employing him. Several days were going to elapse before we could move in, but I gave him the keys to the house then and there. I also gave him ten gourdes, the equivalent of two dollars, which was a large sum of money, and told him to buy for himself what was needful, suggesting a new shirt and a supply of food. He was undernourished, and with that new wealth he could feast for a week; the price of a chicken in Haiti is twenty cents.

Returning some days later, I found him with a new pair of tennis shoes, a magnificently gaudy new scarf knotted round his neck, lying on his back in the grass beneath the shade of a mango tree, blissfully and inoffensively drunk, singing a little happy tune which he made as it went, inviting the birds to come and admire his new clothes. His shirt was as before. His whole shoulder protruded from a rent in it. I examined the cook-pot. It contained the remains of some boiled plantain, and it had apparently contained nothing else in the interval. I have told you, I think, that Louis was a saint. Even so, I fear it is going to be difficult to make you understand Louis, unless you have read sympathetically the lives of the less reputable saints and have also lived in a tropical country like Haiti.

Of course when we furnished the house and moved in, we had additional servants—the dull, competent butler, a middle-aged woman cook, and for *blanchisseuse* a plump little wench with flashing teeth and roving eyes who promptly fell in love with Louis, gave him money, and more intimate favors when he permitted it. Having four servants was not ostentatious in Port-au-Prince, even for us who in New York habitually have none. It was the general custom. We paid the four of them a grand sum total of thirty-one dollars monthly, and they found their own food. The last three were reasonably efficient, as servants, doing generally what they were told; but Louis, who never did what he was told, was nevertheless in actual fact, putting quite aside his fantastic power of holding our affection, the most efficient servant of them all. The things he wanted to do, he did without being ordered, and they were many. For instance, there was the matter of our small sedan. He knew nothing about its mechanical insides and could never learn to change a tire, but he took a passionate pride in keeping it clean and polished. He groomed it as if it were alive. When it came home covered with caked mud he dropped no matter what and labored like a madman. He would never clean up the garden, burn brush, carry stones, but during the first week he anticipated our intentions by appearing with vines and flowers for transplanting, the earth still clinging to their roots, which he had got from God knows where. And these also he attended devotedly as if they were alive in a more than vegetable sense.

He delighted in doing personal things to please us. Sometimes when we thought we needed him he was as tranquilly drunk as an opium-smoking Chinaman or off chasing the moon, but at moments when we least expected anything he would appear with a great armful of roses for Katie or a basket for me of some queer fruit not seen in the markets. On rare occasions, sometimes when drinking, sometimes not, he was hysterically unhappy and could not be comforted. But usually he was the soul of joy. And in the household Louis gradually centered his allegiance and chief concern on me. I mention this because most people, whether servants, kinsfolk, intimate friends, or casual acquaintances, find Katie the more admirable human being of us two. But Louis put me first. He began gradually to give me confidences. He felt, as time passed, that I understood him.

And what has all this to do with the dark mysteries of Voodoo? you may ask, but I suspect that you already know. It was humble Louis and none other who set my feet in the path which led finally through river, desert, and jungle, across hideous ravines and gorges, over the mountains and beyond the clouds, and at last to the Voodoo Holy of Holies. These are not metaphors. The topography of Haiti is a tropical-upheaved, tumbled-towering madland of paradises and infernos. There are sweet plains of green-waving sugar cane, coral strands palm-fronded, impenetrable jungles of monstrous tangled growth, arid deserts where obscene cactus rises spiked and hairy to thrice the height of a tall man on horseback and where salamanders play; there are black canyons which drop sheer four thousand feet, and forbidding *mornes* which rise to beyond nine thousand. But the trail which led among them and ended one night when I knelt at last before the great *Rada* drums, my own forehead marked with blood—that trail began at my own back doorstep and led only across the garden to my yard boy Louis' bare, humble quarters where a tiny light was burning.

In a cocoanut shell filled with oil the little wick floated, its clear-flamed tip smaller than a candle's, and before it, raised on a pile of stones such as a child might have built in play, was a stuffed bag made of scarlet cloth, shaped like a little water-jug, tied round with ribbon, surmounted by black feathers. Louis had come on tiptoe shortly after midnight, seeing me reading late and Katie gone to a dance at the club, whose music floated faintly across from Turgeau in the stillness. He explained that a *mystère*, a *loi*, which is a god or spirit, had entered the body of a girl who lived in a hut up the ravine behind our house, and that everywhere throughout our neighborhood, in the many straw-thatched huts of the ravine, likewise in the detached servant quarters of the plaster palaces of American majors and colonels, hundreds of similar little sacred flames were burning.

Thus, and as time passed, confidence engendering confidence, I learned from Louis that we white strangers in this twentieth-century city, with our electric lights and motor cars, bridge games and cocktail parties, were surrounded by another world invisible, a world of marvels, miracles, and wonders—a world in which the dead rose from their graves and walked, in which a man lay dying within shouting distance of my own house and from no mortal illness but because an old woman out in Léogane sat slowly unwinding the thread wrapped round a wooden doll made in his image; a world in which trees and beasts talked for those whose ears were attuned, in which gods spoke from burning bushes, as on Sinai, and sometimes still walked bodily incarnate as in Eden's garden.

I also learned from Louis, or at least began to glimpse through him, something which I think has never been fully understood: that Voodoo in Haiti is a profound and vitally alive *religion*—alive as Christianity was in its beginnings and in the early Middle Ages when miracles and mystical illuminations were common everyday occurrences—that Voodoo is primarily and basically a form of worship, and that its magic, its sorcery, its witchcraft (I am speaking technically now), is only a secondary, collateral, sometimes sinisterly twisted by-product of Voodoo as a faith, precisely as the same thing was true in Catholic mediaeval Europe.

In short, I learned from Louis that while the High Commissioner, his lady, and the colonel had called and taken tea in our parlor, the high gods had been entering by the back door and abiding in our servants' lodge.

Nor was this surprising. It has been a habit of all gods from immemorial days. They have shown themselves singularly indifferent to polite company, high-sounding titles, parlors, and fine houses . . . indifferent indeed to all worldly pride and splendor. We have built domed temples and vast cathedrals, baited with glories of polychrome and marble to trap them, but when the gods come uninvited of their own volition, or send their messengers, or drop their flame-script cards of visit from the skies, it is not often these gilded temples or the proud of the earth they seek, but rather some road-weary humble family asleep in a wayside stable, some illiterate peasant girl dreaming in an orchard as she tends her sheep, some cobbler in his hut among the Alps. Perhaps in their own far-off celestial sphere the gods are surfeited with glory, and only for that reason visit earth at all. Perhaps they suffer from some divine *nostalgie de la boue*. Always when rich, mighty temples are erected where once the humble stable stood, there is a risk that the bored gods will betake themselves elsewhere without saying *au revoir*. And perhaps it was through some such habit of the gods as this that mortal I, who have stood with bowed head and good intentions in so many of this world's great gilded cathedrals, mosques, and temples, have never felt myself so close to the invisible presence of ultimate mystery as I did later, more than once, beneath straw-thatched roofs in the Haitian mountains. And this despite up-cropping naïvetés, savageries, grotesqueries, superstitious mumbo-jumbo, and at times deliberate witch-doctor charlatan trickeries that must be included too if I am to keep this record honest.

Louis and I began to go wandering in the hills together and sitting under trees, where he would tell me of the names and attributes of the many Voodoo gods—Papa Legba, guardian of the gates, who was the most benevolent; Damballa Oueddo, wisest and most powerful, whose symbol was the serpent; Loco, god of the forests; Agoué, god of the sea; Maîtresse Ezilée, who was the mild Blessed Virgin Mary; Ogoun Badagris, the bloody dreadful One whose voice was thunder. There were dozens of them, it seemed. It was like a nursery lesson in Greek mythology, except that to Louis these were not myths, they were more real than he or I. No need to catalogue all their names here; most of them will fall naturally into the record later. Perhaps before the book is ended I shall try to compile a table of theological Voodoo statistics, but it will not be as congenial a task as sitting with Louis under a palm tree.[2]

One afternoon, quite of his own volition, he began telling me of the ritual ceremonies in which these gods were worshiped, and soon I realized he was eye-witness recounting things quite unknown to the outside world and extraordinarily at variance not only with fiction and stage versions of Voodoo ritual, but with the few records extant of persons who have claimed a direct knowledge. He was telling me, in his own rich creole, of choral processionals all robed in white, of men and women grouped, antiphonally chanting, of a sacred black bull covered with embroidered draperies, glittering with adornments, with lighted candles fastened to its horns, led to the sacrificial altar. . . . "Ah, monsieur," he cried, excited, "it was *belle! belle! belle!*" He was seeing it once more as he sat there. I could tell it in his eyes. He was trying to make me see it. But now, lost in his own memory vision, he could only repeat that it was beautiful, beautiful, beautiful.

Belle was a word Louis seldom used, probably because everything to him was beautiful, just as everything was holy to St. Francis, and a special phenomenon would have to be superlatively beautiful before he felt the fact worth mentioning. Only two phenomena in our immediate lives had hitherto, separately, called forth the adjective: Claire and the peacock. The peacock had been given us by Major Davis, but it was not aware that it belonged to us; it followed Louis about as if he were its mate. "*Oh, la belle bête!*" he exclaimed when it first spread its tail, and he called it by no other name thereafter. When Claire had ap-

[2] See Appendix, page 288.

peared from New York to visit us, Louis had exclaimed with like ecstatic spontaneity, "*Oh la belle dame!*" She will forgive me for suggesting that this was extraordinary. She had beauty, yes, but not of a flagrant kind. Leo Katz, sunken in mystic portrait painting, had limned her as a saint, and might as easily have made her a sibyl or a she-devil, but the social herd in Port-au-Prince, as at home, found her more often strange than surpassingly lovely. Louis was quick enough at remembering names, and hers was easy, but during her entire stay with us he found no other name for her. It was always "the beautiful beast," and always "the beautiful lady."

Claire's face glowed as Louis' sometimes did with the inner light that never shone on land or sea; she also was of that strange company, a little sister of the saints and succubi; and I think it was for this that Louis wisely found her beautiful.

And now in memory he had evoked another vision of unearthly beauty.

I said to him presently, "Louis, it was for this, and for this only, I think, that I came to Haiti. I would give anything in the world to see it. I would risk my life, do you understand?—except that that isn't the way I want to see it."

"Ah, monsieur," said Louis sorrowfully, "if you were only black!"

Several days later Louis said, apropos apparently of nothing, "It's more than a month since I have seen my mother at Orblanche. It takes a day to go and a day to return."

I said, "All right, Louis, but since when have you taken to asking anybody's permission for your goings and returnings?"

"It was not for that," said Louis; "I thought you would come with me."

Chapter II

THE WAY IS OPENED AND CLOSED

Louis was flattered that I should have come with him; I was flattered that he should have asked me. So with our joint egos agreeably inflated we ambled along the narrow donkey path, I on a little saddled pony borrowed from Divesco, he topping me on a bareback mule obtained by his own mysterious devices, and as we rode single file we sang, not always in unison:

'Ti fi pas connais laver passer
Aller caille maman ou;
'Ti fi pas connais laver passer
Rêter caille maman ou.

Chorus (repeated ad lib.):

Angêlica! Angêlica!
Rêter caille maman ou.

It meant, "Little girl, since you don't know how to wash and iron, go on back home to your mamma and stay there." There was another verse in which the girl replies, "Little boy, since you haven't got any pennies in your pocket, you'd better beat it home to your own mamma."

From time to time inspired, Louis and I invented new verses, both indecent and mystical, until we emerged from the trail to the highroad, galloped into Pétionville, and dismounted at the market behind the church where old women sat with their baskets and donkeys. We squabbled and bargained until we had filled a large sack with gifts for Louis' mother. They were not expensive or lordly—such things as Louis might have bought returning to the maternal *caille* alone, dried fish, tobacco leaves, *tablettes* which are brown-sugar candy, gingerbread, a small sack of flour, a bottle of red rum, and (fools that we were) a lot of banana-figs that were crushed to a pulp as we jogged. "No matter," said Louis; "the babies will lick them up."

So down the hills and over the plain of the Cul-de-Sac through fields of green cane, into another woods, to Orblanche, Louis' natal village, a straggling collection of some dozen straw-thatched, wattle-and-mud-walled huts and houses with naked babies and half-naked wenches who cried, "It's Cousin Louis with a white. Welcome, cousin. Welcome, white." It might have been in the friendly heart of Africa.

Louis' mamma, Catherine Ozias of Orblanche, small, black, and wrinkled, lay in her house on a palm-fiber pallet, in a moderately clean white wrapper, ill, but not too ill to arise and bestir herself. She whimpered and sobbed, hugging Louis, as old mothers do, but not excessively. It was only when she stood back to survey him and observed he was wearing shoes that the tears of joy flowed free. For only those who have risen in the world wear shoes in Haiti. And because Louis wore shoes and introduced me as his "friend and protector," she gave thanks to the *bon Dieu* and wanted to kiss my hand. The *bon Dieu* and Blessed Brother Jesus find themselves in strange company in Haiti, both celestial and mortal. The Catholic priests, all save a few of the oldest and wisest rural ones, deplore this, but I suspect that Jesus himself might understand and be well content.[1]

Louis' mother exclaimed over the gifts as they were drawn one by one from the sack. Naked grandchildren crowded shyly in the doorway as she doled out candy and gingerbread. Under a palm-leaf canopy on poles in the yard, a chicken and millet in an iron bowl were set cooking. Louis drew his mother aside and began whispering earnestly with her, nodding in my direction. We went back presently

[1] See Appendix, page 292.

into her house, into its main room, earth-floored, about nine feet by seven in size. We entered through the always-open doorway in which no door had ever hung. Her pallet lay on the earth; there was a little table on which were calabash utensils, also three or four china cups and plates, some tin knives, forks, and spoons; her few other belongings hung from pegs in the mud wall. Partitioned off from this were two other tiny rooms, one open with another pallet lying on the ground, the second closed by a rickety wooden door. To this door Louis and his mother led me, and we entered, shutting it behind us. Built against the wall was a low altar on which were two Voodoo *ouanga* bags surmounted by feathers, a crude wooden serpent symbol, a crucifix, a thunderstone, a French colored lithograph of the Virgin Mary, a calabash bowl with green plantains and other offerings of simple food, and in the altar's forefront a cocoanut-shell lamp with its tiny, floating flame. I wish I could make it clear how real this was despite its, to our eyes, anachronistic naïveté. Forget the details and see only, if you can, that here a sacred flame was burning before sincerely worshiped household gods, just as such flames have burned not only for Louis' savage forbears in the Congo jungle, but before the Lares and Penates of ancient Rome, and still burn today before household shrines in every so-called heathen land and in a few archaic Christian ones where religion is an intimate vital element of daily life.

On the floor beside the altar was a small, cheap painted wooden chest which Louis brought out when we emerged. It contained the somewhat surprising family heirlooms and treasures. He fished out and displayed those which concerned him personally and would therefore be most likely to interest me. They did. There was an old-fashioned engraved certificate of first communion from the parish church at Croix de Bouquet, which Louis handed me as his own. It had come from an ecclesiastical engraver in the Quartier de Saint Sulpice at Paris. It depicted a Gothic interior with mitered mediaeval bishops communing little kneeling blonde girls in hoopskirts and early Victorian pantalettes, little white boys dressed like Frenchified Etonians. How different must the scene have been at Louis' own first communion. I examined the writing. I said, "But look here, Louis, this doesn't say your name, 'Louis, fils de Catherine Ozias'; it says, 'Auguste Jean Baptiste Ozias.' "

"Ah," said Louis, "it's true, but I had long forgotten it. Auguste is my cousin. You see, the priest was in a hurry, he handed them out rolled up and gave me the wrong one, but Auguste has one too, so it's all the same."

And now Louis pulled out of the box a flute. It was a proper black flute with German-silver keys. Writers of fiction generally must stick to probabilities, or at least possibilities, more or less, but in real life there are no such limitations. The impossible happens continually. Louis himself would have been incredible in any fiction, except perhaps that of Dostoevski or Melville. It seemed, as nearly as I could gather, that Louis in his childhood had for a time attended parish school, and that the amiable priests, despairing of teaching him to read and write, but hearing him often singing (and doubtless influenced unknowingly by his kinship with fauns and angels), had given him the old flute and taught him to play it. I am sure that if Louis had been born in an Italian hill village instead of the Haitian jungle, he would have preached to the animals and been canonized. Now he played a melody which I had often heard country people singing or whistling as they worked, and which I was to know later as the invocation to Legba.[2] I said, "Louis, why don't you bring your flute back to town?" He said, "I mean to; I was afraid before that it would be stolen." Where he had slept, how he had lived in the city before he attached himself to us, I wondered.

[2] See Appendix, page 294.

He did bring back the flute and played it sometimes for us, but the best to hear was at a distance when he sat under a far tree in the garden for hours piping to the peacock, which would stand close near him as if enchanted.

Ye patient, pious, and mildly tolerant priests of Croix de Bouquet, would it have caused you pangs to know that the flute you once gave Louis from the goodness of your hearts, which your own consecrated hands taught him to play, was now piping pagan melodies to Legba, serpent gods, and peacocks; to know that his pretty first communion papers engraved in the shadow of Saint Sulpice and brought in Christian vessels across the seas, now lay with ancient thunderstones upon a Voodoo altar?

If so, I believe, your pious pangs would have been in part assuaged could you have seen that selfsame altar as I chanced to return and see it long afterward, late in a Holy Week when all its sacred objects, Christian and pagan together, were stripped from it on the evening of Good Friday, laid as if dead in rows before it upon the ground and covered over with palm fronds, to remain thus buried as Lord Jesus was until the Easter resurrection morn. During Golgotha's tragedy, even the great Voodoo serpent-god Damballa must bow his hooded head. And with the half million Voodoo altars in Haiti, it was and has been, I am told, on each succeeding anniversary the same. Here are deep matters, not easily to be dismissed by crying blasphemy.

In the afternoon Louis and I went to walk by the river and to call upon his uncle, Dort Dessiles, who was a *papaloi*. Louis took him aside as he had his mother, and again whispered earnestly, and I knew they were talking of the conversation I had had with Louis on the hill. Dort Dessiles, naturally, was not wholly trustful. After all, my face was white. I often regretted it in Haiti. Old Dessiles, nevertheless, was friendly, took us to his house for a glass of rum. He wanted to do what Louis asked, but he was afraid.

" . . . Dort Dessiles, who was a *papaloi*."

Louis insisted. He kept saying that I was not *like* a white man, whatever that meant. Finally Dessiles and I had a long conversation. The immediate result was that we three went to another *caille* about a quarter of a mile distant, to lay the matter before a man named Dieron, who was a *hougan*, a sort of Voodoo high priest in the district. His relation to Dessiles, I gathered, was somewhat like that of a bishop to a vicar. When we parted with him the upshot was still uncertain. They had a curious faith in Louis, due, I think, not only to their village and blood relationship, but also in part to Louis' otherworldliness. They accepted me on faith as Louis' friend. They talked with me frankly; they took me back a mile from the road and showed me the local *houmfort* (mystery house) and the peristyle under which blood-sacrifices from time to time took place; but for me, a white man, to be present at these ceremonials—ah, that was a hard matter, over which they shook their heads dubiously. I did not press it. "I am going to be in Haiti a long time," I said; "maybe sometime later if we get to know each other better . . ." And we let it stand at that.

I returned to Port-au-Prince the same night, by the moon, leaving Louis with his family, in his natal village. I guessed that he might accomplish more alone than with me present.

He came back after two days, saying he was sure it could be arranged in the end, and during the next several weeks I made three visits with him to Orblanche, sometimes spending the night there.

It was so well arranged finally—in anticipation—that my part in the preparations became as intimate as that of a city cousin engaged with country kinsfolk in trimming the family Christmas tree. I was to buy sweet cakes, candles, and ribbons. I was taken to admire the black bull chosen a week in advance and now penned up in Dieron's compound. It was to be for the next Saturday night.

Only one thing remained to be done, and it seemed a mere courteous formality. It was to inform Kebreau quietly and unofficially so that he might keep his royal back turned and his royal eyes closed on that night. Kebreau was the brown-skinned Haitian Lieutenant-Chief of Gendarmerie for the Croix de Bouquet district, but unofficially he was political "king" of the Cul-de-Sac plain. Kebreau knew that Dort was a *papaloi*, Dieron a *hougan*. Kebreau knew the location of their *houmfort* and knew that from time to time ceremonials technically against the law occurred there. Kebreau knew everything. But Kebreau was not active in persecuting the religion of his own devoted peasants. I am not suggesting that Kebreau was false to his uniform or that he connived overtly in the breaking of the law; he was one of the most conscientious gendarme officers in Haiti, but he couldn't stamp out Voodoo if he had wished, and why should he try when many of the wisest and most efficient white captains and lieutenants of other rural districts closed their eyes to many things that went on continually around them—when at Leogane, for instance, and in a village just east of Gonaives there were unburned mystery houses, obvious and unmistakable, within clear sight of the great highroad over which the motor cars of white generals frequently passed.[3]

But it was a duty of courtesy to inform Kebreau unofficially, a matter of good faith, as Dort and Dieron explained; so on Thursday morning they were going to tell him.

Thursday night late, a man came in to Port-au-Prince from Orblanche, finding my house and asking for Louis, with the message that everything was spoiled—that Kebreau for some unaccountable reason had told them they must not do it.

I was unhappy, and so was Louis. During the night, lying awake, it occurred to me that Kebreau might have heard they planned to have a white man present, and for that

[3] See Appendix, page 294.

reason had refused to let them go on. I decided, therefore, that there was a bare chance things might be straightened out if I went to see Kebreau myself. I happened to know him personally, and this is how I happened to know him:

Some months previous, Major R. H. Davis, Mr. Halliday, and I had gone on a wild-guinea hunt, motoring out through Kebreau's district, and turning fifteen miles beyond into the thorn-bush desert near Thomazeau, penetrating ten miles from the main highway, on a dirt road over which autos almost never passed. Toward twilight, just as we got back to the car, a torrential rain fell, which lasted most of the night. We had chains and tried to go through, with the result that soon we were bogged to our axles. An old man appeared out of the mud, rain, and darkness, and I said, "*Ou capab' joiend' gros cor' dé bef?*" (Literally: You capable join [find] great rope two bulls?)

"*Non, blanc, pas capab',*" he replied in hopeless tones, but when we showed him six dollars—we chose six because it was the exact amount he could earn by working for a solid month in the canefields—he decided he was *capab'* and disappeared to try. Toward midnight he returned, wading through the mud, with a yoke of oxen and the entire male population of a village. Major Davis stayed at the wheel, trying to low-speed, while Halliday and I got out and pushed behind with the negroes, the old man cracking his whip and shouting at the oxen in front. The engine roared, the oxen tugged, Halliday fell down in the knee-deep goulash mud, got up, cursing, to push again, I fell down too, the negroes laughed, and the car never budged.

The old man gave it up in disgust, and blamed us, saying philosophically, "*Auto bagaï' de ville*" (It's a toy that ought to stay in the city). But another old man, working with his wet black hands in the headlight glare, made a little cross with two sticks and a piece of string fished from his pocket, tied it prayerfully to our tail-light, and with mighty heaving the car came out of the hole. They dragged us eventually to the highway, where the "city toy" went completely dead. Well paid, they departed, and left us to our now hopeless misery. It was a dreary night, and not yet dawn. We were wet through and covered with mud. People now began to pass, like ghosts, with their donkeys on the way to market. We began hailing them, saying, "Are you going to Croix de Bouquet?" When one said, "Yes," we gave him a half gourde (ten cents) and said, "Tell Lieutenant Kebreau at Gendarmerie headquarters to send out and rescue us." We sent a string of messages like that. And Kebreau, not content with sending a truck with a half dozen gendarme privates aboard, also a mechanic, also spades, tackle, and a thermos bottle full of coffee, came out himself in a touring-car to condole us and lend a hand. It was the first time I had ever seen him. He was a magnificent fellow, six feet tall, past middle age, handsome as a bronze statue with his fine Kaiser Wilhelm mustaches and his skin almost the same color as his Sam Browne belt and polished boots. He was respectfully amused, but sympathetic. Furthermore, he took us to his own house at Croix de Bouquet, mud-covered scarecrows that we were, and spread before us a superb breakfast of state—was he not king of the Cul-de-Sac?—with cut-glass decanters of rum, delicious and golden. Our friend Major Davis had an ingrown prejudice against sitting down at table with Haitians, whom he referred to collectively as "darkies" when he was in a good humor and "niggers" when in a less amiable mood, but I observed now that the rain and a salutary fasting had purged him of it. He clinked glasses with Kebreau, told him what a splendid chap he was, and we sat there for two hours lighting each other's cigarettes, and growing more and more friendly.

Now looking back on this adventure, lying in bed, miserable and disappointed, recalling also pleasant subsequent meetings with Kebreau, I made up my mind definitely to go out and see him next morning, and did.

After five minutes' candid conversation with Kebreau, I realized I was encountering some sort of blind obstacle that had no direct connection either with the laws against Voodoo or his personal willingness to forget them, or with the fact that I was a white man. There was something else. He told me frankly that there was something, but concerning its precise nature he remained reticent.

When I returned and reported this to Louis, a light gradually dawned on him. "Ahhh," said he, and "Ahhh" again. "*Moon dit Président jour çi li faché cont' Kebreau, li vlé couper tête li*" (People say President these days is angry against Kebreau and wishes to chop off his head).

That afternoon I dropped in at headquarters to chat with General Turrill, chief of the Gendarmerie d'Haïti. Naturally I did not mention Voodoo, but in the course of our casual talk I said, "By the way, why has Borno got his ax out for Kebreau?"

What a world of irrelevant causes and absurdly disconnected eddying effects we blunder helplessly around in. Big events often upset smaller apple-carts, and it was an absurdly disconnected cause of this sort that had upset mine and Louis'.

United States Senator Shipstead is just a name to me, which I may not be even spelling correctly. The Haitians called him Sheepstead, so I am guessing it would be that. He had come to Haiti on a junket, and Kebreau, so General Turrill told me, had given a big rural barbecue in the senator's honor. Kebreau, as I have explained, was more than an ordinary lieutenant of gendarmerie; he was a powerful politician. At this barbecue, sponsored by Kebreau, Senator Shipstead had made an "agricultural speech" to several hundred peasants. Apparently it was an old warhorse, the same sort of speech he must have made a hundred times at white barbecues in Iowa or wherever he hails from. It was about the importance of the small farmer, and contained reiterated phrases that were interpreted to mean, "Hold on to the land." It sounded innocuous and may have been so intended, but at that moment in Haiti it was taken to be highly charged with specific local significance. The signing of a huge irrigation contract, backed by American capital, was pending, and President Borno, who believed in such developments, was eager to get it signed. But it involved either the purchase or confiscation of thousands of small farms, and Senator Shipstead, whose speech was quoted and made the text of fiery editorials in all the Opposition papers howling that Borno was in league with Wall Street to dispossess and rob his own peasants—Senator Shipstead, the General told me, grinning (he was an old Marine Corps former fighting colonel who didn't give a hoot in hell for politics), had thrown a monkey wrench in the works.

President Borno was highly indignant, the General continued, and Kebreau, whom he held somewhat to blame, was going to have to watch his step very carefully for the next month or so. It was reported that the President had even sent his private spies into the Cul-de-Sac seeking to "hang something" on him which would justify an executive demand that he be kicked out of the service.

If I had ever read the newspapers, or taken any interest in politics, I might have already known most of this and guessed the rest. When I walked out of General Turrill's office, I knew that luck had broken against me.

One of my reasons for recounting this chronicle of disappointment in such detail is that it may throw an interesting sidelight on the legal status of Voodoo in Haiti today; another is that certain otherwise friendly and more than generous reviewers found what they called my "continuous good luck" in the Arabian desert a bit monotonous

"Maman Célie, high priestess of the mysteries."

and too marvelous. But I suffered a hundred untold disappointments and obstacles that had to be deviously circumvented in Arabia. And I feel it best, therefore, to confess that I suffered many similar disappointments in Haiti before I finally reached my goal.

Louis' influence did not extend beyond his natal village in the plain, and my path eventually led up into the mountains. But it was Louis who had set my feet in it. Through him and his uncle Dort I began to understand more definitely what I sought, was able to avoid certain pitfalls, and Louis has my gratitude. Even so, with many a false start and wrong direction, my path was "roundabout" like Peer Gynt's, and more than once the Great Boyg barred it. The trail led me once through deep ravines in which the sun never shone, thence winding narrowly up the edge of a sheer cliff to the door of a little man with a wizened face, a famous little man, a sort of Voodoo hermit-saint, who could have wisely taught me all I wished to know, and more, but who sneered at my sincerity and said, "There is no such thing as Voodoo; it is a silly lie invented by you whites to injure us." Saints are not always amiable. It led once beyond the clouds on Morne Diable to a village whose inhabitants had seen no white face for eight years, and though on that occasion I rode with a doctor whose welcome remedies were freely given them, and though they entertained us hospitably for the night, when we arose next morning to go higher up the mountain, they laid hands on our bridles without violence, and said, "It is forbidden." And once I fled, after being offered hospitality, from the habitation of a leering, evil old woman, full of too eager promises, with greedy fingers already clutching at my pocketbook, who would have cut her own daughter's throat to oblige me, for a price. But also I made friends, occasionally saw strange sights, and there were habitations oft returned to where I became known and welcome.

Chapter III

THE PETRO SACRIFICE

FINALLY I went to live with Maman Célie.

I had come for an earlier first visit weeks before, not entirely as a stranger, to this remote, patriarchal habitation in the mountains, sponsored by a man whom they trusted, and made welcome because I was his friend. But now, on Maman Célie's own suggestion, I had returned alone.

Between Maman Célie and me there was a bond which I cannot analyze or hope to make others understand because in my innermost self its roots went deep beyond analysis or conscious reasoning. We had both felt it almost from our first contact. It was as if we had known each other always, had been at some past time united by the mystical equivalent of an umbilical cord; as if I had suckled in infancy at her dark breasts, had wandered far, and was now returning home.

Such mysterious returnings to a place where one has never been; such strange familiarness of a face that one has never seen; I think these things are within the secret experience of almost every human being, but if one has not at some time felt them, they cannot be explained.

This habitation, lost in the high mountains, was primitive and patriarchal. There were half a dozen thatch-roofed buildings in the cleared compound; the little community was ruled by Maman Célie and Papa Théodore, her venerable, less active husband; its members were their grown sons and daughters, their grandchildren naked from babyhood to puberty, playing in the sunshine among the pigs and goats; the oldest son, Emanuel, was past forty; the youngest unmarried daughter, Catherine, was sixteen. Maman Célie herself I guessed to be far past sixty. Her sweet black face, like that of an old prophetess, was deeply wrinkled, but her thinness and straightness, her vitality, made her seem sometimes curiously young.

Patches of corn, millet, and cotton clung farther downward, above the jungle line, on the mountainside; a full mile below in a green jungle valley were their plantains, banana trees, cocoanut palms, and the clear spring with its rivulet from which donkeys toiled upward, festooned with calabash bottles like ambulant bunches of gigantic yellow grapes, often with children in procession single file behind, each with water-filled calabash balanced on his head.

Many paths led from this spring, winding down over the mountains and far away, but the path to Maman Célie's led upward only to our habitation and ended there. The next nearest family community was on the other side of a deep, mile-wide gorge; we counted them friends and neighbors; we could hear their cocks crowing at dawn, their dogs barking in the evening, and when darkness fell we could see their cook-fires burning; on the drums we could say to them across the chasm, "Come on such and such a day," or "Expect us on such another," exchanging simple messages; but to reach their habitation, scarcely a mile distant as the birds flew, we had to journey seven miles around, down past the spring where the bare gorge narrowed to become a fertile valley, and then up again on the other side, regaining the lost altitude.

Thus we were isolated, not only from the organized world down yonder—the nearest gendarme post, chapel, rural clinic, market, were a long day's journey beyond another range—but even somewhat from our neighbors, of whom there were perhaps fifty little family communities scattered far and wide on our own mountain.

Almost every day, despite our isolation, some of these neighbors trailed up from the common spring, sometimes on donkey-back, more usually in procession afoot, family visiting family; but strangers never came.

So far as the world of urban Port-au-Prince and Americanized Haiti was concerned, I might have been on another planet. Yet I do not wish to exaggerate this isolation. Both Maman Célie and Papa Théodore had been down there. They still went perhaps once a year. She went once, in fact, while I was living among them, being gone nearly a week, but that was a very special journey. In general, this mountain-inclosed life went on as if no Port-au-Prince existed.

It was a life I enjoyed, and they let me share it simply, from day to day. I learned to make *tambors marenguin* (mosquito-drums, so called, though they were stringed instruments of which the mechanical contrivance had survived from Africa) with the brats who were still a little afraid of me because of my white face. I rode often with Emanuel and Rafael, once trying with them to explore the bottom of the gorge. I sometimes lent a hand with them in the fields, if green checker-board squares tilted at an angle of forty-five degrees can properly be called fields; and in the evenings I sat with the rest of the circle while Papa Théodore asked riddles, or told tales of how a wily little negro named Ti Malice, a favorite character in all their fables, had locked up Gros Bouqui in the potato garden, or how he saved his own skin at the expense of Bouqui when they fell among cannibals. Many of these tales were of Congo origin, sometimes modified to the West Indian locale, and sometimes not.

All this I found delightful, but between Maman Célie and me there was something deeper, which grew. I knew, of course, that she was a *mamaloi*. I knew also that the largest building of the habitation, the only one with locked door, was a *houmfort*. She knew likewise that I was profoundly interested in the religion in which she was an active priestess. And she also understood quite definitely that I wished to write about it. There was complete candor and confidence between us. She herself could neither read nor write, but she was keenly intelligent and understood clearly what I was and what books were. She understood, furthermore, instinctively, that there was no latent intention of betrayal,[1] that whatever I might write would not be with intent to do them harm. Instinctively she knew that whatever might grow tree-like from my interest, its roots were buried in soil common to us both.

We talked frequently of the things I had heard first from Louis beneath the palm tree, but Maman Célie made haste slowly. She sometimes said to me, "*Pétit, pétit,*" meaning little by little, or step by step. Perhaps she was wisely waiting until the people of the mountain became thoroughly accustomed to my presence. And finally one day, she said, "There is to be a big, big Petro [2] ceremonial on Saturday and Sunday over yonder at the habitation of Théodore's brother Ernest; all the mountain will be there, and it is understood you are coming too."

Papa Théodore rode in the forefront of our cavalcade, along the narrow trail that wound between inclosing rocky defiles, emerging to follow the edge of the cliff, descending through forests of great sablier trees with their spiked

[1] Voodoo is not a secret cult or society in the sense that Freemasonry or the Rosicrucian cult is secret; it is a religion, and secret only as Christianity was secret in the catacombs, through fear of persecution. Like every living religion it has its inner mysteries, but that is secretness in a different sense. It is a religion toward which whites generally have been either scoffers, spyers, or active enemies, and whose adherents therefore have been forced to practice secrecy, above all where whites were concerned. But there is no fixed rule of their religion pledging them to secrecy, and Maman Célie was abrogating nothing more than a protective custom when she gave me her confidence.

[2] See Appendix, page 295.

trunks, mahogany and towering pines. Behind him rode Maman Célie on a donkey, and I rode third, while Emanuel, Rafael, Marie-Céleste, Catherine, others of the family, followed single file, afoot. Emilie, six months pregnant, rode on a basket-laden donkey.

It was Saturday midafternoon.

In the air all round us, everywhere and nowhere, I became conscious of a steady, slow "boom . . . boom . . . boom . . . boom." It seemed sometimes to come from a great distance, like rolling, far-off thunder beyond hidden valleys and over mountains far away; it seemed sometimes to be low and close at hand, just beyond the next turning; at moments it seemed inside my own head or in my veins like a pulse beating. As we rode farther and the afternoon waned, this steady booming, now louder and closer, became complicated by a hitherto inaudible under-rhythm, an incessant throbbing woven and interwoven around a simple basic motif that emerged thus:

It was not syncopation. It was not remotely like jazz. It was pure counterpoint like a Bach fugue except that the core of it was slow, unhurried, relentless. There was something cosmic in it like the rolling of mighty waters. There was something humanly savage and primitive too in its relentlessness, as darkness inclosed us and lights began to glimmer red up yonder at the head of the gorge.

The habitation to which we came was a compound, unfenced, on a plateau overhanging the gorge, hemmed in by the forest. There were assembled already perhaps a hundred negroes, crowding, moving about like shadows in the red-flickering lights. There were three or four scattered houses, and in the central forefront of the compound was a big open *tunnelle*—the word is misleading, but there is no English equivalent for it. It was a great awning-like roof-canopy, rectangular, of straw thatching, erected on poles. In a corner beneath it were the three drummers, drumming.[3] The man with the tall central drum used one stick and the hard heel of his right palm, which produced the deepest note; the other two with the smaller drums used their hands with virtuoso-like varied rapidity, the flat palm, the bunched, hard tips of their fingers, the fisted knuckles, the rosin-coated thumb drawn across the drumhead, which then emitted a bull-roaring zooming. An old woman stood by and from time to time wiped the sweat from their faces. It was deafening, close at hand, and yet in a curious way seemed not so thunderous as it had from a couple of hundred yards distant down the trail.

Some of the black faces and whitened mud-walls stood out in high lights; other parts of the compound were in dark shadow. We of the family entered Ernest's house for coffee, and then I walked about in the crowd with Maman Célie. There was no one who had not either met or heard definitely of me, and my presence seemed taken for granted. Many greeted me.

A bright moon was now rising over the mountains, and the ceremony was presently to commence. The drums ceased, and for the first time I heard the intermittent bleating of tethered goats.

We ranged ourselves family with family, but serried in close rows, as people sit in church, except that there were no benches. We assembled seated on the ground before the *tunnelle;* I sat between Maman Célie and Rafael in a foremost row, all of us facing the *tunnelle* and the drums.

[3] See Appendix, page 300.

The drums began a new, less deafening rhythm. It was the Damballa ritual march. Its base motif was thus:

The celebrants approached, processionally, singing, from the mystery house. At the head came the *papaloi*, an old man, blue-overalled, bare-footed, but with a surplice over his shoulders and a red turban on his head, waving before him the *açon*, a gourd-rattle wound round with snake-vertebræ. At his right and left, keeping pace with him, two young women held aloft, crossed above his head, two flags on which were serpentine and cabalistic symbols, sewn on with metallic, glittering beads. Behind him marched a young man bearing aloft, horizontally on his upstretched palms, a sword, and next the *mamaloi*, a woman in a scarlet robe and feathered headdress, who revolved as she progressed in a sort of dervish dance; next came marching, two and two, a chorus of twenty or more women robed in white, with white cloths wound bandana-wise on their heads, and as they slowly marched they chanted:

Damballa Oueddo,
Nous p' vini.[4]

It would be best translated, I think, "Oh, Serpent God, we come."[5]

[4] See Appendix, page 302.

[5] Although Damballa, the ancient African Serpent god, remains enthroned as its central figure, this Voodoo ceremony is not the old traditional ritual brought over from Africa, but rather a gradually formalized new ritual which sprang from the merging in earliest slave days of the African

See page 34

" . . . the *mamaloi* in a scarlet robe."

The *papaloi* stands beneath the *tunnelle*, facing us, the chorus of women sits in a semicircle at his right, a chorus of men forms on his left, the *mamaloi* whirls dancing before the drums, which cease as she falls prostrate.

Amid absolute silence, the *papaloi* says solemnly: "*Solei' levé nan l'est; li couché lan Guinea*" (The sun rises in the east and sets in Guinea).

This is the pronouncement of one of the Voodoo nature-mysteries. They have no conception of the earth as a revolving globe. They know that Guinea—their only name for Africa—lies eastward, and that the sun sinks in the opposite direction, in the west. Yet each morning it arises again out of Guinea, and therefore must, in some mysterious way, have returned there. And the secret route it travels symbolizes for them the path by which their own souls go out of their living bodies, in the trance state, and are carried away by the *lois*—a sort of Holy-Ghost-like

tradition with the Roman Catholic ritual, into which faith the slaves were all baptized by law, and whose teachings and ceremonials they willingly embraced, without any element of intended blasphemy or diabolism, incorporating modified parts of Catholic ritual—as for instance the vestments and the processional—into their Voodoo ceremonials, just as they incorporated its Father, Son, Virgin, and saints in their pantheistic theology. Thus indeed all new religions are formed. Fully half the ritual and much of the symbolism of Judaism and Christianity were borrowed from earlier pagan faiths. The cross itself was a sacred symbol before Christ ever died upon it. And these blacks who were brought over from Africa with their own religion, older far than Christianity, were perhaps taking back transformed symbols and ritual practices which had originally been borrowed from their own continent when Moses led Israel out of Egypt. I am contributing nothing new in telling that a crucifix stands today on every Voodoo altar in Haiti. That fact is well known, for *houmforts* have been raided. But the presence of the crucifix has been generally misunderstood. Christian priests have imagined that it involved diabolic and deliberate desecration, as when adherents of the Black Mass, worshiping the devil, turn the cross upside down and spit upon it and recite the Credo backward, mingled with obscenities. They have therefore cried horror and blasphemy and demanded that the *houmforts* be burned, never understanding that the crucifix transplanted to the Voodoo altar is reverenced and held sacred there as it was in the cathedral. True, it becomes the symbol not of *the* God but rather of one god among many, and this in the eyes of some will constitute, I suppose, an almost equally deplorable sacrilege.

emanation from their divinities—to other worlds. "*Li nans Guinea*" (He is in Guinea), they say always of a person stricken into that ecstatic trance.

In response to the priest all sing, including the swaying crowd:

Coté solei' levé?
Li levé nans l'est.

Coté solei' couché?
Li couché lans Guinea!

(Whence does the sun rise?
It rises in the east.

Where does the sun set?
It sets in Guinea!)

Now from the mystery house was led processionally a small black bull, adorned for the sacrifice. And with what a catching of the breath I saw that there were lighted candles on its horns as Louis had foretold, that it was robed and garlanded and glittering!

The bull now stood dazed on a low platform which had been dragged meanwhile beneath the *tunnelle*, and we all knelt before it, while the women clothed in white chanted a wailing, symphonic choral, repeating endlessly the words, "*Mander ou pardon*" (O Lord, forgive our sins).

The bull had become a god or the symbol of a god.[6]

The wailing chant, the throbbing drums, the miraculous

[6] In *The Bacchae* of Euripides, the frenzied women of Thebes who tore Pentheus limb from limb when he spied upon the celebration of their mysteries in a mountain gorge, worshiped Dionysus in the form of a serpent and bull, and "the Orphic congregations of later times, in their most holy gatherings, solemnly partook of the blood of a bull, which was, by a mystery, the blood of Dionysus-Zagreus himself, the 'Bull of God,' slain in sacrifice for the purification of man." See Gilbert Murray's notes on *The Bacchae.* These Voodoo worshipers retained their bull and serpent symbolism from African jungle rites older than the Greek mythology, but the double parallel is interesting.

aliveness of their own belief in wonders to be manifested; the unearthly quality of the great, pale, moon-flooded mountain slopes that towered to the stars, the ghostly ravines and gorges that dropped down to blackness; the red-flickering torches close at hand—all this I remember now as a sort of dream, still more vivid, after a year has passed, than most waking memories. Yet if I should chance to live for twenty years longer, that general memory-picture may fade gradually. But there is one small thing tangled in with this, acid-etched so deeply that it will leave some lines, I think, when my brain lies rotting. It was simple; yet I find it almost impossible to tell. It was the sound of the terrorized, shrill bleating of the white he-goats, tethered out there in the shadows, as it pierced through yet was always dominated, sometimes drowned, by the symphonic female howling choral of the women. It caused something that was elemental male in me, something deeper than anything that the word sex usually defines, to shiver in the grip of an answering, icy terror. Nor had this any remote connection with the fact that I, a white man, knelt there among these swaying blacks who would presently become blood-frenzied. They were my friends. It was a terror of something blacker and more implacable than they—a terror of the dark, all-engulfing womb.

But I forget that I am writing the description of a Voodoo ceremonial in the Haitian mountains, and that excursions among the terrors aroused by elemental nightmares in my own soul are an.unwarranted interruption.

As the sacrificial beasts, goats, kids, sheep, were dragged into the *tunnelle*, the women's choral ceased and a mighty chant arose from every throat:

Damballa Oueddo,
Ou couleuvre moins!

(Damballa Oueddo, our great Serpent-God.)

During an interval, a woman in misery sang alone:

Pas 'joudhui moins gagnin chemin;
Damballa, moins bien prête,
Moins pas 'river.

(It is not today that I will find the path. Damballa, I am ready, but the road is barred.)

I had become gradually aware of an increasing undercurrent of group fear among them, which now outwardly manifested itself in their chants, a fear of their own old, deadly jungle gods, a fear that the blood of beasts alone might not avail:

Ogoun Badagrís,
Ou à manger viande moins,
Ou à quitter zos pour demain?

Me mander ça ou fais moins?
La vie moins est là.

(Ogoun Badagris, will you devour my flesh, and leave my bones for the morrow? I ask what are you going to do with me? My life is in your hands.)

And they sang also:

Zandor, pinga manger petit moins!
Zandor, connais moon par ou!

(Zandor, do not eat my child! Zandor, know your own people.)

It seemed to me presently that in expressing their fears, they somewhat allayed them, that they writhed gradually less in agony, and the harmony was less somber, when they chanted:

Maîtresse Ezilée, vini 'gider nous.
Si ou mander poule, me bai ou.

Si ou mander cabrit, me bai ou.
Si ou mander bef, me bai ou.
Si ou mander cabrit sans cor',
Coté me pren' pr bai ou?

(Maîtresse Ezilée, come and aid us. If a cock is demanded, we will give it. If a goat is demanded, it is here. If a bull will suffice, behold it. But if a goat without horns—a human being—is required for sacrifice, oh, where will we find one?)

They were supplicating Maîtresse Ezilée, who is the Virgin Mary, to intercede with the old African gods, and make them content with the substitution of animal sacrifice for human.

This supplication was followed immediately by a peculiar dance done by the *mamaloi* alone, to the accompaniment of a powerfully accentuated drum rhythm which went thus:

The first three full notes were slow, heavy, explosive booms, and the triplet came as a whirring, light splutter at the end. At each slow "boom," the priestess, holding herself straight and rigid as a lance, yet managed to leap upward like a jack-in-the-box or a figure propelled from a spring-board. At the moments when the whirring triplet recurred, she stood rigid instead of leaping, and a galvanic shudder trembled through her stiff body.

Preparation for the sacrifices, meanwhile, went rapidly forward. A long wooden trough, carved from a tree-trunk, was borne in, coffin-wise, by four men and deposited on the low platform in front of the glittering and bedizened bull. Big wooden bowls, and heavy, common china cups were also brought, and a machete.

Neither in these preparations nor in any part of the all-night ceremonial did Maman Célie take active official part, though I knew that she was the chief *mamaloi* of those mountains. Throughout it all, she remained close beside me. I was destined to see her red-robed finally, but not upon this night.

In the actual slaying of the sacrificial beasts which now began, accompanied by deep chanting, there was no savagery, no needless cruelty, no lust of killing. It was a solemn, ritual business, though when once begun it moved swiftly. A goat was held by the horns, the sharp-edged machete drawn across its throat by the *papaloi*, and the blood gushed into a wooden bowl held by the *mamaloi*, who poured it into the great empty trough before the bull, while the body was tossed out into the shadows. Thus, in turn, the goats and sheep were slain.

And now the bull, before whom, deified, this blood of other beasts had been poured out as an offering, must also die. It was the old riddle of the dying god made carnate and sacrificed miraculously to appease his own bloody godhead. Is it any wonder that the African ancestors of these worshipers, with such traditions of their own, had accepted also the Hebrew-Syriac version of this age-old riddle taught them by the early colonial Christian priests?

For this ultimate sacrifice, the sword was used. Four men with straining muscles sought to uphold the bull, to keep it upright as if it had been a tottering brazen idol, to prevent it from sinking down even in its death-throes, as the *papaloi* plunged the long, pointed blade beneath the bull's shoulder and through its heart. With a deep, choked bellow the bull sagged quivering to its knees, and was held thus by the straining men. The blood did not gush fountain-like as it had from the cut throats of the goats; it spurted in a hard, small stream from the bull's pierced side, where the *mamaloi* knelt with her bowl to receive it and transferred it bowl by bowl to the great common trough.

The *papaloi* and *mamaloi* now both drank ceremonially of the holy blood, and then amid the crescendo excitement and surging forward of the worshipers, the twenty women robed in white danced, leaping and whirling in a group like frenzied maenads, led by the *mamaloi*, while the priest now performed his purifying office, asperged them all, sprinkled them, deluged them, until their white turbans and the shoulders of their robes turned crimson. The worshipers, crowding now and frenzied, yet managed to respect a space in which these women danced, until the priest cried, "All the world approach," and the crowd milled before the altar to be sprinkled by the cleansing sacrificial blood. And brimming cups dipped up by the *papaloi* were now passed spilling from hand to hand, all madly eager, after tasting it themselves, to gain merit with the gods by passing it to the hands of others who might share it; thus, though a pandemonium, it was in the literal sense of the word a "communion," a sharing.

From this swirling, milling ceremony of purification, figures leaped out dancing and screaming glory; here and there in the crowd a still higher, shriller, more unearthly shriek announced the pentecostal, invisible, yet flame-like descent of the *lois*, spirits of the gods and of the *mystères*, entering the bodies of individual dancers. This final phenomenon of ultimate and overwhelming religious ecstasy, as I observed it at this and at other Voodoo ceremonials seen subsequently, never became general or contagious. True, the entire crowd was now becoming frenzied and ecstatic, but they remained *themselves* in *ecstasy*. This other force, which struck a few separate individuals here and there like lightning, swept all self away, and those thus stricken became actually, in the technical, religious sense of the word, *possessed*. No need for me to insist here on the absolute subjective reality of this phenomenon. It has been common to all religions during periods of deep, mystical faith.

Not more than a dozen or at most fifteen scattering individuals that night experienced personally this ultimate and self-destroying illumination, but the coming of the *lois* was a signal to all that the gods had been appeased, and were propitiously disposed, so that they could abandon themselves without fear to joyous, savage exultation.

And now the literary-traditional white stranger who spied from hiding in the forest, had such a one lurked near by, would have seen all the wildest tales of Voodoo fiction justified: in the red light of torches which made the moon turn pale, leaping, screaming, writhing black bodies, blood-maddened, sex-maddened, god-maddened, drunken, whirled and danced their dark saturnalia, heads thrown weirdly back as if their necks were broken, white teeth and eyeballs gleaming, while couples seizing one another from time to time fled from the circle, as if pursued by furies, into the forest to share and slake their ecstasy.

Thus also my unspying eyes beheld this scene in actuality, but I did not experience the revulsion which literary tradition prescribes. It was savage and abandoned, but it seemed to me magnificent and not devoid of a certain beauty. Something inside myself awoke and responded to it. These, of course, were individual emotional reactions, perhaps deplorable in a supposedly civilized person. But I believe that the thing itself—their thing, I mean—is rationally defensible. Of what use is any life without its emotional moments or hours of ecstasy? They were reaching collective ecstasy by paths which were not intrinsically peculiar to their jungle ancestors, but which have been followed by many peoples, some highly civilized, from the earliest ages, and will be followed to the end of time or until we all become mechanical, soulless robots. It is not necessary to look backward to the Dionysian orgies, the bacchanalia, the rites of Adonis, or frenzied David dancing before the Ark of the Covenant. What, after all, were they doing here in these final scenes, when formal ritual had

See page 42

"... blood-maddened, sex-maddened, god-maddened ... danced their dark saturnalia."

ended, that was so different from things which occur in our own fashionable and expensive night clubs, except that they were doing it with the sanction of their gods and doing it more successfully? Savage rhythm, alcohol, and sex excitement—yet there was an essential difference, for here was a mysterious something superadded. Lasciviousness became lust, which is a cleaner thing, and neurotic excitement became authentic ecstasy, the "divine frenzy" of the ancients. There is nothing so stupid and pathetic as an orgy that doesn't quite come off. Perhaps there is a deep mystical truth in the saying attributed to a much-misunderstood voice, "Whatever ye do, do it in My name." Perhaps if we mixed a little true sacrificial blood in our synthetic cocktails and flavored them prayerfully with holy fire, our night clubs would be more orgiastically successful and become sacred as temples were in the days of Priapus and Aphrodite.

Here certainly in these mountains, where sacrificial blood flowed free and all things were done in the name of the gods, the gods magnificently descended.

Next day there was feasting on the bodies of the slain beasts, barbecued whole, or cut up and cooked in iron pots. Nobody felt like going home. Some, still exhausted, danced, not the mad *Rada* of the night, but boisterous, gay Congo dances. It was a time of rejoicing. Everybody was more or less drunken, including Maman Célie.

I notice I have been continually writing "they," using the time-honored pronoun employed by so many otherwise veracious and candid traveler-authors when describing wild happenings which they feel may be regarded dubiously by sisters and aunts back home. Very well: the truth. I drank like the rest, when the bottles were passed my way. I did willingly all else that Maman Célie told me, and now with good appetite stuffed myself with goat flesh and washed down the meats with more white rum, and dozed, replete and vastly contented, in the bright sunshine. It was for this I had come to Haiti. It concerned me personally. It justified something in my soul. I cared not if I never wrote a book. I merely wondered, without worrying—since it is impossible ever to be utterly content—how soon Maman Célie would take me inside her *houmfort*.

Chapter IV

THE "OUANGA" CHARM

"Go bring me a humming bird," said Maman Célie, "and we'll see what can be done."

She was talking to her tall grandson, Paul, Emanuel's boy, who had been moping about the habitation for days because a young, high-breasted black damsel down by the spring, who seemed to him more desirable than all the other young black damsels on the mountain, had tossed her crinkly head and sent him about his business.

It was through this idyllic episode of the humming bird that I discovered Maman Célie to be a sorceress, as well as a priestess of Voodoo. The two functions do not necessarily concur.

It seemed to me, however, that she had set her grandson a somewhat difficult task. I had seen humming birds occasionally down yonder among the tropical flowers and fig-banana groves, tiny, fragile, iridescent, darting sprites, as incorporeal as soap-bubbles, as swift to disappear at a threatened touch. To catch one of them seemed almost as difficult as trapping a sunbeam. I knew vaguely that naturalists made use of delicate and cunningly constructed nets, and I had heard with equal vagueness of tiny shot-guns spraying microscopic pellets, but Paul was equipped only with his natural wits.

Next day he returned with the humming bird. He had trapped it with a sort of birdlime made of a sticky, gummy sap. It was already dead and Maman Célie hung it up to dry in the sunshine. Meanwhile she persuaded Paul to show me, reluctantly, a former love-charm she had fabricated for him, but which apparently had failed of its purpose, though he still wore it next his skin in a little sack strung round his neck. She explained its construction and use. Two needles of equal length are stood upright, side by side, baptized with suitable incantations, and are given the names of the youth and his unwilling girl. The two in this particular case were called Paul and Ti-Marie. The needles are then left side by side, parallel but reversed, so that the point of each presses against the eye of the other. The point is symbolic of the phallus and the eye symbolic of the vulva. The reverse doubling simply increases the potency of the charm; it has no perverse significance. The needles are placed between twigs from the roots of the *bois chica* tree, whittled smooth and straight, and then wound round with thread. Like all charms of every sort in Haiti, it was called a *ouanga*. There are love-*ouangas*, hate-*ouangas*, birth-*ouangas*, protective-*ouangas*, and murder-*ouangas*.[1] Sometimes they work, and sometimes they don't. Apparently this one hadn't worked, and Paul now centered all his hopes in the humming bird.

Aware of my curiosity about these matters, Maman Célie permitted me to see her make the new *ouanga*. It was a less weird, less cabalistic business than one might guess, though midnight and moonlight were in it, as she crouched, crooning her incantations, but there was nothing mysteriously dreadful. In a little wooden mortar, which they call *pilon*, she ground the dried body of the humming bird into a dust-like powder, droning, "Wood of the woods, bird of the woods, woman you were created by God. Bird of the woods, fly into her heart. I command you in the name of the three Marys and in Ayida's name. *Dolor, Dolori, passa.*" There was much more of it, untranslatable and cryptic. And with the dried powder of the humming bird she mixed a few dried drops of her grandson's blood, also of his semen, likewise the pollen of jungle flowers.

[1] See Appendix, page 302.

When all this had been duly ground together into dust-like fineness, she transferred it to a leather pouch made (as Spanish shepherds often do to hold their love-charms) from the scrotum of a he-goat, and gave it to Paul next day.

I was told, for I did not see it, that on the following Saturday evening, at the *danse Congo*, as Ti-Marie swayed past him laughing, he threw the dust full in her face, and that half blinded, with the dust in her eyes and nostrils and mouth, she spat like a young wildcat, and cried out that she would kill him—but she lay with him that night in the forest, and on Monday morning he fetched her home. Doubtless a deeper magic than Maman Célie's was also at work, but I think it would be a mistake to assume *a priori* that without Maman Célie's incantations and the humming bird, Ti-Marie would have yielded.

There were two other occasions when I saw her magic work effectively. I saw her, by processes which she considered magical, cure a dying girl [2] and catch a thief.[3] She said and believed that it was magic. Words are merely labels, and we do not always explain the inner essence of things by rejecting the old labels and inventing new ones. The Lady of Shalott gazed in her crystal mirror to behold scenes far away, and that was sorcery; now we experiment with Television, and that is science. The Witch of Endor was a witch, but Svengali is a hypnotist. Old Nostradamus working over his crucibles called it alchemy when he sought to transform lead to gold, but now the Germans are engaged in the same experiment and call it advanced chemistry. I realize that there is a flaw in these parallels. But the scientific-minded Carrel, after his long stay at Lourdes, came away convinced that there were invisible powers unknown to any science at work there, and that the probable power of immaterial emanations to produce constructive or de-

[2] See Appendix, page 302.
[3] See Appendix, page 306.

structive changes in material substances, for instance the human body, was a thing which saints still knew more about than savants. When such things occur at holy shrines, they are called miracles; when they occur in a psychological laboratory, they are called science; when they occur in the Haitian jungle, they are called Voodoo magic. These words are all tags, labels, nothing more. Life and the forces of life remain shrouded in eternal mystery.

Maman Célie's sorcery was principally benevolent, as when she presently began gathering materials for the construction of a *ouanga* packet for me—it seemed that I was to have one of my very own, like that of Louis, which was the first I had ever seen, down in my back yard at Port-au-Prince—and that it was to preserve me safe from all harm amid these mountains. It was to be used also, she told me, in the special ceremonial that would occur when I was finally led into the *houmfort* to face certain of the ultimate Voodoo mysteries. I would need it then, she assured me earnestly.

How much I believed in that *ouanga* packet, and in what manner I believed what I did believe, are questions difficult to answer. I suspect that generally in such matters it is easier to believe in things which are sinister, perhaps dangerous, than it is to believe in things which are benevolent. It is always easier to fear ghosts, hobgoblins, and demons than it is to feel the hovering presence of guardian spirits. How many millions of people have been terrorized by ghosts and sworn trembling afterward to their reality, compared with the few score in the history of the world who, like Saint Augustine and Joan of Arc, have conversed with angels. I knew that certain other *ouanga* packets in this Voodoo sorcery, horridly devised, were sometimes as definitely deadly as the murderer's knife or poison. There is no question about that. Every white man who has lived long enough with primitive peoples, no matter what his hard scientific background, no matter how rational the texture of his mind, has come finally to an often reluctant admission of the fact.[4] One may find the semi-scientific explanation of how so-called black magic can kill, in the fifteen volumes, more or less, of Frazer's *Golden Bough;* the condensed edition in two volumes has been emasculated. But if one has ever lived, I mean geographically, outside the limits of our well-ordered rule-of-thumb world where every effect is politely assumed to trace back to respectably explicable causes, it will scarcely be necessary to read Frazer to understand that I am not treating here of superstition. Superstition would have had naught to do with my fleeing from that mountain if word had come to my ears that these people were secretly contriving for me the black death-*ouanga*, and even fleeing I might not have been safe. White men have died in London—and the records are in Scotland Yard—because some monk in the mountains of Thibet marked them to die, and sat droning in his far-off cell among the Himalayas. A subtle poison leaving no trace? Who knows? How can one be ever sure?

But the *ouanga* packet they were now preparing to make for me was to be bright-colored, friendly and protective, and for those very reasons I found it more difficult to view it seriously, to separate it from obvious elements which were merely superstition. Yet had I not accepted it seriously I should have been wrong, for into its making went something more than aromatic leaves and powders; into it went also the imponderable will-to-protect of a community, so that whatever it was or was not magically, it not only deserved respect but had an actual potency-value as the sacred symbol and earnest of their protection.

It was the realization of this, I think, that enabled me to see, somewhat with their eyes, as more than mummery, the ceremony of this *ouanga* packet's making.

In a small, bare room inside Maman Célie's dwelling-house, from which a sleeping-pallet and other common

[4] See Appendix, page 307.

household gear had been removed, a large cowhide was spread, hairy side upward, on the earthen floor, and around it in a circle sat solemnly a dozen negroes whom I knew, mostly of our immediate household. There were eight men and four women. It was night time. The only light flickered upward on their faces from small candles arranged as a geometric pentagram on the cowhide. Barring the doorsill were two crossed machetes, their broad, naked blades inscribed with white chalk symbols, the swirling serpent, the phallic staff, the enmeshed triangles.

Spread in the center of the candle pentagram, on the cowhide, was a square red cloth, like a napkin, which was to be the covering of my *ouanga* packet. Bright ribbons, red and yellow, lay beside it, and also feathers brilliantly dyed. In little, separated piles upon the cowhide were balsam leaves, leaves of the castor-bean plant, roots of the lime tree; a saucer of flour, a saucer of ashes, a bottle of *clairin*, a bottle of perfume, a tiny iron crucifix.

Maman Célie and I sat on one side in the circle, Papa Théodore facing us. While they chanted almost in undertones, "*Papa Legba, ouvri barrière pour li; tout Mystère 'gider li*" (Legba, open the gate for him and every Mystery protect him), old Théodore took some of the roots and leaves, mixed them in a brazier, charred them over a fire now kindled on a plate before him, then pounded them together in a mortar. The two machetes were taken from the doorsill and planted upright in the ground, flanking him on each side. A *bocor* (magician) filled his mouth with *clairin* and sprayed it, sputtering, over all the paraphernalia on the cowhide, to drive away evil spirits. While Papa Théodore continued rhythmically pounding his materials in the mortar, the *bocor* began picking up balsam leaves and castor-bean leaves, one by one, marking each with a chalked cross and depositing it on the napkin, until a new pile was made there. Atop these leaves he now laid the crucifix, also a tuft of hair (tied together with thread) which had been

"—but marked for death by the Voodoo curse, they died."

cut previously from the central crown of my head; a paring from my right thumb-nail, and a small square cut from a shirt which had been worn next my skin.[5] Something of this sort runs through all primitive magic, whether the purpose be benevolent or evil. Articles intimately connected with the individual to be affected, a part of his own body such as hair or nail-paring if it can be procured, or a piece of clothing saturated with his perspiration or grease, are used variously as a substitution for himself. One of the most dreaded forms of Haitian-African magic includes the dressing of a corpse in a garment of the person marked for vengeance and then exposing it to rot away in some secret place in the jungle. Men have gone stark mad seeking that jungle-hidden horror, and others have died hopelessly, searching. Fear, hunger, thirst, jungle-terror, one may say. Names again, tags, labels. But marked for death by the Voodoo curse, they died. In the case of the death-*ouanga* packet, poisonous leaves are used with other corroding and defiling substances.[6] Frazer contends that for magic of this sort to operate fatally without supplementary human agency the victim must *know* and *believe*. Probably this is true. But in the case of unbelievers they sometimes make use of appallingly pragmatic methods to instill faith. I am told that when some years ago "Bank" Williams, the saturnine, cynical, fearless Yankee manager of the bank which is Haiti's treasury, was thus marked for death, on one occasion a dog died in agony lapping pure water from the seemingly innocent clean bowl in which his morning coffee might have been poured had not the bowl been suspected, and on another occasion, deadly poison was found inside an egg whose shell had apparently never been broken. He survived, I am told, because he fought the devil with fire; for weeks, until definite events made his death no longer desired, every particle of food that passed his lips, every garment that

[5] See Appendix, page 308.
[6] See Appendix, page 308.

touched his skin, first went through the hands of an old wrinkled woman from Martinique who knew every trick of black magic and served him with single-hearted fidelity.

So there was an additional element beyond anything that could be connected with credulity, superstition, or a belief in supernormal agencies that caused in me this knowledge that Voodoo magic was pragmatically effective, whether for good or evil; that caused me to believe in a definite sense that this bright, protective charm which they were engaged in preparing for me now constituted a real and actual protection. There is a queer point involved here which I find difficulty in putting into words. It will doubtless seem to many readers superstitious when I aver that I actually believe the protective virtue would have been destroyed in this charm unless I myself had faith in it. But, suppose I had sat there deeming their whole performance, well, say—silly, or funny? Suppose I had viewed it as futile, childish charlatanism? I do not mean, "Suppose I had laughed or sneered in their faces." I do not mean anything as clearly defined as that. These people were intuitively sensitized to shades of unexpressed feeling, almost like animals. Is it sure that if I had felt a humorous or contemptuous scorn, even secret and unexpressed, I should have been as well protected by this *ouanga*, as safe thereafter among these people in the mountain? I tell you that my believing gave it power. And connected with this truth are many deep collateral truths concerning the power of all magic, miracles, and prayer.

When Papa Théodore had finished pounding the charred aromatic herbs, the *bocor* took a pinch of the substance between his fingers and sprinkled it, muttering incantations, on the pile of green leaves surmounted by the crucifix and the objects which had been a part of myself, of my living body. All arose, and slowly circling, took similarly a pinch of the charred mixture and sprinkled it. I, last of all, was instructed to do likewise. When we were reseated, the *bocor*, with a small glowing brand from the fire, touched off successively three little piles of gunpowder on the cowhide to drive away evil spirits; then he and Papa Théodore drew the two cabalistically marked machetes from the earth and clashed them violently together above all our heads.

Maman Célie handed me a copper coin and instructed me to place it on the packet. And now, before it was tied up, she told me to make a prayer (wish). I hesitated, then stood with both arms stretched straight out before me, palms downward, as I had seen them do and said in English:

"May Papa Legba, Maîtresse Ezilée and the Serpent protect me from misrepresenting these people, and give me power to write honestly of their mysterious religion, for all living faiths are sacred."

Chapter V

GOAT-CRY GIRL-CRY

ON the afternoon of the Friday set for my blood baptism, more than fifty friends and relatives gathered at the habitation of Maman Célie. There was no reason to suppose that we might be disturbed, but as an extra precaution a gay *danse Congo* was immediately organized to cover the real purpose of our congregation. Maman Célie had told me that I would get no sleep that night; so despite the noise I napped until after sunset, when she awakened me and led me across the compound to the *houmfort*.

Through its outer door, which Emanuel stood guarding like a sentinel and unlocked for us, we entered a dim, windowless, cell-like anteroom in which were tethered the sacrificial beasts, a he-goat, two red cocks and two black, an enormous white turkey, and a pair of doves. Huddled there in a corner also was the girl Catherine, Maman Célie's youngest unmarried daughter; why she was there I did not know, and it is needless to say that I wondered.

From this dim, somewhat sinister antechamber we passed through an open doorway into the long, rectangular mystery room, the temple proper, which was lighted with candles and primitive oil lamps that flickered like torches. Its clay walls were elaborately painted with crude serpent symbols [1] and anthropomorphic figures. Papa Legba, guardian of the gates, god of the crossroads, was represented as a venerable old black farmer with a pipe between his teeth; Ogoun Badagris, the bloody warrior, appeared as an old-time Haitian revolutionary general in uniform with a sword;

[1] See Appendix, page 310.

Wangol, master of the land, drove a yoke of oxen; Agoué, master of the seas, puffed out his cheeks to blow a wind and held in the hollow of his hand a tiny boat; the serpent symbols stood for the great Damballa Oueddo, almighty Jove of the Voodoo pantheon, and his consort Ayida Oueddo.

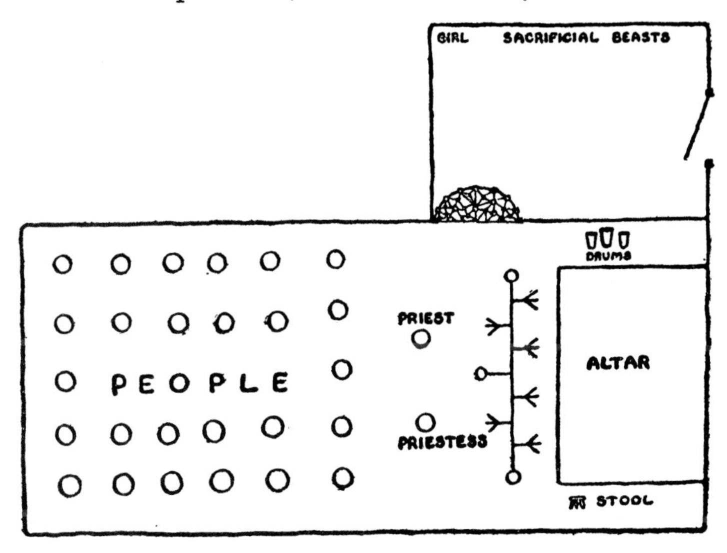

At the near end of the room, close to the doorway through which we had entered, was the wide, low altar, spread over with a white lace tablecloth. In its center was a small wooden serpent, elevated horizontally on a little pole as Moses lifted up the serpent in the wilderness; around this symbol, which was ancient before the Exodus, were grouped thunderstones, Christian crucifixes made in France or Germany, necklaces on which were strung snake vertebrae, others from which hung little medallions of the Virgin Mary. On the corner of the altar nearest me, my *ouanga* had been placed. Grouped also on the altar were earthen jugs containing wine, water, oil; platters of vegetables and fruits, plates containing common bread, and plates containing elaborate sweet fancy cakes, bought days before down in the plain. There were bottles of expensive French-labeled grenadine and orgeat, a bottle of rum, kola-champagne, etc. There were also three cigars, not of the rough sort the peasants smoke, but fat and smooth in their red-gilt bands. With a naïve but justifiable rationality, these worshipers, whose gods were vitally, utterly real, saw no anachronism in offering to their deities the best of everything that could be procured. Maman Célie herself, accompanied by Papa Théodore, had gone by narrow trails across mountains and valleys, leading a donkey down to the modern city, shopping there for their celestial guests and returning with the donkey's panniers heavy laden.

On the altar also was a cone-like mound of cornmeal surmounted by an egg, and before the altar candles were burning, and wicks floating in cocoanut shells of oil. At the left were the three *Rada* drums, at the right was a low wooden stool placed for me.

At the other end of the mystery room, so that a ten-foot open space was left before the altar, were seated on the ground the eighteen or twenty people, all close relatives or trusted friends, who were to witness the ceremony. When I entered, they were swaying and singing:

Papa Legba, ouvrí barrière pour moins!
Papa Legba, coté petits ou?
Papa Legba, ou oué yo!
Papa Legba, ouvrí barrière pour li passer!

(Father Legba, open wide the gate!
Father Legba, where are thy children?
Father Legba, we are here.
Father Legba, open wide the gate that he may pass!)

The *papaloi*, a powerful clean-shaven black man of middle age with red turban and a bright-colored embroidered stole over his shoulders, traced with cornmeal this cabalistic design on the bare earth before the altar:

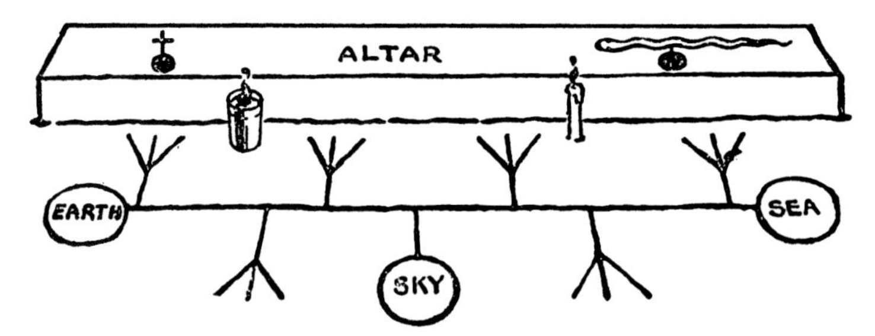

It measured perhaps twelve feet from end to end. The circles, it was afterward explained to me, represented, from left to right, earth, sky, and sea. (Adepts of the esoteric will read here earth, air, and water, or if of a certain school will read earth, air, fire, and water, accepting the central sky-circle as a symbol also of the sun.) All these matters indeed entered into it, but the simpler interpretation was dominant. The forked marks, all connecting, with lines interjoining them with the three circles, thence radiating toward the altar and reversely toward the worshipers, were symbols of the invisible paths through which the gods and mysteries would move.

Into the earth circle the *papaloi* poured oil, flour, and wine, while the people chanted, "*Wangol maît' la terre*" (Wangol is master of the earth). Into the sky circle he poured rum and ashes, while they chanted, "*Damballa Oueddo, ou maît' la ciel*" (Damballa Oueddo, thou art master of the sky). Into the sea circle he poured water, while they sang, "*Papa Agoué, li maît' la mer*" (Father Agoué, he is master of the sea).

A number of solos interspersed this general chanting. It was impossible to retain them all in memory. I could not make pencil notes there; not even Maman Célie was able afterward to repeat them all for me, and the next day some of the singers were gone. There was one song to Papa

Agoué, however, which I partly remembered because it had seemed to me beautiful, and later I rode to find the singer and transcribe it. It was:

Agoué, woyó! woyó!
Maît' Agoué reter lans la mer;
Li tirer canot.

Bassin blé
Reter toi zilet;
Nèg coqui' lans mer zorage;
Li tirer canot là.

Agoué, woyó! woyó!

(Hail to Father Agoué
Who dwells in the sea!
He is the Lord of ships.

In a blue gulf
There are three little islands.
The negro's boat is storm-tossed,
Father Agoué brings it safely in.

Hail to Father Agoué!)

When this singing and pouring of libations were ended, the *papaloi* sealed the open doorway by tracing thus across its earthen sill:

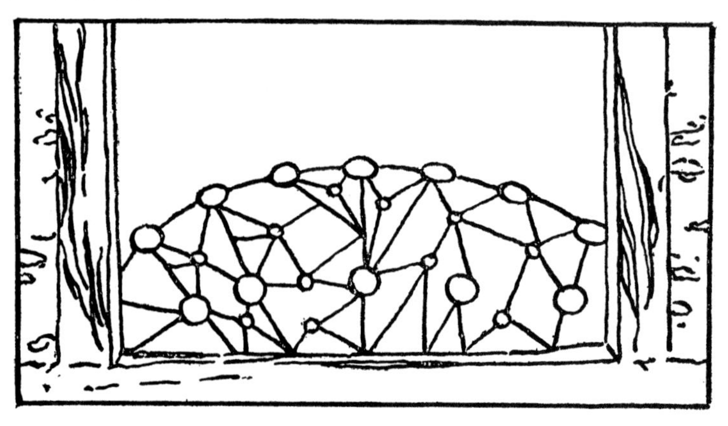

See page 55

"At the left of the altar were the *Rada* drums."

Evil or unwelcome forces which sought to enter would become entangled in the lines and go wandering from circle to circle like lost souls among the stars.

This done, he began the real service, for which all thus far had been but a preparation. He stood with arms raised before the altar and said solemnly, "*Lans nom tout Loi et tout Mystère*" (In the name of all the Gods and all the Mysteries).

Maman Célie advanced at a sign from the *papaloi* and was invested by him, with the scarlet robe and headdress of ostrich feathers black and red, as *mamaloi* or priestess. This was accompanied by a shrill chant:

Ayida Oueddo, ou couleuvre moins!
Qui lé ou filer ou cou z'éclai!

(Ayida Oueddo, my serpent goddess,
When you come it is like the lightning flash!)

At the same time now I heard through the chanting a sharp long-drawn continuous hissing. It was Maman Célie, hissing like a snake, drawing and expelling the breath through her teeth.

I looked for Maman Célie's familiar sweet, gentle face, but beneath the black and scarlet plumes I saw now only what seemed a rigid mask. I felt that I was looking into the face of a strange, dreadful woman, or into the face of something which I had never seen before. As I watched, the cheeks of this black mask were deeply indrawn so that the face became skull-like, and then alternately puffed out as if the skull had been covered with flesh and come alive.

As the chanting died away, she whirled three times and flung herself prostrate before the altar with her lips pressed against the earth.

Emanuel, without donning sacerdotal garb, but now acting as a sort of altar servant, brought in the two red cocks.

Each was handled gently, almost reverently, by the *papaloi*, as he knelt holding it and with white flour traced on its back a cross. One of the small sweet cakes was crumbled, and each cock must peck at it from the *mamaloi's* hand. This was awaited patiently. At the moment when each bird consented to receive the consecrated food, the priestess seized it and rose wildly dancing, whirling with the cock held by its head and feet in her upstretched hands, its wings violently fluttering. Round and round she whirled while the drums throbbed in a quick, tangled, yet steady rhythm. With a sudden twist the cock's head was torn off and as she whirled the blood flew out as if from a sprinkling-pot. The other birds, the black cocks and the dove, were dealt with similarly. As she danced with the white living doves, it was beautiful, and it seemed to me natural also that they should presently die. Blood of the doves was saved in a china cup.

A thing which had a different, a horror-beauty like a mad Goya etching, occurred when the black priestess did her death dance with the huge white turkey. Though far from feeble, possessed of great vitality, she was a slender woman, slightly formed, whose nervous strength lay not in muscular weight. When the turkey's wings spread wide and began to flap frantically above her head as she whirled, the great bird seemed larger and more powerful than she; it seemed that she would be dragged from her feet, hurled to the ground, or flown away with fabulously into the sky. And as she sought finally to tear off its head, sought to clutch its body between her knees, it attacked her savagely, beating her face and breasts, beating at her so that she was at moments enfolded by the great white wings, so that bird and woman seemed to mingle struggling in a monstrous, mythical embrace. But her fatal hands were still upon its throat, and in that swanlike simulacre of the deed which for the male is always like a little death, it died.

So savage had this scene been that it was almost like an

anticlimax when the sacrificial goat was now led through the doorway to the altar, but new and stranger things, contrasting, were yet to happen before other blood was shed. He was a sturdy brown young goat, with big, blue, terrified, almost human eyes, eyes which seemed not only terrified but aware and wondering. At first he bleated and struggled, for the odor of death was in the air, but finally he stood quiet, though still wide-eyed, while red silken ribbons were twined in his little horns, his little hoofs anointed with wine and sweet-scented oils, and an old woman who had come from far over the mountain for this her one brief part in the long ceremony sat down before him and crooned to him alone a song which might have been a baby's lullaby.

When it was finished, the *papaloi* sat down before the little goat and addressed to it a discourse in earnest tones. He told the little goat that it would soon pass through the final gates before us all, instructed it in the mysteries, and pleaded with it concerning its conduct on the other side. But before it passed through the gate, he explained, certain magical changes, making its path easier, would occur on this side. Therefore it need have no fear. Upon its forehead he traced a cross and circle, first with flour and afterward with blood of the doves. Then he presented to it a green, leafy branch to eat.

This goat had by now become inevitably personal to me. I had conceived an affectionate interest in him while the old woman was singing. I recalled what had happened to the other creatures at the moment they touched food, and I had an impulse to cry out to him, "Don't do that, little goat! Don't touch it!" But it was a fleeting, purely sentimental impulse. Not for anything, no matter what would happen, could I have seriously wished to stop that ceremony. I believe in such ceremonies. I hope that they will never die out or be abolished. I believe that in some form or another they answer a deep need of the universal human soul. I, who in a sense believe in no religion, believe yet in them all, asking only that they be alive—as religions.[2] Codes of rational ethics and human brotherly love are useful, but they do not touch this thing underneath. Let religion have its bloody sacrifices, yes, even human sacrifices, if thus our souls may be kept alive. Better a black *papaloi* in Haiti with blood-stained hands who believes in his living gods than a frock-coated minister on Fifth Avenue reducing Christ to a solar myth and rationalizing the Immaculate Conception.

And so I did not cry out.

And the goat nibbled the green leaves.

But no knife flashed.

In the dim, bare anteroom with its windowless gray walls, the girl Catherine had remained all this time huddled in a corner, as if drugged or half asleep.

Emanuel had to clutch her tightly by the arm to prevent her from stumbling when they brought her to the altar. Maman Célie hugged her and moaned and shed tears as if they were saying good-by forever. The *papaloi* pulled them apart, and some one gave the girl a drink of rum from a bottle. She began to protest in a dull sort of angry, whining way when they forced her down on her knees before the lighted candles. The *papaloi* wound round her forehead red ribbons like those which had been fastened around the horns of the goat, and Maman Célie, no longer as a mourning mother but as an officiating priestess, with rigid face aided in pouring the oil and wine on the girl's head, feet, hands, and breast.

All this time the girl had been like a fretful, sleepy, annoyed child, but gradually she became docile, somber, staring with quiet eyes, and presently began a weird song of

[2] See Appendix, page 313.

lamentation. I think she was extemporizing both the words and the melody. She sang:

Cochon marron saché chemin caille;
Moins mandé ça li gagnin.
"Nans Léogane tout moon malade O!"

Béf marron saché chemin caille.
Moins mandé ça li gagnin.
"Nans gros morne tout moon malade O!"

Cabrit marron saché chemin caille.
Moins mandé ça li gagnin.
"Nans Guinea tout moon malade O!"

M'pas malade, m'a p'mourri!

(The wild pig came seeking me;
I said why have you come?
"Every one is sick in Léogane!"

The wild bull came seeking me;
I said why have you come?
"Every one is sick in the mountains!"

The wild goat came seeking me;
I said why have you come?
"Every one is sick in Africa!"

So I who am not sick must die!)

And as that black girl sang, and as the inner meaning of her song came to me, I seemed to hear the voice of Jephtha's daughter doomed to die by her own father as a sacrifice to Javeh, going up to bewail her virginity on Israel's lonely mountain. Her plight in actuality was rather that of Isaac bound by Abraham on Mount Moriah; a horned beast would presently be substituted in her stead; but the moment for that mystical substitution had not yet come, and as she sang she was a daughter doomed to die.

The ceremony of substitution, when it came, was pure effective magic of a potency which I have never seen equaled in Dervish monastery or anywhere. The goat and the girl, side by side before the altar, had been startled, restive, nervous. The smell of blood was in the air, but there was more than that hovering; it was the eternal, mysterious odor of death itself which both animals and human beings always sense, but not through the nostrils. Yet now the two who were about to die mysteriously merged, the girl symbolically and the beast with a knife in its throat, were docile and entranced, were like automatons. The *papaloi* monotonously chanting, endlessly repeating, "Damballa calls you, Damballa calls you," stood facing the altar with his arms outstretched above their two heads. The girl was now on her hands and knees in the attitude of a quadruped, directly facing the goat, so that their heads and eyes were on a level, less than ten inches apart, and thus they stared fixedly into each other's eyes, while the *papaloi's* hands weaved slowly, ceaselessly above their foreheads, the forehead of the girl and the forehead of the horned beast, each wound with red ribbons, each already marked with the blood of a white dove. By shifting slightly I could see the big, wide, pale-blue, staring eyes of the goat, and the big, black, staring eyes of the girl, and I could have almost sworn that the black eyes were gradually, mysteriously becoming those of a dumb beast, while a human soul was beginning to peer out through the blue. But dismiss that, and still I tell you that pure magic was here at work, that something very real and fearful was occurring. For as the priest wove his ceaseless incantations, the girl began a low, piteous bleating in which there was nothing, absolutely nothing, human; and soon a thing infinitely more unnatural occurred; the goat was moaning and crying like a human child. I believe that through my Druse and Yezidee accounts I have earned a deserved reputation for being not too credulous in the face of marvels. But I was in the presence now of a thing that could not be denied. Old magic was here at work, and it worked appallingly. What difference does it make whether we call it supernatural or merely supernormal? What difference does it make if we say that the girl was drugged—as I suspect she was—or that both were hypnotized? Of course they were, if you like. And what then? We live surrounded by mysteries and imagine that by inventing names we explain them.

Other signs and wonders became manifest. Into this little temple lost among the mountains came in answer to goat-cry girl-cry the Shaggy Immortal One of a thousand names whom the Greeks called Pan. The goat's lingam became erect and rigid, the points of the girl's breasts visibly hardened and were outlined sharply pressing against the coarse, thin, tight-drawn shift that was her only garment. Thus they faced each other motionless as two marble figures on the frieze of some ancient phallic temple. They were like inanimate twin lamps in which a sacred flame burned, steadily yet unconsuming.

While the *papaloi* still wove his spells, his hands moving ceaselessly like an old woman carding wool in a dream, the priestess held a twig green with tender leaves between the young girl and the animal. She held it on a level with their mouths, and neither saw it, for they were staring fixedly into each other's eyes as entranced mediums stare into crystal globes, and with their necks thrust forward so that their foreheads almost touched. Neither could therefore see the leafy branch, but as the old *mamaloi's* hand trembled, the leaves flicked lightly as if stirred by a little breeze against the hairy muzzle of the goat, against the chin and soft lips of the girl. And after moments of breathless watching, it was the girl's lips which pursed out and began to nibble at the leaves. Human beings, normally, when eating, open their mouths and take the food directly in between their teeth. Except for sipping liquids they do not use their lips. But the girl's lips now nibbling at the leaves were like those of a ruminating animal. Her hands, of course, were flat on the ground so that in a sense she perforce must have eaten without using them, somewhat in the manner of a quadruped; but in a castle near the edge of the Nefud desert I once watched closely a woman eating whose hands were tied behind her back, and that woman, opening her mouth and baring her teeth, took the fragments of food directly between her teeth, as any normal human being would. But this girl now pursed her lips and used them nibbling as horned cattle do. It sounds a slight thing, perhaps, in the describing, but it was weird, unnatural, unhuman.

As she nibbled thus, the *papaloi* said in a hushed but wholly matter-of-fact whisper like a man who had finished a hard, solemn task and was glad to rest, "*Ça y est*" (There it is).

The *papaloi* was now holding a machete, ground sharp and shining. Maman Célie, priestess, kneeling, held a *gamelle*, a wooden bowl. It was oblong. There was just space enough to thrust it narrowly between the mystically identified pair. Its rim touched the goat's hairy chest and the girl's body, both their heads thrust forward above it. Neither seemed conscious of anything that was occurring, nor did the goat flinch when the *papaloi* laid his hand upon its horns. Nor did the goat utter any sound as the knife was drawn quickly, deeply across its throat. But at this instant, as the blood gushed like a fountain into the wooden bowl, the girl, with a shrill, piercing, then strangled bleat of agony, leaped, shuddered, and fell senseless before the altar.

At the moment the knife flashed across the goat's throat, the company had begun to chant, not high or loud but with a sort of deep, hushed fervor, across which the girl's inhuman bleating had shrilled sharp as another invisible blade. Now they continued chanting while the celebrants performed their various offices. They chanted:

See page 63

"... and as she sang, she was
a daughter doomed to die."

Damballa Oueddo odan q'icit
Mandé ça la! Oué!
Ayida Oueddo odan q'icit
Mandé ça la! Oué!

(Damballa and Ayida, behold the deed we have done as you commanded.)

The body of the goat was thrown as a ritually useless and no longer sacred thing through the door into the anteroom. The body of the unconscious girl, spattered with blood, was lifted carefully into Emanuel's arms and carried away, followed by two old women versed in magic who would attend her recovery. If Maman Célie, her face still like a terrible, inspired mask, bestowed one fleeting glance on either body, I did not see it. She was revolving slowly before the altar with the bowl in her outstretched arms and now held it to the *papaloi*, who received it, drank, then placed it on the altar, and with a little china cup poured libations within each of the three cabalistic circles on the earth. They also sang an invocation to Ybo, another of the ancient gods.[3]

There was a pause, a lull, in which I who had been for hours too utterly absorbed to give myself a thought, recalled that all this ceremonial was leading up to an event which concerned me more deeply than any other present. The time had now come. A very old black man, deeply wrinkled, with a beard that was like Spanish moss turned snowy white, who had been sitting silent all the while, took from a bag at his feet a white cloth which he wound around his head, and a white embroidered garment like a cassock which he put over his shoulders. He invested himself without the aid of other hands as a black pope or emperor might have done. He was not of our mountain. He had come riding upon a donkey from beyond the great Morne. Maman Célie had

[3] See Appendix, page 318.

summoned him and had paid the expenses from her own purse. It was a thing for which she would never permit me to repay her. As he arose and beckoned me to kneel at last before the altar, there was absolute silence. He was Voodoo of the Voodoo, but as he laid his hand upon my head it was neither in creole that he spoke, nor French, nor even the almost forgotten language of old Guinea. I heard as in a dream, low, clear, and deep as the voices of old men rarely are, "*In nomine Patris, et Filii, et Spiritus Sancti. Amen.*"

And when still kneeling there with my eyes closed, I heard as from a great distance and as an echo from years long past his sure voice intoning that most marvelous and mysterious of all Latin invocations, "Rosa Mystica . . . Tower of David . . . Tower of Ivory . . . House of Gold . . . Gate of Heaven," it seemed to me that I heard too the rolling of mighty organs beneath vaulted domes. . . .

Oil, wine, and water were poured upon my head, marks were traced upon my brow with white flour, and then I was given to eat ritually from the cakes upon the altar, to drink from the wine, rum, and syrups there. Parts of many cakes were crumbled together in a little cup and were put into my mouth with a spoon; likewise were mingled a few drops from each of the many bottles.

This, it seemed, had been a preliminary consecration rite in sincere inclusion of the Christian divinities, saints, and powers. Now the Voodoo chanting recommenced, and for the first time my own name was mingled with the creole and African words. They were beseeching Legba to open wide the gates for me, Damballa and Ayida to receive me. A sort of mad fervor was again taking possession of them all. The old *hougan*, shouting now so that his voice could be heard above the singing, demanded once more silence, and placing both hands heavily upon my head, pronounced a long mixed African and creole invocation, calling down to witness all the gods and goddesses of ancient Africa.[4] Still commanding

[4] See Appendix, page 318.

silence, he dipped his hand into the wooden bowl and traced on my forehead the bloody Voodoo cross.

Then he lifted the bowl, hesitated for a queer instant as if in courteous doubt—it was a strange, trivial thing to occur at such a moment—and then picked up a clean spoon. Maman Célie interfered angrily. So the bowl itself was held to my lips and three times I drank. The blood had a clean, warm, salty taste. In physical fact, I was drinking the blood of a recently slain goat, but by some mysterious transubstantiation not without its parallels in more than one religion other than Voodoo, I was drinking the blood of the girl Catherine who in the body of the goat had mystically died for me and for all miserable humanity from Léogane to Guinea.[5]

One small thing yet remained to be done. I had been told that it would be done, and its meaning explained to me. I had been told also that for no white man alive or dead had it ever been done before. The *papaloi* took from the altar an egg which had surmounted a little pyramid of cornmeal, and holding it aloft in his cupped hands, pronounced incantation. As the blood had represented the mystery of death, sacrifice, and purification, likewise fertilization as it was poured upon the earth, the egg now represented rebirth, productivity, fertility, re-creation. Maman Célie, the priestess, took it from the hands of the *papaloi*, traced with it a new cross on my forehead, and dashed it to the earth. My knees were spattered. Then the priestess tore off her feathered headdress, and Maman Célie, the old woman, sank down beside me, put her arms around me, and cried, "Legba, Papa Legba, open wide the gates for this my little one."

[5] See Appendix, page 319.

Chapter VI

THE GOD INCARNATE

IF Maman Célie treated me as one of her own sons, no more, no less, mending my clothes, wrapping up my head in a mess of herbs and soapsuds (whether I would or no) when she thought I had caught *danghi* fever, scolding me on some occasions—but loving me—and showing me respect, thank God, on none, the attitude of the other members of this patriarchal family group at my adopted home in the mountains was slightly different. It was not that I was a *blanc*, a white man; they had come to care nothing about that; it was rather that after all our intimacy they deemed me still *gros moon*, important "company," an honored guest. The big peristyle, an open straw-roofed pavilion, inclosed only by a waist-high lattice fence to keep out the pigs and dogs that roved by night, was my guest chamber. I slept on a cot with sheets and the children made my bed. Marie-Céleste, an unmarried daughter, spied upon my awakenings, brought me black coffee. The grown sons generally insisted on helping saddle and unsaddle my horse. The young naked brats who toddled and crawled about regarded me still with a slight awe because of my boots and because they were forbidden to enter the peristyle. A table with a checkered cloth, knives, forks, and china plates was laid for me in the peristyle. Usually Maman Célie and Papa Théodore dined with me, but sometimes I dined alone.

Thus accustomed by habitude to all these little considerations, I was roundly surprised one evening, and, I am afraid, ungraciously annoyed at the outset, when the following thing occurred.

Capitan Despine, a *gros nègre* whom I knew well, had ridden up to the habitation on a friendly call, and had been invited to stop and dine with me in the peristyle. We were seated alone at the table. Papa Théodore was occupied, and was to have coffee and rum with us later. It was during a lull in a hard week-end. No one had slept the previous night, and this may explain the fact, perhaps, that the nerves of all of us were a bit on edge. I know that I welcomed the lull and Despine's amiable, unexciting matter-of-factness with his talk of cotton crops and rural gossip. Dinner was late, and I was hungry.

Marie-Céleste had just brought to the table a steaming bowl of chicken stew, boiled plantains, and freshly baked hot biscuit.

As I was helping Despine's plate, Rafael, the second son of the family, a man about forty, entered the peristyle. He was an unassuming fellow who had always treated me with friendly deference.

Now he strode to our table and said gruffly, sharply, "*Lever ou, tout suite, s'ou plais.*" (Get up, immediately, please).

Despine pushed back his chair preparatory to arising. But I sat still and motioned Despine to do the same. Whatever it was, it could wait until we had eaten. I saw the chicken getting cold. I said as much to Rafael, with a slight impatience. He stared a moment, confused, uncertain, then said, "*Mais mystère p'vini*" (But a mystery approaches).

But I was in a wrong mood. I was hungry and tired.

I saw Rafael glancing toward the gate of the peristyle, and just inside it was a barefoot man in ragged overalls and a torn straw hat, a field laborer of the poorest class who moved slowly as if sleep-walking. Behind him outside the peristyle was a hushed group of strained black faces. Moods are uncontrollable. I was not impressed. Of course all this, which I am deviously telling, actually occurred within fifteen or twenty seconds.

Then suddenly something happened to my friend Rafael, and it was well that my eyes had turned back to him. The muscles of his black neck and shoulders swelled like those of a gorilla, his clenched, rigid hands came up slowly toward my throat, like those of a galvanized, trembling automaton, and he said hoarsely, in creole: "*Up! It is a god who comes. . . .*"

I realized my danger almost too late. Had I not then leapt instantly to my feet, Rafael would have throttled me.

As if sleep-walking still, the peasant in ragged overalls slowly approached our dinner table. Save for him and the three of us who now stood withdrawn, the peristyle was empty, but faces thronged all round it. There was no chanting, shrieking, as when the ordinary *mystères* or *loïs* descend. There was thick silence. The man now stood over our table, staring at it as if dreaming. In addition to the food there was a bottle of rum and a clay water jug. He picked up the rum bottle, hesitating, and set it down again. With his fingers he took up a piece of the stewed chicken, started to lift it toward his mouth, and put it back into the dish. He stared about him as if not knowing what to do. Curiously enough then, he saluted us vaguely, and shuffled toward the gate. Meanwhile Maman Célie and Papa Théodore had been called. Bundled in her arms, she was carrying her own priestess' headdress of bright, dyed ostrich feathers, the *papaloi's* embroidered stole, and a long ceremonial necklace, taken from the altar, on which were strung big beads, crucifixes, bullets, thimbles, charms, human teeth, and medals. They did not kneel before the man. They bowed low to him, from the waist, so that the upper parts of their bodies were horizontal. Then both lay prostrate before him and kissed his feet. Then they stood erect before him and began dressing him as they would an inanimate idol, while he stood docile, still as if dreaming. They draped the bright-colored stole and a surplice over his shoulders, tore the band into which the ostrich feathers were sewn so that it would fit his head, loaded him with necklaces. The women in the crowd now stripped off their own necklaces, rings, bracelets, and offered them with outstretched arms across the peristyle railings. Rings and bracelets which were too small to be pushed on his fingers or over his hands were strung together on a cord and hung round his neck. Maman Célie and Papa Théodore now fell back as if waiting to see what the man would do. He stood there alone in the lighted, vacant space, bedizened like an idol, doing nothing whatsoever, except, I noticed, that his black expressionless face began to stream with perspiration, though the night in these high mountains was cool. Maman Célie found time to whisper in my ear that a powerful and in some of his manifestations dreadful one of the elder gods, Ogoun Badagris, had entered the body of this man; that they were grateful for the presence of the god, but also frightened. And it was for this reason, I realized, that Rafael would surely have attacked me had I not leapt from the table at his last command. It was never satisfactorily explained to me how the incarnation had been identified as Ogoun Badagris. It was from some words the man had said and some gestures he had made when the trance-state had first fallen upon him, but those who had heard and seen the stroke, which had occurred outside in the compound, were not of Maman Célie's household, and were reluctant afterward to talk about it.

Again the man-god, hesitating, approached the table, where our chicken stew had long since grown cold. The god still wished food and drink, though apparently he did not care for this of ours; but it was a favorable sign. A procession was formed to the *houmfort*. Maman Célie and Papa Théodore walked close at the right and left hand of the god, a half pace behind him; it looked as if the man-god was leading the procession, but I think really they were propelling him gently toward the door of the temple. Meanwhile the crowd began singing:

Ogoun viní caille nous;
Li gran' gout, li gagnin soif.
Grand me'ci, Ogoun Badagris!
Manger, bweh!

(Ogoun is in our house; he is hungry and thirsty, and we are grateful. Eat and drink, Ogoun Badagris.)

This joyfully, impromptu. And then more solemnly, because they were still a little frightened, they intoned the formal ritual chant:

Ogoun Badagris, ou général sanglant;
Ou saizí clé z'orage, ou scell'orage;
Ou fais katáou z'eclaï.

(Ogoun Badagris, bloody warrior, you hold the key to the storm-clouds; you lock them up; you loose the thunder and lightning.)

When we first entered the *houmfort*, crowding in as many of us as could, wise Maman Célie did a little thing that seemed to me natural and lovely. It was the sort of thing that made her Maman Célie—that made her different from all the rest. Hastily crouching before the altar, with a quick side glance at the dread Ogoun Badagris who still seemed to be vaguely dazed in his then present incarnation, she surreptitiously removed the large Damballa snake staff which had occupied the position of central honor, and pushed over into its place a thunderstone, which was the special symbol of the god who had dropped down to visit us.

The mystery room and the anteroom were crowded to suffocation, but a little space was left from which they pressed back as if it had been inclosed by invisible ropes, before the altar where Ogoun Badagris stood alone. The people were so crowded that only those in the front ranks

" . . . they were staring fixedly as entranced mediums stare into crystal globes.'

could kneel. Some mothers had brought in brats who peered wide-eyed, frightened, from behind skirts to see the marvel. Like Moses peering from the cleft on Sinai, they were able to glimpse only the hinder parts of the god. I was standing aside, near the altar, looking over Maman Célie's shoulder. The only lighting was from candles on the altar. When I looked at the man's face, his head surmounted by ostrich plumes, his neck loaded with beads, his shoulders covered by the bright-colored vestments, I saw only a dazed peasant masquerading in fantastic garments. But when I looked at his black hands, black as if they had been carved from basalt or unpolished ebony, all the fingers and thumbs loaded with glittering rings and bangles, it did something curious, almost hypnotic, to my mental and emotional processes. My rational faculties ceased temporarily to function, and it seemed to me that I was in the presence of something indeed mysteriously superhuman. And when this creature at last bent forward and began to move those black, jeweled hands, vaguely groping toward the objects on the altar, it was for me as if some monstrous, black, bedizened idol had come alive. I was a little afraid of it. We were all a little afraid of it, I think, even Maman Célie. We were chanting in two endlessly repeated, monotonous minor chords. I was singing without at first having realized it. Something had got inside me. And because I was in that semi-hallucinatory state, I saw presently—as truly, I think, as any mortal eyes have ever seen it, for truth of this sort is purely subjective in the last analysis—a god descended to earth and made incarnate, accepting and devouring (for devouring is the only word when gods or beasts slake their hunger) the meats arrayed for him upon his own sacrificial altar.

He was indeed anhungered and athirst. He did not seat himself before the altar as if it were a table. No book of etiquette has ever been written for the immortal gods. He climbed ponderously upon the altar, and crouching there like an animal, began eating and drinking ravenously but without haste. Clutching a whole handful of little cakes, he crammed some of them into his mouth, then dropped the rest to lift with both hands a wooden bowl of congealing goat's blood, and drank deep. Thus alternating, he ate his fill of the fruits and meats, drinking from the dozen various bottles which stood open on the altar, ranging at random from grenadine to rum and orgeat. He seemed utterly self-contained, utterly unconscious of the presence of any of us. He was the god, and we were less than nothing in his presence.

Yet when he had finished, he deigned to notice us. He arose, stood before the altar, and for the first time began to speak. My knowledge of creole is practical and fairly thorough, but I could not follow him. I could follow perhaps a third of what he said, or less. There were many words and phrases of definite African origin, a very few of which I knew, but much of it was jargon, a speaking "in strange tongues," as the modern Apostolic sectarians speak when the Pentecostal flame descends. As an entirety, however, it was far from senseless. It involved, as Maman Célie verified for me afterward, predictions and definite commands relating to protective agricultural measures against the *avalasse*, the approaching spring storms and torrents. It related also to other definite matters which I regret can have no place in this chronicle.

When the events which I have described were finished, we emerged beneath the stars, and the god, replete with food and quietly drunken, lay down to sleep alone in his silent temple. But when morning came, the god had departed. Only an humble ragged negro lay there dozing at the foot of the altar.

The small intimate sequels of more or less unusual occurrences hold sometimes an interest which makes them worth recording. My first concern next day was to find Rafael and offer apology. He bore me no malice. He said that, of course, I hadn't understood, and that part of the fault was really his for not having explained more clearly. But it had all happened so quickly. Anyway, he said, it was lucky that I had jumped up in time, for something *funeste* might have happened. I was surprised that he knew such a lugubrious word; it isn't usual creole. I am sure, since he used that particular word, he was not referring to the mere physical fact that he had been on the hairbreadth verge of strangling me. I have no wish to exaggerate the episode. It was the only occasion among them when I was in bodily danger, and it came about as a sort of accident, through my own stupidity.

I was interested in the young black man whose body had been for a time the abode of Ogoun Badagris, and curious to see how he would now be treated by the others. I observed that he was shown no special attention, and had gained no prestige or merit. He was like a common, empty cup, in which a rare elixir had for a brief period chanced to be contained. No odor of godhead clung to him. The man himself had no recollection whatsoever of anything which had occurred. Not even the rings, beads, and necklaces remained which the women had showered for his adornment. These were reclaimed from a basket, to be cherished as sacred.

My horse stood saddled for the last time beside the peristyle.

Good-by, Théodore; good-by, Emanuel, Rafael, Catherine, Marie-Céleste—good-by to you all of the mountain.

And now farewell, Maman Célie . . . farewell, old priestess of dark mysteries . . . farewell, old mother whom I love. . . . I feel your arms around me and your wrinkled cheek wet with tears.

Part Two: BLACK SORCERY

Chapter I

THE ALTAR OF SKULLS

In downtown Port-au-Prince, diagonally across the street from Mohr & Laurin's, where Marine Corps officers, their wives, and occasional tourists go to buy jazz records and cocktail shakers and to have their Kodak films developed, there is a small pharmacy with a large gilded lion suspended from an iron strut projecting over the sidewalk.

Above this pharmacy is located the clinic of Dr. Arthur C. Holly, who has the largest practice of any negro doctor in the Haitian capital. Mornings, from ten to noon, he treats charity patients, and his waiting-room is crowded. In the afternoon he treats the rich and well-to-do by appointment.

His desk is cluttered with the latest medical journals; his laboratory and operating-room are scientifically equipped; there are few abler physicians, black or white, in the West Indies.

But when Dr. Holly goes home at night, to his lovely villa, set among palm trees and flower gardens, behind a high brick wall with a tall grilled gate at the entrance to the driveway, he discards medical journals and buries his nose in a totally different sort of literature—Paracelsus, Eliphas Levy, Frazer, Swedenborg, William James, Blavatski—for Dr. Holly is profoundly, studiously interested in comparative religion, folk-lore, mysticism, and magic. His own new book on these subjects, when it is finished and published in France, will be a permanent contribution.

I am not betraying a confidence, nor will these statements harm my friend when they are read in Haiti, for his patients and the public know that these two sides of Dr. Holly are kept, as it were, in watertight compartments, and that when they go to him for diagnosis he consults no oracles save those of strictly modern science.

Most cultivated urban Haitians either fear or pretend to deny the existence of magic and Voodoo, but to Dr. Holly they have been for many years a rich field for scholarly and esoteric research. The peasants, whom he treats without charge, give him their confidence, and he is on intimate terms with half the *papalois* of Haiti, some of whom have been his patients.

To my friend Holly I went one day concerning vague tales of a witchcraft cult in the peninsula, called *le culte des morts*—hoping that if it existed, he might put me in touch with some of its exponents. He was surprised that I should have heard of it.

"These people," he said, "are necromancers (users of corpses for magical purposes), though the word necromancy does not exist in our creole vocabulary. What you ask is difficult, and your Voodoo friends will not be able to help you. The practice is not widespread; most orthodox members of the Petro and Legba Voodoo cults hate and will have no dealings with them. It is barely possible, however, that something may be arranged."

In my investigation of the *culte des morts*, there were failures, refusals, difficulties, disappointments, frustrations.

But one day a boy appeared at my house with a note—I had no telephone—asking me to go down to Dr. Holly's office. I went immediately and found him talking with a country girl, a coal-black, smooth-skinned negress, who seemed to me particularly mild and childlike. He introduced us politely. Her name was Classinia—Mam'selle Classinia. She stood up, almost as tall as I, accepted my hand awkwardly, and noncommittal, soft-voiced, amiable but not friendly, said, "*Bon jou', blanc.*"

Dr. Holly explained that I was his trusted friend, a

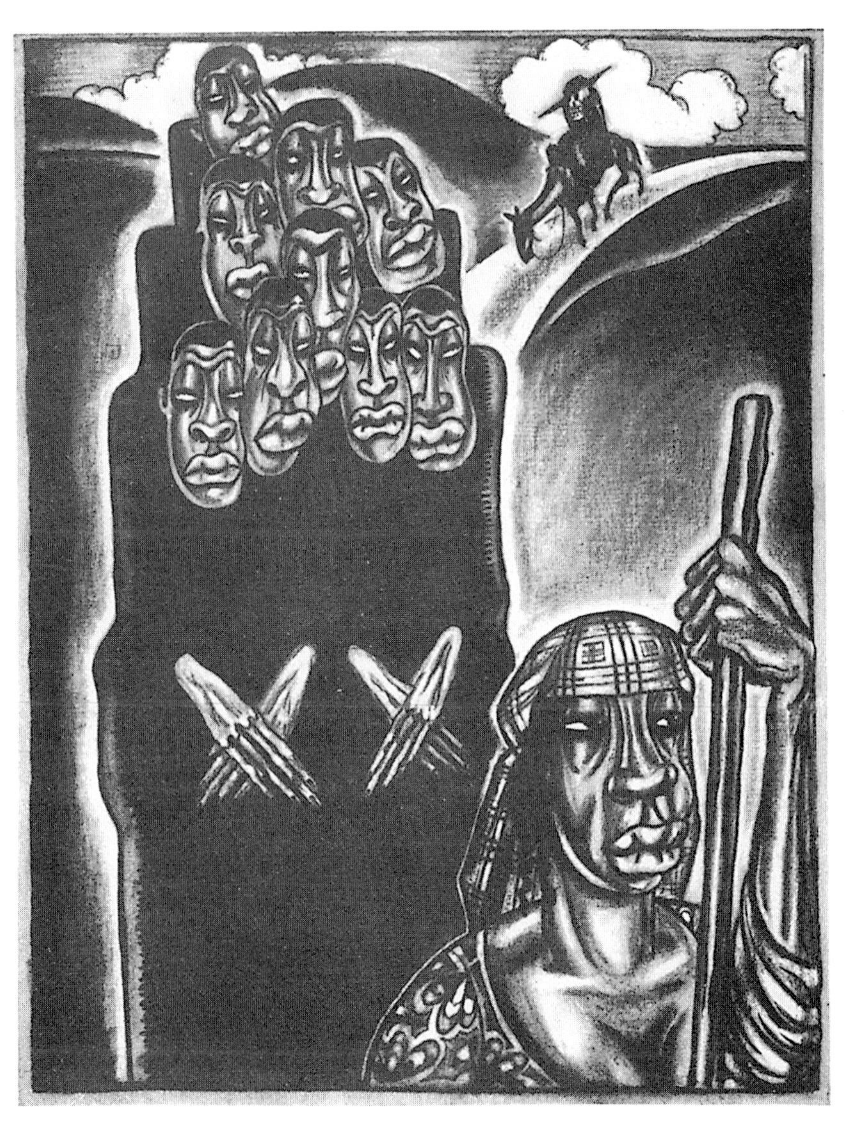

See page 97

" . . . Croyance, leading the nine dead men and women."

white *bocor* who had gone round the world studying the "mysteries" in old Guinea and in countries even farther distant.

"*Oui, papa,*" she agreed blandly, and "*Oui, papa,*" she acquiesced again when Dr. Holly announced that Mam'selle Classinia was a "Nebo" of the *culte des morts*, and that on Saturday afternoon I was going to visit her habitation in the hills. . . .

Dr. Holly had no intention of accompanying me. Since the coming of the American administration he has felt, because of his professional position, that he must forego being present at even technical infractions of the legal prohibition against *sortilège*. As a fellow student of these matters, and as a fellow author, he could help me in obtaining data, but only as far as it involved no infringement of the statutes on his part.

I arrived at the habitation before dusk. An old man and woman were expecting me, but Classinia was not there. She would return presently, they told me. They gave me coffee and I sat smoking, while they went about their occasions. Presently, as darkness fell, people began appearing until two or three dozen had arrived. They looked at me suspiciously, and their grudging salutations were not friendly, but after the old woman had whispered among them, they seemed satisfied, at least not aggressively unpleasant. Time passed, and nothing happened. At last, about nine o'clock they went into the house, and a quarter of an hour later the old man, who seemed to be head of the place—perhaps Classinia's father—emerged and took me inside.

The narrow oblong room was bare except for a common table with a red and white checkered tablecloth on which were laid skulls, bones, a shovel, a pick-ax; there was a wooden cross painted like a totem pole, wreathed by a feather boa. Before it were rows of lighted tapers, slender, brown, crudely-made candles, of the sort placed on graves and in the niches of tombs. There were no Voodoo symbols or sacred objects of any sort. This was not Voodoo, nor was it religious. There was additional light from a smoking tin lamp fastened to a post which supported the roof.

Huddled upon the floor, body to body, some crouching and others prostrate, were a score or more of black men and women, swaying, writhing, moaning.

Before the altar of skulls, facing us, stood three human figures, grotesque, yet indescribably sinister. All three who stood there were women. The tall central figure, the former mild Classinia, now completely changed, wore a soft white muslin skirt, above it a man's long-tailed black frock coat, and on her head a man's high silk hat; her eyes were hidden by dark, smoked goggles. Why it was that as simple a thing as smoked goggles seemed horrible, I cannot tell, unless because they made the face impersonal, inscrutable. Grotesquely in the corner of her mouth, as if stuck into the mouth of a wooden dummy, was an unlighted cigar.

Thus symbolically clothed, she was no longer a woman, but Papa Nebo, the male-female hermaphroditic oracle of the dead. The dark goggles meant that death was blind.

This metamorphosed creature which had been the girl Classinia, but which was now neither man nor woman, or was both, was flanked on either side by two "wives."

At the right stood one woman without special garb, but holding in her hand a heavy bag. Her title was Gouédé Mazacca. In the bag she carried an afterbirth and part of a navel cord, wrapped in the poisonous leaves of the manchineel tree.

At the left stood another woman with a high white turban wound awry. She was poised, motionless like a statue, but with her arms thrust forward, and her hands clutching a half-empty rum bottle and a bludgeon. Her feet were planted wide apart, her head was thrown back, and there was a sort of shameless abandon in the whole posture of her body. She was called Gouédé Oussou, the Drunken One, possibly from a corruption of the creole phrase, *ou soule* (thou art drunk). She was not actually drunk, for no drunken woman could have held that posture for a moment, and she stood fixedly.

There, then, before the altar piled with human bones, stood these three silent figures, in the dull smoky light, while the huddled, groaning, contorted bodies lay prostrate before them on the earthen floor.

These moaning peasants meant to establish contact through the oracle—for various purposes, some innocent, some evil—with persons recently or long since dead. After a period of writhing and groaning, during which one or two of the prostrate forms emitted loud wails, Gouédé Mazacca called out and Gouédé Oussou repeated after her, "*Papa Nebo attend!*" which could mean either "Papa Nebo is waiting to hear you," or "Listen, Papa Nebo." I think it meant the former.

Two or three who had been lying face down got simultaneously to their knees with black hands clutched, outstretched; strained, eye-closed faces, muttering; but only one, a middle-aged man, spoke out loudly.

His son was sick; he feared that the dead mother had put a *ouanga* on the son to make him join her in the grave, and he was begging that the boy be spared. His pleas were whimpering, simple, yet full of terrified emotion. The boy was needed for the spring planting. The family would be in poverty if he grew sicker and died. The habitation would fall in ruin.

When he had finished and waited, a hush fell, broken only by low moans. And the sexless oracle of death began to speak—if any such word as speech could be applied to the dreadful sounds that came from its throat—a series of deep, rasped gutturals, strung together on meaningless vowel monotones:

"*Hgr-r-r-r-u-u-u-u-hgrr-r-r-o-o-o- Hgr-r-r-a-a-a-a-a Oh-h-h-h-uu-uu-uu-uu- Bl-bl-bl-ghra-a-a-a- Ghu-u-u-u-u-u*—"

It was like the prolonged death-rattle from a windpipe choked with phlegm or blood; it was those horrid sounds in skillful savage simulacre.

The oracle was talking with the dead, in the subhuman vernacular of death itself—or at least so it must have seemed to the ears of the waiting listeners.

And it seemed to them that the dead made answer, but through what process of transmission was not altogether clear, for when the oracle paused it was Gouédé Mazacca, she of the afterbirth and poisonous leaves, who said in plain blunt creole:

"Let your son go hang his own garments on a tree near the mother's grave, and plant six candles at the foot of the tree, with three upon the grave itself, and she will be content."[1]

"*Merci, Maman, merci*," whimpered the father.

Other ghastly colloquies followed, always through the death-rattle mumbling of the oracle, ending with blunt pronouncement of Gouédé Mazacca or Gouédé Oussou. There was a dead woman who for spite had made a certain spring go dry; an old farmer who was on his deathbed had forgotten where he had hidden the earthen pot of coins which were the family savings. Similar reasons motivated most of these appeals, though one kneeling woman merely wanted to know whether her father was content with the offerings she placed upon his grave. And one or two, who perhaps had tried the ordinary *ouangas* in vain, clamored for aid from the tomb in wreaking some personal vengeance. Various instructions were given and translated, offerings to be put on graves, exorcisms to be pronounced, *ouangas* to be made with parts of human corpses.

Here was ample scope for the charlatanry and profitable fraud which I had been told the superstitious peasants universally suffered at the hands of rapacious sorcerers. Yet I had the feeling that while Classinia with her family and

[1] See Appendix, page 321.

these other death-cult women obviously reaped profit from their ceremonies—since all who came left gifts of various sorts upon the altar—the chief actors believed in what they were doing, just as did the supposedly "victimized" audience.

I noted that when it was over, Classinia and her two assistants were stupefied, tired, "washed-out," almost to the point of exhaustion, as if they had been under prolonged and violent nervous stress. These people gave me no personal confidence, nor were they particularly friendly. They had permitted me to see what I had just seen only because they had been instructed to do so, and had been assured that I was "safe"—not connected in any way with the gendarmerie or "government."

Upon the three chief sorceresses of this cult, Papa Nebo, Gouédé Mazacca, and Gouédé Oussou—whoever personally they may happen to be—devolves the function of providing new dead bodies when they are needed.[2]

Certainly no white man, certainly not I, and I imagine few Haitians, has ever seen the conjurations which take place between midnight and dawn in some lonely, isolated little country graveyard. The account I am going to give is not even the "first-hand" report of another eye-witness. The man who supplied me the details had never seen it. He had got it directly, however, from a woman who he believes did see it. I am inclined also to believe that it is accurate, but I cannot vouch for it.

The three women carry with them a spade, a pick-ax, a white candle, and a small bag of wild acacia leaves. Arriving among the graves they light the candle and set it at the foot of the wooden cross which usually stands in every country graveyard. If no cross is there, they make one, and set the candle before it. Next they kneel, and taking two stones from a grave, knock them together to awaken Baron

[2] See Appendix, page 321.

Samedi, who is the spirit of the graveyard. Baron Samedi is a big black man with a long white beard. He usually remains invisible, but makes his presence felt by some sign. Without his consent it is dangerous to open a grave. The women pray for this permission and promise, if it is granted, to return with gifts of food, fruit, and copper coins. They then toss the acacia leaves toward him and say:

"*Dormi pa'fumé, Baron Samedi!*" (Sleep sweetly, Baron Samedi!)

Baron Samedi, ruler of the cemetery, granting his protection, retires into the earth.[3]

Next they say, "*Exège Morti amo vini*" (probably a corruption of the dog-Latin formula, *Exurgent mortui et acmo venuient*). Distorted old ecclesiastical phrases are frequently used in Haitian sorcery. They say also, "*Mortoo tomboo miyi!*"—a jargonized creole, meaning, "Dead in the tomb, to me!"

Now they set about their grave-robbing with pick and spade. They dig up the body for which they have come and carry it away with them.

The necromantic uses which they make of various parts of the corpse are thoroughly authenticated in many verifiable cases. The facts have appeared even in American military reports of the Caco guerilla uprisings. They rub grease made from the brains upon the edges of machetes and tools, so that they will be intelligent and cut more accurately; on the head of the hammer so that it will know always where to strike; upon the sights of a gun so that the bullet will reach its mark. The heart they dry and use to give courage to weak persons who eat small portions of it or carry bits of it in a tiny bag strung around their necks. From other parts of the body are concocted *ouangas*, *caprelatas*, philters, charms for various purposes, benevolent and malevolent. The skull and bones become a

[3] See Appendix, page 323.

part of the permanent altar paraphernalia.[4] This *culte des morts* is a limited witchcraft group. In America the word Voodoo has come to mean indiscriminately any negro sorcery, secret ceremony, or old African witch-doctor practice. In Haiti the word is similarly loosely used sometimes even by natives, so that when they wish to distinguish sharply they are likely to use the word *Rada* as the name of their religion, and *Service Petro* or *Service Legba* for their ceremonial religious rites. This *culte des morts* is not *Rada.*

While the corpse sorcerers and their adherents are a group limited and feared, it is true that all Haitian peasants are on curiously intimate terms with their dead and seem almost totally devoid of that special, unreasoning terror of graveyards, ghosts, "haunts," and dead bodies (merely as such) which is traditional among rural negroes—and some white people too—in the United States.

Riding through the mountains between Morne Rouis and Les Verettes late one night I heard shouting, singing, and sounds of *bamboche* in a group of habitations hidden by a clump of banana trees in a ravine below the trail. If the drums had been going, I should have guessed it to be an ordinary Congo dance. I dismounted and led my horse zigzagging downward.

One of the compounds with its huts was lighted by tin lamps and resin torches, the yard thronged with people. All the little neighborhood, apparently, had gathered there. Baskets of gingerbread, biscuit, and dried fish, a cook-pot simmering over the embers, indicated they were making a night of it. The women and girls were bedecked in their Sunday best—gold earrings, bead necklaces, bright kerchiefs. In a corner, near a torch stuck in the bamboo fence, some men were playing cards, and a second group were noisily shooting craps.

Others crowded round me in amiable welcome—"*Bon soir, blanc,*" or "*Bon soir, lieutenant,*" or "*Bon soir, doc-*

[4] See Appendix, page 331.

teur"—feeling me friendly, but guessing variously what I might be. They offered me *clairin*, raw white rum, in tin cups. I drank a little and said, "*Oui, me'ci. Mais ça ou fais, tout moon icit?*"

"*Grand moon li mort*" (The old man is dead), they replied. "*Entrer donc oué li*" (Come in and see him).

They escorted me indoors to view the remains. The room was crowded. All the home-made chairs in the neighborhood had been borrowed, also old boxes and stools. There was a table piled with more gingerbread, a basket of dried herring, bonbons, brown-sugar candy, a five-gallon jug of *clairin* already half emptied. Family, cousins, friends, were seated around, eating, drinking, wailing, singing, and having, all in all, a grand good time.

Over against the wall, in the place of honor, which meant nearest the food and rum-jug, sat the dead man in a clean blue smock and blue cotton trousers with shoes on his feet and his Sunday straw hat on the back of his woolly gray head. They had propped him up in a position as lifelike as possible and had fastened him in the chair so he wouldn't topple over. His head had dropped sideways, but there was nothing repellent about his old wrinkled face. He seemed just a kindly old man, rather stiff in the joints, who had come to the party and then gone to sleep.

I suppose nine-tenths of what one thinks one sees in any material phenomenon, shocking or the reverse, lies not primarily in the visual impression, but in the contributory psychology. I suppose this dead man, really, looked as any corpse would look propped up in a chair. That he seemed so casual, so devoid of shocking or macabre grotesqueness, was doubtless because the living people there accepted him so casually. They expected me to salute him as I did the rest of the company, and when rum was poured out they politely offered the dead man a cupful too. When I produced packages of cigarettes, a youth, probably son or grandson, said, "Perhaps papa would like a smoke," lighted a cigarette from his own, and went and stuck it between the old man's lips. It did not seem rude or shocking. It seemed mildly humorous, rather. And I think it was mildly humorous to them, for presently, as the cigarette burned of itself, a smiling wench nudged another and cried, "*Garder tonton fimer! Ça li fait plaisi'!*" (See Uncle smoking! He seems to like it!)

And several exclaimed delightedly, "*Oui, c'est ve'tab'! Li fime!*"

Another cried, "*Bai li bweh*" (Give him a drink).

There was no mockery in this, but rather a sort of faintly humorous affection. Also they believed that his spirit was still hovering around and would enjoy these little attentions.

They wanted me to stay the night with them and attend the funeral next day—it was to be a dancing funeral [5]—but I had seen dancing funerals before and wanted to get on to Les Verettes.

After taking leave of the company and of the old man, whose cold hand I clasped in saying *adieu*, which seemed to please them, I gave the widow a couple of small bills to help defray expenses of the *bamboche*, and rode away reflecting that Haitian peasants are difficult for the civilized mind to understand. . . .

If, for example, the little scene I have just described seems out of key with things which have preceded it and things which are to follow, I beg readers not to tax me with the inconsistency. The Haitian peasants are thus double-natured in reality—sometimes moved by savage, atavistic forces whose dark depths no white psychology can ever plumb—but often, even in their weirdest customs, naïve, simple, harmless children.

[5] See Appendix, page 332.

Chapter II

". . . DEAD MEN WORKING IN THE CANE FIELDS"

PRETTY mulatto Julie had taken baby Marianne to bed. Constant Polynice and I sat late before the doorway of his *caille*, talking of fire-hags, demons, werewolves, and vampires, while a full moon, rising slowly, flooded his sloping cotton fields and the dark rolling hills beyond.

Polynice was a Haitian farmer, but he was no common jungle peasant. He lived on the island of La Gonave, where I shall return to him in later chapters. He seldom went over to the Haitian mainland, but he knew what was going on in Port-au-Prince, and spoke sometimes of installing a radio.

A countryman, half peasant born and bred, he was familiar with every superstition of the mountains and the plain, yet too intelligent to believe them literally true—or at least so I gathered from his talk.

He was interested in helping me toward an understanding of the tangled Haitian folk-lore. It was only by chance that we came presently to a subject which—though I refused for a long time to admit it—lies in a baffling category on the ragged edge of things which are beyond either superstition or reason. He had been telling me of fire-hags who left their skins at home and set the cane fields blazing; of the vampire, a woman sometimes living, sometimes dead, who sucked the blood of children and who could be distinguished because her hair always turned an ugly red;[1] of the werewolf—*chauché*, in creole—a man or woman who

[1] See Appendix, page 332.

See page 104

"... strange tales are told of Voodoo in the boudoir and salon."

took the form of some animal, usually a dog, and went killing lambs, young goats, sometimes babies.

All this, I gathered, he considered to be pure superstition, as he told me with tolerant scorn how his friend and neighbor Osmann had one night seen a gray dog slinking with bloody jaws from his sheep-pen, and who, after having shot and exorcised and buried it, was so convinced he had killed a certain girl named Liane who was generally reputed to be a *chauché* that when he met her two days later on the path to Grande Source, he believed she was a ghost come back for vengeance, and fled howling.

As Polynice talked on, I reflected that these tales ran closely parallel not only with these of the negroes in Georgia and the Carolinas, but with the mediaeval folklore of white Europe. Werewolves, vampires, and demons were certainly no novelty. But I recalled one creature I had been hearing about in Haiti, which sounded exclusively local—the *zombie.*

It seemed (or so I had been assured by negroes more credulous than Polynice) that while the *zombie* came from the grave, it was neither a ghost, nor yet a person who had been raised like Lazarus from the dead. The *zombie*, they say, is a soulless human corpse, still dead, but taken from the grave and endowed by sorcery with a mechanical semblance of life—it is a dead body which is made to walk and act and move as if it were alive. People who have the power to do this go to a fresh grave, dig up the body before it has had time to rot, galvanize it into movement, and then make of it a servant or slave, occasionally for the commission of some crime, more often simply as a drudge around the habitation or the farm, setting it dull heavy tasks, and beating it like a dumb beast if it slackens.

As this was revolving in my mind, I said to Polynice: "It seems to me that these werewolves and vampires are first cousins to those we have at home, but I have never, except in Haiti, heard of anything like *zombies*. Let us talk of them for a little while. I wonder if you can tell me something of this *zombie* superstition. I should like to get at some idea of how it originated."

My rational friend Polynice was deeply astonished. He leaned over and put his hand in protest on my knee.

"Superstition? But I assure you that this of which you now speak is not a matter of superstition. Alas, these things—and other evil practices connected with the dead—exist. They exist to an extent that you whites do not dream of, though evidences are everywhere under your eyes.

"Why do you suppose that even the poorest peasants, when they can, bury their dead beneath solid tombs of masonry?

"Why do they bury them so often in their own yards, close to the doorway?

"Why, so often, do you see a tomb or grave set close beside a busy road or footpath where people are always passing?

"It is to assure the poor unhappy dead such protection as we can.

"I will take you in the morning to see the grave of my brother, who was killed in the way you know. It is over there on the little ridge which you can see clearly now in the moonlight, open space all round it, close beside the trail which everybody passes going to and from Grande Source. Through four nights we watched yonder, in the peristyle, Osmann and I, with shotguns—for at that time both my dead brother and I had bitter enemies—until we were sure the body had begun to rot.

"No, my friend, no, no. There are only too many true cases. At this very moment, in the moonlight, there are *zombies* working on this island, less than two hours' ride from my own habitation. We know about them, but we do not dare to interfere so long as our own dead are left unmolested. If you will ride with me tomorrow night, yes, I will show you dead men working in the cane fields. Close even to the cities, there are sometimes *zombies*. Perhaps you have already heard of those that were at Hasco. . . ."

"What about Hasco?" I interrupted him, for in the whole of Haiti, Hasco is perhaps the last name anybody would think of connecting with either sorcery or superstition.

The word is American-commercial-synthetic, like Nabisco, Delco, Socony. It stands for the Haitian-American Sugar Company—an immense factory plant, dominated by a huge chimney, with clanging machinery, steam whistles, freight cars. It is like a chunk of Hoboken. It lies in the eastern suburbs of Port-au-Prince, and beyond it stretch the cane fields of the Cul-de-Sac. Hasco makes rum when the sugar market is off, pays low wages, twenty or thirty cents a day, and gives steady work. It is modern big business, and it sounds it, looks it, smells it.

Such, then, was the incongruous background for the weird tale Constant Polynice now told me.

The spring of 1918 was a big cane season, and the factory, which had its own plantations, offered a bonus on the wages of new workers. Soon heads of families and villages from the mountain and the plain came trailing their ragtag little armies, men, women, children, trooping to the registration bureau and thence into the fields.

One morning an old black headman, Ti Joseph of Colombier, appeared leading a band of ragged creatures who shuffled along behind him, staring dumbly, like people walking in a daze. As Joseph lined them up for registration, they still stared, vacant-eyed like cattle, and made no reply when asked to give their names.

Joseph said they were ignorant people from the slopes of Morne-au-Diable, a roadless mountain district near the Dominican border, and that they did not understand the creole of the plains. They were frightened, he said, by the din and smoke of the great factory, but under his direction they would work hard in the fields. The farther they were sent away from the factory, from the noise and bustle of the railroad yards, the better it would be.

Better indeed, for these were not living men and women but poor unhappy *zombies* whom Joseph and his wife Croyance had dragged from their peaceful graves to slave for him in the sun—and if by chance a brother or father of the dead should see and recognize them, Joseph knew that it would be a very bad affair for him.

So they were assigned to distant fields beyond the crossroads, and camped there, keeping to themselves like any proper family or village group; but in the evening when other little companies, encamped apart as they were, gathered each around its one big common pot of savory millet or plantains, generously seasoned with dried fish and garlic, Croyance would tend *two* pots upon the fire, for as every one knows, the *zombies* must never be permitted to taste salt or meat. So the food prepared for them was tasteless and unseasoned.

As the *zombies* toiled day after day dumbly in the sun, Joseph sometimes beat them to make them move faster, but Croyance began to pity the poor dead creatures who should be at rest—and pitied them in the evenings when she dished out their flat, tasteless *bouillie.*

Each Saturday afternoon, Joseph went to collect the wages for them all, and what division he made was no concern of Hasco, so long as the work went forward. Sometimes Joseph alone, and sometimes Croyance alone, went to Croix de Bouquet for the Saturday night *bamboche* or the Sunday cockfight, but always one of them remained with the *zombies* to prepare their food and see that they did not stray away.

Through February this continued, until Fête Dieu approached, with a Saturday-Sunday-Monday holiday for all the workers. Joseph, with his pockets full of money, went to Port-au-Prince and left Croyance behind, cautioning her as usual; and she agreed to remain and tend the *zombies,* for he promised her that at the Mardi Gras she should visit the city.

But when Sunday morning dawned, it was lonely in the fields, and her kind old woman's heart was filled with pity for the *zombies*, and she thought, "Perhaps it will cheer them a little to see the gay crowds and the processions at Croix de Bouquet, and since all the Morne-au-Diable people will have gone back to the mountain to celebrate Fête Dieu at home, no one will recognize them, and no harm can come of it." And it is the truth that Croyance also wished to see the gay procession.

So she tied a new bright-colored handkerchief around her head, aroused the *zombies* from the sleep that was scarcely different from their waking, gave them their morning bowl of cold, unsalted plantains boiled in water, which they ate dumbly uncomplaining, and set out with them for the town, single file, as the country people always walk. Croyance, in her bright kerchief, leading the nine dead men and women behind her, past the railroad crossing, where she murmured a prayer to Legba, past the great white-painted wooden Christ, who hung life-sized in the glaring sun, where she stopped to kneel and cross herself—but the poor *zombies* prayed neither to Papa Legba nor to Brother Jesus, for they were dead bodies walking, without souls or minds.

They followed her to the market square, before the church where hundreds of little thatched, open shelters, used on week days for buying and selling, were empty of trade, but crowded here and there by gossiping groups in the grateful shade.

To the shade of one of these market booths, which was still unoccupied, she led the *zombies*, and they sat like people asleep with their eyes open, staring, but seeing nothing, as the bells in the church began to ring, and the procession came from the priest's house—red-purple robes, golden crucifix held aloft, tinkling bells and swinging incense-pots, followed by little black boys in white lace robes, little black girls in starched white dresses, with shoes and stockings, from the parish school, with colored ribbons in their kinky hair, a nun beneath a big umbrella leading them.

Croyance knelt with the throng as the procession passed, and wished she might follow it across the square to the church steps, but the *zombies* just sat and stared, seeing nothing.

When noontime came, women with baskets passed to and fro in the crowd, or sat selling bonbons (which were not candy but little sweet cakes), figs (which were not figs but sweet bananas), oranges, dried herring, biscuit, casava bread, and *clairin* poured from a bottle at a penny a glass.

As Croyance sat with her savory dried herring and biscuit baked with salt and soda, and provision of *clairin* in the tin cup by her side, she pitied the *zombies* who had worked so faithfully for Joseph in the cane fields, and who now had nothing, while all the other groups around were feasting, and as she pitied them, a woman passed, crying,

"*Tablettes! Tablettes pistaches! T'ois pour dix cobs!*"

Tablettes are a sort of candy, in shape and size like cookies, made of brown cane sugar (*rapadou*); sometimes with *pistaches*, which in Haiti are peanuts, or with coriander seed.

And Croyance thought, "These *tablettes* are not salted or seasoned, they are sweet, and can do no harm to the *zombies* just this once."

So she untied the corner of her kerchief, took out a coin, a *gourdon*, the quarter of a *gourde*, and bought some of the *tablettes*, which she broke in halves and divided among the *zombies*, who began sucking and mumbling them in their mouths.

But the baker of the *tablettes* had salted the *pistache* nuts before stirring them into the *rapadou*, and as the *zombies* tasted the salt, they knew that they were dead and made a dreadful outcry and arose and turned their faces toward the mountain.

See page 99

"No one dared to stop them, for they were corpses walking in the sunlight."

No one dared stop them, for they were corpses walking in the sunlight, and they themselves and all the people knew that they were corpses. And they disappeared toward the mountain.

When later they drew near their own village on the slopes of Morne-au-Diable, these dead men and women walking single file in the twilight, with no soul leading them or daring to follow, the people of their village, who were also holding *bamboche* in the market-place, saw them drawing closer, recognized among them fathers, brothers, wives, and daughters whom they had buried months before.

Most of them knew at once the truth, that these were *zombies* who had been dragged dead from their graves, but others hoped that a blessed miracle had taken place on this Fête Dieu, and rushed forward to take them in their arms and welcome them.

But the *zombies* shuffled through the market-place, recognizing neither father nor wife nor mother, and as they turned leftward up the path leading to the graveyard, a woman whose daughter was in the procession of the dead threw herself screaming before the girl's shuffling feet and begged her to stay; but the grave-cold feet of the daughter and the feet of the other dead shuffled over her and onward; and as they approached the graveyard, they began to shuffle faster and rushed among the graves, and each before his own empty grave began clawing at the stones and earth to enter it again; and as their cold hands touched the earth of their own graves, they fell and lay there, rotting carrion.

That night the fathers, sons, and brothers of the *zombies*, after restoring the bodies to their graves, sent a messenger on muleback down the mountain, who returned next day with the name of Ti Joseph and with a stolen shirt of Ti Joseph's which had been worn next his skin and was steeped in the grease-sweat of his body.

They collected silver in the village and went with the name of Ti Joseph and the shirt of Ti Joseph to a *bocor* beyond Trou Caiman, who made a deadly needle *ouanga*, a black bag *ouanga*, pierced all through with pins and needles, filled with dry goat dung, circled with cock's feathers dipped in blood.

And lest the needle *ouanga* be slow in working or be rendered weak by Joseph's counter-magic, they sent men down to the plain, who lay in wait patiently for Joseph, and one night hacked off his head with a machete. . . .

When Polynice had finished this recital, I said to him, after a moment of silence, "You are not a peasant like those of the Cul-de-Sac; you are a reasonable man, or at least it seems to me you are. Now how much of that story, honestly, do you believe?"

He replied earnestly: "I did not see these special things, but there were many witnesses, and why should I not believe them when I myself have also seen *zombies?* When you also have seen them, with their faces and their eyes in which there is no life, you will not only believe in these *zombies* who should be resting in their graves, you will pity them from the bottom of your heart."

Before finally taking leave of La Gonave, I did see these "walking dead men," and I did, in a sense, believe in them and pitied them, indeed, from the bottom of my heart. It was not the next night, though Polynice, true to his promise, rode with me across the Plaine Mapou to the deserted, silent cane fields where he had hoped to show me *zombies* laboring. It was not on any night. It was in broad daylight one afternoon, when we passed that way again, on the lower trail to Picmy. Polynice reined in his horse and pointed to a rough, stony, terraced slope—on which four laborers, three men and a woman, were chopping the earth with machetes, among straggling cotton stalks, a hundred yards distant from the trail.

"Wait while I go up there," he said, excited because a chance had come to fulfill his promise. "I think it is Lamercie with the *zombies*. If I wave to you, leave your horse and come." Starting up the slope, he shouted to the woman, "It is I, Polynice," and when he waved later, I followed.

As I clambered up, Polynice was talking to the woman. She had stopped work—a big-boned, hard-faced black girl, who regarded us with surly unfriendliness. My first impression of the three supposed *zombies*, who continued dumbly at work, was that there was something about them unnatural and strange. They were plodding like brutes, like automatons. Without stooping down, I could not fully see their faces, which were bent expressionless over their work. Polynice touched one of them on the shoulder, motioned him to get up. Obediently, like an animal, he slowly stood erect—and what I saw then, coupled with what I had heard previously, or despite it, came as a rather sickening shock. The eyes were the worst. It was not my imagination. They were in truth like the eyes of a dead man, not blind, but staring, unfocused, unseeing. The whole face, for that matter, was bad enough. It was vacant, as if there was nothing behind it. It seemed not only expressionless, but incapable of expression. I had seen so much previously in Haiti that was outside ordinary normal experience that for the flash of a second I had a sickening, almost panicky lapse in which I thought, or rather felt, "Great God, maybe this stuff is really true, and if it is true, it is rather awful, for it upsets everything." By "everything" I meant the natural fixed laws and processes on which all modern human thought and actions are based. Then suddenly I remembered—and my mind seized the memory as a man sinking in water clutches a solid plank—the face of a dog I had once seen in the histological laboratory at Columbia. Its entire front brain had been removed in an experimental operation weeks before; it moved about, it was alive, but its eyes were like the eyes I now saw staring.

I recovered from my mental panic. I reached out and grasped one of the dangling hands. It was calloused, solid, human. Holding it, I said, "*Bonjour, compère.*" The *zombie* stared without responding. The black wench, Lamercie, who was their keeper, now more sullen than ever, pushed me away—"*Z'affai' nèg' pas z'affai' blanc*" (Negroes' affairs are not for whites). But I had seen enough. "Keeper" was the key to it. "Keeper" was the word that had leapt naturally into my mind as she protested, and just as naturally the *zombies* were nothing but poor, ordinary demented human beings, idiots, forced to toil in the fields.

It was a good rational explanation, but it is far from being the end of this story. It satisfied me then, and I said as much to Polynice as we went down the slope. At first he did not contradict me, even said doubtfully, "Perhaps"; but as we reached the horses, before mounting, he stopped and said, "Look here, I respect your distrust of what you call superstition and your desire to find out the truth, but if what you were saying now were the whole truth, how could it be that over and over again, people who have stood by and seen their own relatives buried have, sometimes soon, sometimes months or years afterward, found those relatives working as *zombies*, and have sometimes killed the man who held them in servitude?" [2]

"Polynice," I said, "that's just the part of it that I can't believe. The *zombies* in such cases may have resembled the dead persons, or even been 'doubles'—you know what doubles are, how two people resemble each other to a startling degree. But it is a fixed rule of reasoning in America that we will never accept the possibility of a thing's being 'supernatural' so long as any natural explanation, even far-fetched, seems adequate."

"Well," said he, "if you spent many years in Haiti, you would have a very hard time to fit this American reasoning into some of the things you encountered here."

As I have said, there is more to this story—and I think it is best to tell it very simply.

[2] See Appendix, page 334.

In all Haiti, there is no clearer scientifically trained mind, no sounder pragmatic rationalist, than Dr. Antoine Villiers. When I sat later with him in his study, surrounded by hundreds of scientific books in French, German, and English, and told him of what I had seen and of my conversations with Polynice, he said:

"My dear sir, I do not believe in miracles nor in supernatural events, and I do not want to shock your Anglo-Saxon intelligence, but this Polynice of yours, with all his superstition, may have been closer to the partial truth than you were. Understand me clearly. I do not believe that any one has ever been raised literally from the dead—neither Lazarus, nor the daughter of Jairus, nor Jesus Christ himself—yet I am not sure, paradoxical as it may sound, that there is not something frightful, something in the nature of criminal sorcery if you like, in some cases at least, in this matter of *zombies*. I am by no means sure that some of them who now toil in the fields were not dragged from the actual graves in which they lay in their coffins, buried by their mourning families!"

"It is then something like suspended animation?" I asked.

"I will show you," he replied, "a thing which may supply the key to what you are seeking," and standing on a chair, he pulled down a paper-bound book from a top shelf. It was nothing mysterious or esoteric. It was the current official *Code Pénal* (Criminal Code) of the Republic of Haiti. He thumbed through it and pointed to a paragraph which read:

"*Article* 249. Also shall be qualified as attempted murder the employment which may be made against any person of substances which, without causing actual death, produce a lethargic coma more or less prolonged. If, after the administering of such substances, the person has been buried, the act shall be considered murder no matter what result follows." [3]

[3] See Appendix, page 335.

Chapter III

TOUSSEL'S PALE BRIDE

WHAT proportion of the Haitian upper classes believe secretly in sorcery and Voodoo is impossible to ascertain and difficult to guess. "Not one in a thousand," I have been told. "Nine hundred and ninety-nine in every thousand," I have also been told, and both answers came from Haitians who were themselves of that class. Yet I am convinced that neither answer was approximately correct.

I believe, and this is ventured simply as an opinion, that very few of them adhere to Voodoo as a religion, but that a great majority of them fear its magic.

Strange tales, however, are told in Port-au-Prince of both these phases of Voodoo in the boudoir and salon, and whenever this subject becomes the topic of more or less confidential speculation, some one is always certain to recall and tell the story of how—and why—Père Béranger, a Catholic priest as distinguished for his mundane elegance and the exquisite diction of his classical French sermons as for his inner piety, astounded his fashionable congregation one Sunday morning by mounting the pulpit and denouncing them in blunt jungle creole.

Before coming to that, however, I must revert for a moment to the peasants. If you stroll through any market, even in the cities, where country women are assembled with their produce, you will see here and there among them some woman fantastically garbed. She will be wearing usually a white dress, but an irregular shoulder of the dress may be black or glaring red, not dyed so, but a sort of huge, crazy-quilt patch sewn on. Another may wear a dress made entirely of large, angular, crazy-quilt cotton patches in clashing colors; another a bodice perpendicularly divided off center, so that two-thirds of the upper body is clothed in white, the other third, as if sliced off, in black. The effect is not gay or holiday-like, but conspicuous and grotesque. A woman thus garbed is usually sullen or defiant if she is questioned or eyed too curiously. Others may be seen more rarely, particularly on mountain trails, wearing coarse burlap sacks, with holes cut in the top for head and arms to come through. These are all penitential garments imposed by the *papaloi*, either as a penance for some offense committed against the Voodoo gods, or to aid in the working of some charm, the averting of some impending evil, or the bringing about of some desired happening. The white Catholic priests, knowing the significance of these garments, generally bar peasants so clothed from entering a church or chapel. I recall one morning when, with Père Pessel, *curé* of Trouin, walking with Dr. Parsons and me along a mountain trail near his chapel, we met a peasant girl of his flock in piebald garments. Père Pessel was a tolerant old priest, but he became very angry, seized the girl by the arm, shook her, and talked to her bitterly. This explanation is necessary, to make clear what follows.

The story of how Père Béranger denounced his more exalted city congregation concerns a certain Madame Tel. No need to distress this proud lady by using her family name, which is distinguished among the aristocracy of the Haitian capital; but she was a beautiful creature, and neither the fact that she was married nor the fact that she was an exemplary devout member of Père Béranger's congregation—it was said that he used to lend her the mystical works of Saint Theresa, and that she sometimes had pious fits of melancholy in which she considered renouncing all vanities to enter a Carmelite convent—none of these things, I am told, eclipsed her dominating charm in worldly social gatherings, but rather, by adding an element of mysterious soulfulness, enhanced it.

The story is that one night Madame Tel appeared late at a grand ball, more beautiful than usual, in a new gown from Paris, extremely becoming but slightly less décolleté than was customary. This occasioned no surprise, for Madame Tel set fashions rather than slavishly followed them. She was eagerly sought by aspiring partners amid the brilliant crush, and her dance-card was soon filled. She refused champagne, but danced ravishingly, with abandoned grace and a strange light in her starry eyes. Late in the evening—or early in the morning rather, since midnight was long past—she fell in a dead faint and was carried, still unconscious, to a couch in a retiring-room, followed by sympathetic ladies. Her bodice and corset were loosened, and sewn tightly next to her own delicate golden skin they found another bodice of roughly woven sisal fiber, an abrasive plant of the cactus family, from which coarse rope is made.

And sewn upon this inner bodice, which was harsher than any penitential shirt of haircloth or thistles worn by nuns in Saint Theresa's time, so the ladies whispered afterward, were the telltale Voodoo patches.

Of course the scandal was whispered about, and eventually came to the ears of Pére Bèranger. Furthermore, there had been other whisperings, less sensational in their dénouement but almost equally disturbing to his piety, of other ladies who had been said to wear coarse sacking, colored patches, or little *ouanga* bags beneath their finery. And Pére Bèranger, perhaps, had an exaggerated vision of all his flock repairing secretly by moonlight to the jungle. At any rate, when he mounted with dignity into the pulpit on Sunday morning, after mass, to preach, and his distinguished congregation sat attending the customary eloquent phrases of Fénelon-like French purity which usually characterized his exquisite discourse, he clutched the rail, leaned forward, threw his dignity to the winds, and out of his mouth, inspired by righteous wrath, rolled sentence after sentence of the bluntest, lowest, most idiomatic creole dialect conceivable.

They must have imagined, at his first words, that either they or he had gone mad. It was as if the fashionable rector of All Saints' on Fifth Avenue had suddenly begun to address his parishioners in slang of the Bowery underworld, or as if the vicar of Saint Germain had assaulted the ears of his Parisian congregation with a volley of argot from the Halles. Yet here it was even worse; it carried an additional, special, vigorous insult and indictment. In the parallel cases just drawn from fancy there would be many ears to which the slang and argot were incomprehensible. But in Haiti everybody *knows* creole, though among the upper classes it is considered bad form to admit a fluent knowledge of it or make use of it in refined circles. Therefore, at the outset, by this dramatic stroke, Père Béranger was stripping them.

"You sit there in your silks and high-heeled shoes," he thundered, "but God only knows what you're wearing underneath. . . . Ladies? Baahh! Superstitious savages, slicked up outwardly . . . heathen, pagan, snake-worshiping, idolaters, some of you. . . . How do you expect to limp straddle-legged into heaven with one foot in the church and the other in the *houmfort? . . .*"

They say that he passed from invective to pleading, that he discoursed, always in creole, for more than half an hour. It must have been a noble oration.

But I am sure that pious Père Béranger was over-outraged, over-credulous, over-frightened, over-quick to generalize. And concurrently, with less excuse, I should be blamable if I implied or created the impression that the Haitian upper world was mysteriously honeycombed with Voodoo. Such generalities have been asserted in print, but, as generalities, they are not dependable. I had many close friends among Haitians of this class, and aside from striking individual exceptions, it seemed to me that almost universally they believed less in Voodoo than I myself did, that it concerned them less than it did me, concerned them in fact not at all—unless one of them should happen to be threatened with specific danger from it—and that in many cases they were quite ignorant about it, either indifferently ignorant or ignorant with curiosity, depending on their temperaments. I recall one night a family dinner at the Baussans'; Pradel was there, also Léonce Borno, nephew of the president and now consul-general in New York; a niece also, I believe of the president, a Mlle. Mathon. I had returned from the mountains, and in answer to their questions was telling them of one of the simpler Legba ceremonies, something of the ritual processions and dancing, the chants, the names and attributes of various Voodoo deities—and all of them listened as fascinated and surprised as if I had been telling them of exotic customs in some far-off land of which they had vaguely heard but never visited. These things were totally outside their charming civilized world, and I think this group was representative of what I mean to convey.

But nevertheless, mysterious and strange occurrences sometimes came to light in connection with people more or less high up in the city as well as with peasants in the jungle. And then one was compelled almost to doubt this very point I have been striving fairly to make—to wonder how many *other* strange things might be occurring which never came to light. My Haitian friends are sensitive on this subject. It may please them if I draw a certain parallel between Port-au-Prince and New York. Once in a blue moon, an accident or intervention of the law reveals to an astonished American public that in such-and-such a feudal thick-walled mansion on Manhattan, or huge isolated country estate in Westchester or Nyack, things utterly monstrous and chimeric have been secretly occurring—things madly fantastic and outside the civilized age we fondly think we are living in—things which make Caligula and

Gilles de Retz mere amateurs. "How impossible!" we exclaim when we learn of such a case, "how astounding!" But the next inevitable reflection is, "How many of these other thick-walled, many-chambered vast modern castles which we pass every day atop the bus, and yet know nothing more of their ultimate interiors than if they were on lost mountain-tops in China, may also contain mysteries that will never be revealed?" And how much more inevitable, even though perhaps unfair, are similar reflections in Haiti with its ever-present background of Voodoo and ancient jungle sorcery.

The strangest and most chimeric story of this type ever related to me in Haiti by Haitians who claimed direct knowledge of its essential truth is the tale of Matthieu Toussel's mad bride, the tale of how her madness came upon her. I shall try to reconstruct it here as it was told to me—as it was dramatized, elaborated, perhaps, in the oft re-telling.

An elderly and respected Haitian gentleman whose wife was French had a young niece, by name Camille, a fair-skinned octoroon girl whom they introduced and sponsored in Port-au-Prince society, where she became popular, and for whom they hoped to arrange a brilliant marriage.

Her own family, however, was poor; her uncle, it was understood, could scarcely be expected to dower her—he was prosperous, but not wealthy, and had a family of his own—and the French *dot* system prevails in Haiti, so that while the young beaux of the *élite* crowded to fill her dance-cards, it became gradually evident that none of them had serious intentions.

When she was nearing the age of twenty, Matthieu Toussel, a rich coffee-grower from Morne Hôpital, became a suitor, and presently asked her hand in marriage. He was dark and more than twice her age, but rich, suave, and well educated. The principal house of the Toussel habitation, on the mountainside almost overlooking Port-au-Prince, was not thatched, mud-walled, but a fine wooden bungalow, slate-roofed, with wide verandas, set in a garden among gay poinsettias, palms, and Bougainvillaea vines. He had built a road there, kept his own big motor car, and was often seen in the fashionable cafés and clubs.

There was an old rumor that he was affiliated in some way with Voodoo or sorcery, but such rumors are current concerning almost every Haitian who has acquired power in the mountains, and in the case of men like Toussel are seldom taken seriously. He asked no *dot*, he promised to be generous, both to her and her straitened family, and the family persuaded her into the marriage.

The black planter took his pale girl-bride back with him to the mountain, and for almost a year, it appears, she was not unhappy, or at least gave no signs of it. They still came down to Port-au-Prince, appeared occasionally at the club soirées. Toussel permitted her to visit her family whenever she liked, lent her father money, and arranged to send her young brother to a school in France.

But gradually her family, and her friends as well, began to suspect that all was not going so happily up yonder as it seemed. They began to notice that she was nervous in her husband's presence, that she seemed to have acquired a vague, growing dread of him. They wondered if Toussel were ill-treating or neglecting her. The mother sought to gain her daughter's confidence, and the girl gradually opened her heart. No, her husband had never ill-treated her, never a harsh word; he was always kindly and considerate, but there were nights when he seemed strangely preoccupied, and on such nights he would saddle his horse and ride away into the hills, sometimes not returning until after dawn, when he seemed even stranger and more lost in his own thoughts than on the night before. And there was something in the way he sometimes sat staring at her which made her feel that she was in some way connected with those secret thoughts. She was afraid of his thoughts and afraid of him. She knew intuitively, as women know, that no other woman was involved in these nocturnal excursions. She was not jealous. She was in the grip of an unreasoning fear. One morning when she thought he had been away all night in the hills, chancing to look out of a window, so she told her mother, she had seen him emerging from the door of a low frame building in their own big garden, set at some distance from the others and which he had told her was his office where he kept his accounts, his business papers, and the door always locked. . . . "So, therefore," said the mother, relieved and reassured, "what does this all amount to? Business troubles, those secret thoughts of his, probably . . . some coffee combination he is planning and which is perhaps going wrong so that he sits up all night at his desk figuring and devising, or rides off to sit up half the night consulting with others. Men are like that. It explains itself. The rest of it is nothing but your nervous imagining."

And this was the last rational talk the mother and daughter ever had. What subsequently occurred up there on the fatal night of the first wedding anniversary, they pieced together from the half-lucid intervals of a terrorized, cowering, hysterical creature, who finally went stark, raving mad. But what she had gone through was indelibly stamped on her brain; there were early periods when she seemed quite sane, and the sequential tragedy was gradually evolved.

On the evening of their anniversary, Toussel had ridden away, telling her not to sit up for him, and she had assumed that in his preoccupation he had forgotten the date, which hurt her and made her silent. She went away to bed early and finally fell asleep.

Near midnight she was awakened by her husband, who stood by the bedside, holding a lamp. He must have been some time returned, for he was fully dressed now in formal evening clothes.

"Put on your wedding dress and make yourself beautiful," he said; "we are going to a party." She was sleepy and dazed, but innocently pleased, imagining that a belated recollection of the date had caused him to plan a surprise for her. She supposed he was taking her to a late supper-dance down at the club by the seaside, where people often appeared long after midnight. "Take your time," he said, "and make yourself as beautiful as you can—there is no hurry."

An hour later when she joined him on the veranda, she said, "But where is the car?"

"No," he replied, "the party is to take place here," and she noticed that there were lights in the outbuilding, the "office" across the garden. He gave her no time to question or protest. He seized her arm, led her through the dark garden, and opened the door. The office, if it had ever been one, was transformed into a dining-room, softly lighted with tall candles. There was a big old-fashioned buffet with a mirror and cut-glass bowls, plates of cold meats and salads, bottles of wine and decanters of rum.

In the center of the room was an elegantly set table with damask cloth, flowers, glittering silver. Four men, also in evening clothes, but badly fitting, were already seated at this table. There were two vacant chairs at its head and foot. The seated men did not arise when the girl in her bride-clothes entered on her husband's arm. They sat slumped down in their chairs and did not even turn their heads to greet her. There were wine-glasses partly filled before them, and she thought they were already drunk.

As she sat down mechanically in the chair to which Toussel led her, seating himself facing her, with the four guests ranged between them, two on either side, he said, in an unnatural strained way, the stress increasing as he spoke:

"I beg you . . . to forgive my guests their . . . seeming rudeness. It has been a long time . . . since . . . they have . . . tasted wine . . . sat like this at table . . . with . . . with so fair a hostess. . . . But, ah, presently . . . they will drink with you, yes . . . lift . . . their

See page 118

"Antoine Simone, president of the republic, was active in black sorcery."

arms, as I lift mine . . . clink glasses with you . . . more . . . they will arise and . . . dance with you . . . more . . . they will . . ."

Near her, the black fingers of one silent guest were clutched rigidly around the fragile stem of a wine-glass, tilted, spilling. The horror pent up in her overflowed. She seized a candle, thrust it close to the slumped, bowed face, and saw the man was dead. She was sitting at a banquet table with four propped-up corpses.

Breathless for an instant, then screaming, she leaped to her feet and ran. Toussel reached the door too late to seize her. He was heavy and more than twice her age. She ran still screaming across the dark garden, flashing white among the trees, out through the gate. Youth and utter terror lent wings to her feet, and she escaped. . . .

A procession of early market-women, with their laden baskets and donkeys, winding down the mountainside at dawn, found her lying unconscious far below, at the point where the jungle trail emerged into the road. Her filmy dress was ripped and torn, her little white satin bride-slippers were scuffed and stained, one of the high heels ripped off where she had caught it in a vine and fallen.

They bathed her face to revive her, bundled her on a pack-donkey, walking beside her, holding her. She was only half conscious, incoherent, and they began disputing among themselves as peasants do. Some thought she was a French lady who had been thrown or fallen from a motor car; others thought she was a *Dominicaine*, which has been synonymous in creole from earliest colonial days with "fancy prostitute." None recognized her as Madame Toussel; perhaps none of them had ever seen her. They were discussing and disputing whether to leave her at a hospital of Catholic sisters on the outskirts of the city, which they were approaching, or whether it would be safer—for them—to take her directly to police headquarters and tell their story. Their loud disputing seemed to rouse her; she seemed partially to recover her senses and understand what they were saying. She told them her name, her maiden family name, and begged them to take her to her father's house.

There, put to bed and with doctors summoned, the family were able to gather from the girl's hysterical utterances a partial comprehension of what had happened. They sent up that same day to confront Toussel if they could—to search his habitation. But Toussel was gone, and all the servants were gone except one old man, who said that Toussel was in Santo Domingo. They broke into the so-called office, and found there the table still set for six people, wine spilled on the table-cloth, a bottle overturned, chairs knocked over, the platters of food still untouched on the sideboard, but beyond that they found nothing.

Toussel never returned to Haiti. It is said that he is living now in Cuba. Criminal pursuit was useless. What reasonable hope could they have had of convicting him on the unsupported evidence of a wife of unsound mind?

And there, as it was related to me, the story trailed off to a shrugging of the shoulders, to mysterious inconclusion.

What had this Toussel been planning—what sinister, perhaps criminal necromancy in which his bride was to be the victim or the instrument? What would have happened if she had not escaped?

I asked these questions, but got no convincing explanation or even theory in reply. There are tales of rather ghastly abominations, unprintable, practiced by certain sorcerers who claim to raise the dead, but so far as I know they are only tales. And as for what actually did happen that night, credibility depends on the evidence of a demented girl.

So what is left?

What is left may be stated in a single sentence:

Matthieu Toussel arranged a wedding anniversary supper for his bride at which six plates were laid, and when she looked into the faces of his four other guests, she went mad.

Chapter IV

CÉLESTINE WITH A SILVER DISH

Two burnt matches crossed and fastened together with a bit of scarlet thread lay unnoticed one afternoon in the spring of 1921 on the great marble staircase of the new presidential palace at Port-au-Prince.

On the top steps of that same white marble staircase, very much noticed, stood his Excellency Sudre Dartiguenave, president of the Black Republic.

Below on the lawn a fanfare of bugles sounded, and at the foot of the staircase the motor of the presidential limousine purred softly, waiting to convey his Excellency to a reception in his honor at the French legation. President Dartiguenave was a bachelor beau, and there were always a lot of pretty women of various colors at these French legation functions in the gay capital of Haiti.

Faultlessly attired in frock coat, pin-striped trousers, pearl-gray spats, and patent leathers, twirling his imperial waxed mustache with kid-gloved fingers, Sudre Dartiguenave, who liked to be told that he resembled Napoleon III (in bronze, of course), strolled slowly down the great marble steps of the presidential palace to the accompaniment of bugle fanfares. At his left was young Captain Jones of the United States Marine Corps, blond, glittering and magnificent in his special uniform as Commander of the Palace Guard. At his right was Ernest Lalo, suave, charming brown-skinned Haitian poet and friend of Maurice Rostand. Outside the iron palings in the Champs de Mars, crowds hearing the bugles had stopped to glimpse the presidential sortie.

How the two burnt match-ends fastened together with a bit of thread happened to lie there tiny on the immense white staircase seems almost less of a mystery than how President Dartiguenave chanced to spy them. . . .

But he did spy them, directly on a step beneath him, as his foot was poised, and he recovered his balance with some difficulty, recoiling upward as if he had been about to tread on a tarantula.

Then, hoping that his eyes had deceived him, he bent over in a somewhat undignified posture to examine the menacing object more closely. Having thus verified his original suspicion, he asked advice of nobody, neither his American bodyguard nor his Haitian poet friend, nor the black senators and white Marine Corps officers who waited below. He turned and retraced his steps up the great marble staircase, reëntered the palace, and retired to the presidential bed chamber, where with the aid of Captain Jones, who was sympathetic if skeptical, he took off his patent leather shoes, and took off his collar, paced up and down the floor in his stocking feet, and then sat for a long time staring out of the window. . . .

Two small charred sticks crossed and fastened together with a bit of string, black or red, are not uncommon in Haiti. One frequently sees them, usually laid on a new grave, some say for a black curse, others say so that the spirit can kindle a little blaze and warm its hands in the cold other-world; but whatever their purpose, not even the relatives dare remove them without first consulting a *bocor* or a *papaloi*. Americans have also sometimes seen them nearer home than in a graveyard. When they occur on the doorstep of a kitchen, it is usually necessary to go looking for a new cook. President Dartiguenave, however, had more nerve than that. It was not necessary for the American treaty officials to go looking for a new president. But he did not attend the reception at the French legation, nor did he stir from the palace for three whole days, and unless he was more foolhardy than I think, he took certain needful precautions, for matters of this sort sometimes go deeper than white men ever dream.

Haiti, of course, buzzes continually with exaggerated tales of "Voodoo in the palace" and other political high places,[1] and many of them are untrue, but some very queer things have actually happened within quite recent years. One of the queerest occurred in 1910, prior to the contretemps of Dartiguenave and the burnt match-ends. It was under the régime of President Antoine-Simone. It also occurred in bright sunshine with martial music, but it involved much more than a couple of burnt match-ends.

Antoine-Simone was no sophisticated product of mixed aristocratic blood, French culture, and European universities. He was of black African savage stock, peasant born, an old-fashioned black revolutionary "general" from the south, former chief of a *section rurale.* With a rag-tail "army" he erupted from Jacmel in 1908, defeated the government forces of Nord Alexis, and installed himself in the old wooden palace which was in the Champs de Mars on the site of the present new one. He continued to wear his general's uniform with huge gold epaulettes and revenged the smiles and sneers of the Port-au-Prince *élite* by making himself an *opéra bouffe* tyrant, forcing all Haitians and even foreigners to stop stockstill in the street and uncover their heads when he passed in his carriage.

He installed in the palace with him as first lady of the land his daughter Célestine. She also was a black peasant, not beautiful except for her superb peasant's figure; she had none of the culture or refinement of the exquisite mulatto creatures who form the cream of Port-au-Prince's feminine society—but Célestine was a personality. Although under thirty, she was reputed to be secretly the *grande mamaloi* of all Haiti, its supreme high priestess.

[1] See Appendix, page 335.

And not only Célestine herself but her father, Antoine-Simone, president of the Republic, was reputed to be active in black sorcery. It was commonly said that magical rites and practices occurred even within the confines of the palace walls, and probably they did.

On the surface, however, both the president and his daughter were devout Catholics, and attended mass regularly at the cathedral. So also were most of the officials and attendants at the palace.

One day Colonel X——, of Aux Cayes, a black member of the presidential household, fell seriously ill. It was a bona-fide illness, with nothing sinister or mysterious about it. He had been suffering intermittently from cirrhosis of the liver for years. When it became apparent that he was going to die the gentlemen of the clergy were called in to hear his confession, anoint him with holy oils, and perform their other sad, consoling offices, which they did with considerable ceremony, seeing that he was a member of the presidential entourage. And that night, surrounded by members of his family who had come from Aux Cayes, with nurses and physicians properly in attendance, Colonel X—— died. And all this was sad but wholly natural, without mystery of any sort.

The solemn obsequies which followed two days later also seemed to be natural and proper. That is to say, the open coffin with the mortal remains of the late colonel exposed to the view of mourning relatives and friends lay all day Wednesday in the palace, and on Thursday morning the same coffin, now closed with the lid screwed down, was conveyed with considerable pomp in a hearse with plumes to the cathedral, where it presently lay before the high altar covered with a black pall on which was laid a great silver crucifix, while a high requiem mass was sung for the soul of the dead.

And while the solemn strains of the Kyrie Eleison, the Credo and the Agnus Dei sounded through the cathedral,

President Antoine-Simone and his daughter Célestine knelt and crossed themselves devoutly with the rest.

Presently the mass concluded with the Dies Irae, the funeral cortège set out for the cemetery. They do these things superbly in Latin America. Leading the way went the palace band, resplendent in gold braid, playing the Dead March from *Saul*. At a suitable distance followed the ecclesiastical procession, a tall black acolyte bearing the crucifix aloft in the sunshine, a procession of little black altar boys in their white lace surplices, swinging censers; then the priests, the celebrant of the mass with his servants, deacons and subdeacons in their rich funeral vestments of black and silver.

Next came the plumed hearse drawn by six horses, also plumed, and after it the carriages, in the first of which rode the president of the Republic and his daughter, Célestine, with discreet, sad, solemn faces.

It was after the coffin had actually been lowered into the grave that trouble began to brew—and how it started has never been quite clear. Some say that one of the pallbearers didn't like the "feel" of the coffin, others that relatives of the dead man had become suspicious, others that the priest celebrant had smelt an ancient odor which was not that of sanctity.

As I say, it occurred only after the coffin had been lowered into the grave, sprinkled with holy water, marked with the sign of the cross. As the final solemn "*Requiescat in pace*" was about to be pronounced, there was a sharp pause, a quick consultation among the priests, doubt, suspicion, horror reflected on their faces, then a stern whispered order, and the coffin was dragged up from holy ground.

No one had a screw-driver, but the lid was pried open with a machete borrowed from a peasant in the crowd, exposing to view not the whole interior of the coffin, but the head and shoulders of the deceased.

Now the head which the priests and others who crowded close beheld was black and bearded, but in no other respect did it resemble that of the late Colonel X——, or of anything human. It was surmounted by two horns, like those of the devil himself. In short, it was the head of a great he-goat—a pagan, hairy, dreadful, dead he-goat which the innocent, now outraged priests had been blessing and sprinkling with holy water and marking with the sign of the cross and committing to holy ground—a goat which had lain beneath a crucifix before the high altar in the cathedral, a goat for which a solemn requiem mass had been chanted —a consecrated goat which His Worship the Archbishop himself had only been prevented from following to the grave because of a slight cold in the head.

The scandal, of course, was tremendous. Its percussions even reached Rome. The archbishop sent for President Antoine-Simone, with threats of excommunication and anathema, and the president went apologetically, dutifully to make his explanations, for Haiti is a Catholic country, and not even its president can flout the church. I doubt that Antoine-Simone had meant to flout the church. Rather he had probably sought to compound his own black magic with white, in which he believed with equal sincerity.

The president's explanation was plausible, and of course a lie. It had been a malicious plot contrived by his political enemies to bring him into disgrace. They had gained access to the palace by night and substituted the goat in the coffin. By the way, what disposition had his worship made of the goat? The goat had been exorcised and burned. The president stroked his own short, goatlike beard reflectively, and made no comment.

It was deemed wise to accept the explanation, but no one believed it, for this was not the first time that the odor of the goat had permeated the presidential palace. The actual explanation of this whole fantastic occurrence is, up to a point, simple enough. Célestine and Antoine-Simone were steeped in Voodoo magic. For purposes known specifically only to themselves, they had required, for some extraordinary rite, the body of a goat which had been blessed and made holy by the church. The requirement, fantastic as it sounds, is not without frequent parallels in Haiti. Precisely what they had proposed to do with the sanctified goat is beyond my knowledge.

Antoine-Simone, deposed by revolution in 1911, fled to Jamaica and died there some years ago, but Célestine is still alive in Haiti. She who was once the dreaded mistress of the palace lives in complete retirement on a small farm near Aux Cayes. She does not like Americans; I made several unsuccessful efforts to see her. I wanted to ask her about the famous MacDonald pearl necklace, which is the reason why she doesn't like Americans. Perhaps she was suspicious that I wanted to ask her about the silver dish.

The story of the silver dish is based on the evidence of two credible eye-witnesses, one a Frenchman who may still be seen and talked with at the Cape, the other a Haitian now dead. I talked with numbers of people about it and found none who questioned its approximate truth. It is current among the Haitians themselves; so they will forgive me for including it.[2]

The old wooden palace stood in the center of the Champs de Mars, amid extensive gardens, surrounded by a fence, with a clear lawn at the front, but winding pathways amid tropical foliage with pergolas and little summer-houses in the rear. At the rear also were the presidential stables, and these stables were sometimes used for purposes other than the stabling of horses. Senators, officialdom, foreign consuls, and respectable visitors came in at the front gates past the sentry-boxes, but through the stables were habitually admitted persons of all sorts with whom Antoine-Simone had business which concerned him rather than the Republic of

[2] See Appendix, page 336.

Haiti, and these, when known and trusted by the stable sentries, made free of the back gardens.

One moonlight night in the spring of 1909—it was during Easter week—the Frenchman who now lives at the Cape was sitting in one of the little vine-covered summer-houses with his Haitian friend, holding a long private conversation. They were in that particular secluded spot because they did not want to be seen or overheard. They had come late, separately, to the previously arranged rendezvous, and sat there talking until long after midnight.

Toward one o'clock in the morning they heard a tramping of feet from the direction of the palace, and presently saw a black sergeant with two squads of soldiers marching toward the stable yard, along a pathway of the deserted gardens. They passed close to the summer-house. Behind them, at a little distance, came Célestine. She was barefooted, in a scarlet robe, and carried in her hands a silver dish.

In a small, open moonlit glade close to the summer-house, the sergeant halted his eight men and lined them up at attention, as if on a parade ground. Except for his low-voiced commands, not a word was spoken. Célestine, in her red robe which fell loose like a nightgown to her bare feet, laid the great silver platter on the grass.

The sergeant handed Célestine a forked bent twig, a sort of crude divining-rod, and stepped back a little distance. Célestine, holding the wand loosely before her, facing the eight soldiers standing at attention, began a gliding, sidestepping dance, singing her incantations of mixed African and creole in a low voice alternating from a deep guttural contralto to high falsetto, but never raised loudly, pointing the wand at each in turn as she glided to and fro before them.

The men stood rigid, silent as if paralyzed, but following her every movement with their rolling eyeballs as she glided slowly from end to end of the line.

For a long ten minutes that seemed interminable, Célestine glided to and fro, chanting her incantation, then suddenly stopped like a hunting-dog at point before one man who stood near the center of the row. The wand shot out stiff at the end of her outstretched arm and tapped him on the breast.

"*Ou là soule, avant!*" ordered the sergeant. (You there, alone, step forward.)

The man marched several paces forward from the ranks, and halting at command, stood still. The sergeant, who seemed unarmed, drew the man's own knife-bayonet from its scabbard, grasped the unresisting victim by the slack of his coat collar, and drove the point into his throat.

While this was taking place, the other seven men stood silent obediently at attention. The victim uttered not a single cry, except a gurgling grunt as the point went through his jugular, and slumped to the grass, where he twitched a moment and lay still.

The sergeant knelt quickly over him, as if in a hurry to get the job finished, ripped open the tunic, cut deep into the left side of the body just below the ribs, then put the knife aside, and tore out the heart with his hands.

Black Célestine in her red robe, holding the gleaming platter before her, returned alone beneath the palm trees to the palace, barefooted queen of the jungle, bearing a human heart in a silver dish.

Part Three:
THE TRAGIC COMEDY

Chapter I

A BLIND MAN WALKING ON EGGS

In the opening chapter of this book, I mentioned a High Commissioner and his lady. I seem to have left them seated with Katie and the colonel on a front veranda while I climbed over the back fence with Louis and ran away to the mountains.

I propose now a return by way of the front gate, to the dichromatic social world of Haiti's urban capital, under our own benevolent American protectorate.

The High Commission, with its resident Marine Corps —its colonels, majors, wives, and machine guns—its civilian treaty experts and technicians borrowed from the Navy— has introduced a number of constructive changes in the social-economic life of Haiti.

Among these changes are excellent roads, sewers, hospitals, sanitation, stabilized currency, economic prosperity, and political peace.

But we are more than crass materialists.

The most interesting and pervasive of the American innovations is the belated lesson in race-consciousness which we have been at pains to teach the Haitian upper classes.

These urban Haitians, free, vain, independent, and masters in their own land for a long hundred years or more, had accumulated money, education, a literature, an aristocratic tradition, and had somehow forgotten that God in His infinite wisdom had intended the negroes to remain always an inferior race. Indeed, as many Americans in Haiti will testify, there were members, whole families and social groups among the upper class, who were proud of being Haitians, proud actually of being negroes.

And one of the most difficult problems of the American occupation has been to teach these people their proper place. It has been difficult, because the Haitians have refused to accept this lesson graciously. It has been doubly difficult because a very important minority among the Americans have complicated the problem by treating the Haitians as if they were white.

Consequently this needful reform has not been quite so successful as the stamping out of malaria, but notable progress has been made.

I should say that only a rhinoceros could be unconscious of his skin in Port-au-Prince today.

And this would hold true regardless of whether the rhinoceros' inch-thick hide were black or white, for a situation has developed so fantastic as to be unthinkable in most parts of the United States; there are Haitians who draw a reverse color line and dare to despise white people.

Katie and I had encountered this topsy-turvy reversal of natural phenomena on the first days of our arrival in Port-au-Prince, and had found it somewhat bewildering.

It was a queer and in a way quite interesting experience, to be distrusted and occasionally despised for impersonal reasons connected solely with the pigmentation of one's skin.

I felt like a blind man walking on eggs for the first day or two in Haiti. Then I dropped in to see Christian Gross, the American Chargé d'Affaires, who had lived for years in Paris. We had mutual friends. To Mr. Gross I am indebted for the beginning of my first real orientation. The tangled social scene under the American occupation, I learned from him, was in some respects more simple than I could possibly have guessed. It seemed to have certain fixed, definite rules. What made it difficult was that there were many irregularities, exceptions to these rules. In this respect it was like Latin grammar.

Early in our conversation he mentioned putting my name up at the American club and offered me a guest card meanwhile. I suggested that this might prove embarrassing later to my American friends, since I had letters to numerous Haitians and hoped to be invited to their clubs and homes.

"It isn't so bad as that," he said. "I am a member at Mariani (the fashionable Haitian country club), and so are a number of other Americans. If you suffer embarrassment later, it will not be with us but with your Haitian friends, for although you may be invited to their clubs and entertained delightfully if they like you personally, you cannot reciprocate by inviting any Haitian to our club—not even the president of the Republic. Amusing, isn't it? We hold an open annual tennis tournament, in which both Haitians and Americans play; but it has to be held every year at Mariani because no Haitian may enter our club."

It sounded to me more or less insane, and I ventured to say so.

"As a matter of fact," he continued, "there is no general social mingling between the Americans and Haitians, except on formal official occasions. The Marine Corps, which is still here as an armed force, has almost no social contact with the Haitians—and this by a cordial, mutually reciprocated consent. Outside of the Marine Corps there are many exceptions to the general rule, and even a few within it."

By the way, changing the subject, where were we stopping? At the Belvidere. Mr. Gross advised me, purely as a matter of comfort, pending our house-hunting, to move up on the hill to the Hotel Montagne; we'd find it cooler and more spacious; it was an old converted palace, with a fine view of the city and bay.

Meanwhile, he said, this might be as good a moment as any to step upstairs to the office of the High Commission and pay my respects informally to General John H. Russell.

My last personal contact with a military High Commissioner had been a somewhat similar call on General Sarrail in Syria, and I suppose it was from my vivid recollection of his Ruddygore cheeks, fierce mustache, gold braid, medals, and clanking spurs—or perhaps it was merely from reading *The Nation*—that I rather expected to meet a military martinet. Instead, I found a phlegmatic gentleman in civilian clothes, with a vague resemblance to Punch, except that his chin was more of the bulldog type. I learned that General Russell, whose mission in Haiti carries the rank of ambassador, had chosen never to wear his Marine Corps uniform. He seemed to me, in our first brief chat, a man without sparkle, wit, or special intelligence, but solidly endowed with character and common sense. I found no reason later to alter materially these impressions.

Mr. Gross telephoned to the Hotel Montagne, arranging for our immediate accommodation, and suggested that he would drop by in the late afternoon and take us to the club, where we might find a game of tennis if I liked.

We wound upward toward the Hotel Montagne, passing beautiful villas, set behind walls amid palm trees, with glimpses through grilled gates of lovely lawns and tropical gardens. Immediately beyond this hill with its palaces and estates rose the tangled slopes of Morne Hôpital, the jungle mountain creeping down to the edge of the city, primitive and eternal as if patiently biding its time to reclaim its own.

The hotel itself was a rectangular three-storied palace, curiously ecclesiastical in architecture. There were bits of stained-glass window here and there, stone balustrades and cornices which shouted, "*Pax vobiscum.*" I wondered if it had been built by a bishop. Madame Shea, the proprietress, who had a tired smile, and a chattering marmoset on the end of a silver chain, told us that it had been built by a black president with material stolen from the half-finished cathedral, as a home for one of his mulatto mistresses.

He had certainly done well by his *mulatresse*. A big veranda, now the dining-terrace, looked out through tropical foliage with clambering pink Bougainvillaea blossoms upon a panorama of sea and mountains which neither Algiers nor the Bay of Naples could surpass. Haiti, thus viewed, was a paradise. From an upper terrace, adjacent to which Madame Shea installed us in a clean, airy bed-chamber, we could see the towering peaks of Santo Domingo's central range, a hundred miles away.

In the later afternoon, Mr. Gross appeared and took us in his roadster to the American club, on Turgeau, another villa-dotted slope ten minutes distant. It was children's day, and all the little American children with their nurses were scattered about the lawn, while a band in the pergola played "Katinka." General Russell was already on the court, volleying down the sidelines against a lank, familiar-looking figure who turned out to be William Beebe. I played singles with a Major R. H. Davis of the Marine Corps, while Mr. Gross and Katie met the wives of various officers and treaty officials on the terrace. Before sunset the band played the Haitian national anthem. All the little American children with their nurses arose and stood charmingly at attention—all the American grown-ups too, including General Russell, my opponent Major Davis, and the other officers in flannels on the tennis courts, who stopped their play and snapped smartly to salute for the Haitian national tune. I wondered whether this gracious demonstration of esteem would comfort me if I were an aristocratic Haitian, barred from this club's sacred portals by a Jim Crow rule which probably no Haitian had dreamed could exist in his own free republic until we came down to befriend them.

It may seem that I am over-emphasizing this color question, but it would be futile to attempt any true picture of the urban Haitian scene today without giving it the all-pervasive, equivocal, and frequently acute predominance which it actually has.

Major Davis and I had grown friendly during our tennis game. He invited me home with him to dinner; we found our respective wives on the veranda, who had met and were also friendly. His house, a wide-porticoed mansion with enormous rooms and acres of formal garden, had been built, I believe, by another revolutionary president. On this first evening, the Major and I formed one of those sudden friendships destined to last because it was based on violently candid disagreement, openly arrived at. We disagreed fundamentally and vigorously on every subject from Henry Ford to religion, women, the meaning of marriage, the art of Picasso, and the future of the Chinese, until our wives cried, "For heaven's sake, shut up, the two of you!" He promised to take me guinea-hunting. He advanced the dictum meanwhile that "all writers and artists were more or less nuts," and when, as he had been praising the wisdom of Congress, I declared, to annoy him, that "all congressmen were fatheads and most of them crooks," he replied without rancor that his own father was a congressman and that I was a God-damned Bolshevik, just as he had suspected from the first. The only thing we agreed on was the quality of his sixteen-year-old Haitian rum.

Inevitably we touched upon what Major Davis called "the nigger question." Mrs. Davis had been asking about life among the Arabs. The Major said, "Well, of course, you'll never be able to get as close as that to the Haitians; you won't want to; of course you'll meet them and see them, as we all have to do sometimes, but you won't want to be intimate." I said, "Why not? I understand that they are interesting, that many of them are well worth knowing." He replied, "Yes, but after all they *are* niggers. You can't get away from that."

And so we were off, full steam ahead. "If you had a daughter, etc., etc.," said Major Davis; and, "Suppose your own sister, etc., etc.," to which I replied, without knowing whether I was telling the truth or not, that if I had a daughter I'd rather she'd, etc., etc., including the subsequent baby, with a good Haitian if she loved him, than with a bad blond Nordic she didn't love.

"You're as crazy as hell," said the Major, "and besides you haven't got a daughter." But he didn't throw me out of his house. He invited me to have another drink, and during the months which followed he invited us back many a time to his house, despite the fact he knew we might have been dining or dancing with Haitians the previous evening. I am anxious to present Major Davis fairly, because he seems to me important as being typical of most Marine Corps officers in Haiti today. I never saw him commit a brutal act, never even an intentionally offensive gesture toward any Haitian. There is no question involved here of swaggering about in Prussian boots and pushing people off the sidewalk. Reports of that sort, in my sincere belief, after living in Haiti with my eyes open, are propagandist rot. We had to kill a few of them at first, for various reasons. But that is all fortunately ended. Our attitude now in Haiti is superior, but kindly.

Chapter II

A NYMPH IN BRONZE

LÉONCE BORNO, Haitian consul-general in New York, had written concerning us to his kinsman, Georges Baussan, Haiti's leading architect, who had designed the new national palace.

One morning soon after we were installed in the Hotel Montagne, a barefooted black wench tapped at our door and presented Monsieur Baussan's card on a silver tray. I mention the tray because this same wench had deemed her own dark and not too clean paw adequate for the cards of previous white callers. These amusing little variations do not occur by accident in Haiti. They frequently fill Americans with impotent or explosive rage. Pretense that the servants are dumb affords a fictitious safety-valve.

I found Monsieur Baussan on the terrace, tropically attired in white linen, tentatively twirling his watch-chain, standing at a distance and with his back turned to some elderly American women who were rocking and buzz-buzzing.

Haitians were no longer "encouraged" to stop at the Hotel Montagne, but the big terrace-veranda was neutral ground.

Monsieur Baussan was a *griffe*, that is to say brown-skinned, midway between black and mulatto; he was past middle age, a large man, heavy, handsome, with fine mustaches, kinky hair; in his intelligent face there was an expression of veiled sadness, which, combined with his bulk and the slight yellow tinge in the whites of his eyeballs, made me think of a fine Saint Bernard dog.

Monsieur Baussan was tentative. Above all he was tentative. He was tentative even after I had insisted on his taking the better chair and offered a light for his cigarette.

M. Baussan was only a microscopic shade less tentative when Katie presently appeared. He remained tentative indeed to the last, when, after chatting for some twenty minutes, he said good-by. It was not coldness or uncordiality. It was subtle, studied self-protection. It was curious, slightly uncomfortable, and very interesting.

Three afternoons later, we returned Monsieur Baussan's call. The high-walled gardens and villa were only a stone's throw from the hotel. Monsieur had not yet returned from his office, but would be coming soon. Madame Baussan, mulatto, slender, pretty, and much younger than her husband, received us with shy grace, on a luxurious rug-strewn veranda. The furniture was mostly of pale-green painted wicker, for coolness; there were also pieces of native mahogany. On tables and taborets were strewn recent Paris fashion magazines, a *Mercure de France*, a number of French and German novels, recent journals in those two languages, a piece of embroidery on which Madame had been stitching. I observed no English or American publications. Apparently, the culture of the Baussan family derived exclusively from the Continental.

A butler came presently, uncalled, with grenadine in tall glasses, the edges of their rims frost-crusted with crystals of rose-colored sugar. "Would Monsieur prefer a brandy and soda? *Non?* Perhaps later then, when Monsieur Baussan arrived. He should be coming any moment now."

I ventured to disclose that when Madame had received us, I had mistaken her for a daughter of the family. She was not displeased. She explained that for her husband this was a second marriage. The first Madame Baussan had died some years before, leaving three daughters and a son, now grown. They were off at a *thé dansant* this afternoon, but another day . . . Meantime she would like us to see her own children. They appeared presently with a maid, who stood in the doorway shooing them forward—Pierrot, about four, a little, coatless Lord Fauntleroy in velvet knickers and wide Windsor collar, woolly-haired and dark-skinned, who sucked his thumb and ran to mamma—six-year-old Marcelle, lighter and curly-haired, who made a pretty curtsy and was rewarded with a bonbon, while Master Pierrot could have none until he came back and shook hands with the visitors. Eventually he climbed into Katie's lap, and his little sister, observing this, lisped, as if she had found the solution of something that had been vaguely puzzling her mind, "*C'est une dame française alors, Maman?*"

It occurred to me that an analysis of the implications behind that infantile and apparently trivial question might have a more important bearing on the final solution of the Haitian problem than all the tons of senatorial investigation, inquiries, and reports.

Madame Baussan meanwhile replied simply in answer to the apparently so simple query, "*Mais non, Marcelle, c'est une dame américaine.*"

Monsieur Baussan now arrived and seemed pleased to see us. We strolled about the garden, where he pointed out pomegranate trees, breadfruit, cocoanut, and less familiar fruit-bearing sapodillas, caimitiers, and *cœurs-de-bœuf*. He called a yard-boy who climbed one of the cocoanut trees, barefooted, like a monkey or a jumping-jack, up the smooth, tall trunk, and clinging among the fronds, twisted off heavy cocoanuts in their thick, green-yellow husks, which dropped and plopped violently on the lawn. The boy slid down, found a machete, and chopped through husk and shell with a single glancing blow; the butler brought glasses with ice, into which the sweet, cloudy milk was poured, with a dash of rum. To me it was sickly and unpleasant. I tried some without the rum and found it worse. Monsieur Baussan thought it might be an acquired taste, but said that he also cared little for it.

Through a gate in a brick wall we entered the rose garden, which sloped down a hillside, There were acres of roses, white, yellow, red, covering the slope; the soft evening air was fragrant with their odor. It appeared that my host was an *amateur des roses*. He had eight hundred bushes, including varieties which had come from all parts of the world. He told me with pride that it was the finest rose garden in Haiti, perhaps in the whole West Indies. Madame plucked an armful, and to see her bending among the buds and full-blown flowers was charming. She herself was like a yellow rose. Her pale golden skin was faintly flushed with pink. Her cheeks were like the petals of a pale yellow rose.

When we returned to the veranda, Madame Baussan spread out the multicolored roses in her lap, and began removing thorns from their long stems. Katie said, "Oh, but that is too much!" Madame replied, "No, only these white ones have thorns; all the other varieties are *sans épines*."

Was she being amiably matter-of-fact, or was this the quintessence of a subtlety, cynical and barbed, yet elusive as the musk of the plucked roses?

Madame was smiling, and we could not guess. Nor could we guess whether there was any intangible connection between this episode and the fact that Monsieur Baussan, almost as if to announce the termination of tentative protective subtleties, suddenly recollected that there was to be a ball at Bellevue (the ultra-exclusive Haitian town club) on the following evening, and said they would be charmed if we cared to attend it as their guests.

Next morning we received cards to the ball, inscribed with the names of Monsieur and Madame Baussan. It was being given for the officers of the Royal Swedish battleships on world-tour, which lay at anchor in the bay.

Arriving at the Bellevue next evening, it might have been any club on a gala night at Nice, Marseilles, New Orleans, except for the darker skins of the arriving guests; there were jammed limousines, traffic policemen with special details holding back the crowds which craned their necks as the fashionable *élite* descended from their cars to the canvas-covered pavement and trailed up the staircase beneath a striped canopy.

Except in the foyer of the Paris opera house during the war, I have never seen anything so brilliant and formal, yet so gay, as the picture presented by the great main ballroom as we stood for a moment in its doorway while our host was being sought.

Here was assembled the native aristocracy of Haiti, its brains, wealth, and beauty, its inner circle; and recalling that these people had come up from plantation slavery in the brief cycle of a century, it was very interesting.

It became immediately apparent that this aristocracy was principally mulatto, but by no means entirely so. Here and there were coal-black dowagers seated proudly at their ease, coal-black demoiselles dancing; over yonder former President Légitime, with a powerful head like that of an aged Roman senator carved in ebony. But these stood out sharply. Between these pure blacks and the dominant pale mulatto tone with its lighter shades of quadroon and octaroon, there was a considerable element of brown like my friend Monsieur Baussan, who had appeared meanwhile and was escorting us to a terrace opening on the ballroom, where we found Madame Baussan with Seymour Pradel, the leading lawyer and bachelor beau of Port-au-Prince society; also a Monsieur Roi whose face, although it was so dark as to be almost black, with its aquiline nose, thin lips, and finely molded skull, showed not the slightest trace of what is loosely associated with the word negroid. It required no poring over the historical pages of Moreau de Saint Méry to understand that the seventeenth-century slavers had been, to say the least, careless in selecting their supposed "human cattle" for West Indian export. Here flowed the blood of warriors and chiefs. Revolt, uprising, massacre, were bound to follow the enslavement of such types as these. Came presently, asking Katie to dance, young Maurice de Joie, with the face of an Iroquois who had stepped from the pages of Fenimore Cooper to masquerade in modern evening clothes, and proud as Satan of a descent traced back, Madame told me, to one of the great African princely families on the southern edge of the Sahara.

Madame Baussan and I strolled among the tables on the terrace, toward the dance floor. She designated various individuals or groups, pausing occasionally for introductions. Except for the Swedish naval officers in their resplendent glittering full dress, there were few whites present—Mr. Edwards, the British consul-general, with his lady, small family groups from the other European legations—an American naval commander, Dr. Paul Wilson, head of the Haitian General Hospital. Dr. Wilson was in civilian clothes. There is a rule at the Club Bellevue that no American in military uniform may enter its doors—*histoire* of an evening ten years ago when General Smedley Butler was told, after too pointedly folding his hands behind his back, or something of the sort, that his presence was socially objectionable.

While dancing with Madame Baussan, I noticed, gliding in the arms of the tall flaxen-haired Swedish admiral, a tall, pale-brown-skinned lithe creature of whom my hostess said proudly in answer to my query, "That is Thérèse, our daughter."

There was no crush on the floor, so that I was able to observe her closely. She was slightly darker than mulatto. She was a tall, strong, slender hamadryad in pale bronze. She was like a pale bronze nymph come to life from the Luxembourg gallery, but fitted in the Rue de la Paix with a scant clinging frock of old rose shot with gold, pale gold stockings, and high-heeled slippers. Her figure was revealed candidly as the current world-wide fashion is. Her legs, her ankles, arched instep, and long, slender feet were Louis Quinze rather than sculptural. It was interesting because of the general Anglo-Saxon belief that persons of partial African descent invariably lack grace in this particular.

As Mlle. Thérèse glided close beside us in the arms of the blond Swedish admiral she said, "*Tu t'amuses bien, Maman.*" Big, sultry brown eyes flashed, wide-set beneath a low forehead; there was a touch of cruelty, *sauvagerie*, I thought, in the wide, short chin, cobra-like cheek bones, the mouth like a slashed red fruit; a touch of negroid too in the chin and slightly retroussé nose, a touch also which suggested the face of Faustina on old Roman golden coins, Pola Negri as the wife of Pharaoh. Her hair, bobbed in an almost Egyptian style, was crinkly. She was too wise in her sure beauty to straighten it by pomades or tricks. She was Africa, yet not quite Africa, Africa of the poets rather than of the ethnologists and explorers.

Later I was presented to Mlle. Thérèse and we danced. Her conversation, French, was the usual banal social patter. There was a restraint and poise in her talk and in her dancing, yet in her 'cello-like contralto voice and the swaying of her body there lurked potentialities neither banal nor restrained. Shut behind the fashionable convent culture, the Paris-gowned sophistication, the facile small talk, something was asleep, yet not asleep, like a caged panther dreaming.

Sitting opposite Mlle. Thérèse at midnight, with Monsieur Baussan at the head of a long table, glittering with long-stemmed champagne glasses, massed roses, and pink trailing vines of Belle Mexicaine, I reflected on the strange biological-hereditary processes that had culminated in his daughter. It occurred to me that in terms of cold science, if not by more conventional standards, she represented a fusing of the highest selective elements in both the white and negro races. I shall try to explain presently what I mean by "highest." Assuming that these highly selective elements were fused in her, I wondered whether she represented some ultimate future type, superior perhaps to anything that either race alone could breed, and which, a thousand years or ten thousand years hence, might become the dominant superior world-type. I wondered whether even now, an unprejudiced, detached ethnologist visiting the earth from another planet would not deem Mlle. Thérèse superior in physical beauty and strength, in richness of potentiality, perhaps also in pigmentation, to any purely white or purely negro type.

The first French colonial planters and slave-owners were pre-Napoleonic aristocrats, viscounts and marquises, gentleman adventurers. The slaves were not imported from thick-lipped Congo stock alone, but from diverse and widely scattered African peoples, including the royal Dahomey strain and many of tall Zulu warrior caste. Slightly decadent but authentic aristocratic blood, cross-breeding with strong, rich primitive blood, makes an excellent biological mixture. The French colonial masters chose mistresses and concubines from their slave girls. They chose the prettiest, healthiest, and most desirable. It was deplorable morally if you like, but it was biologically sound. It was probably also agreeable.

As a cross-strain in the white blood of Mlle. Thérèse, who now sat opposite me toying with her champagne glass, there may also have been blood of the buccaneers, the pirates and adventurers of the golden days in the Spanish Main.

As I sat speculating about Mlle. Thérèse in terms of her ancestors—the slave-owning marquis with his jeweled snuff-box, the swashbuckling buccaneer captain in plumed hat and lace, the pretty dark-skinned slave mistresses and concubines—it occurred to me how very interested, and perhaps astonished, the ghosts of her various ancestors would be if they could come back on this stroke of midnight and see the ultimate product of their fusing, this rather gorgeous, poised, modern creature with her crinkly hair, Egyptian-bobbed, and high-heeled gold slippers, dancing with the tall blond Swedish admiral—belle of the ball at Bellevue.

Chapter III

"THE TRUTH IS A BEAUTIFUL THING"

"You will be entertained this afternoon," said my white friend Ash Pay Davis, "for I've invited Ernest Chauvet to call and meet you. We'll loosen up with a few rum cocktails and weep together over Haiti's tragic fate."

"Who is Ernest Chauvet?" I asked, and Ash Pay sketched Chauvet's background quickly.

Chauvet was the chief thorn in the flesh of the American occupation, owner and editor of the *Nouvelliste*, violently anti-American and consequently anti-Borno. Every little while President Borno threw him in jail, where he enjoyed himself hugely, devoured whole roast turkeys, drank champagne, and thumbed his nose at the wide world outside. But even his bitterest political enemies, including some of the American treaty officials whom he belabored and traduced outrageously in his editorial column, liked him as an individual because of his wit, gay amiability, and cynical candor. Most of the little Americans feared and despised him, but it seemed that he was on terms of curious intimacy with some of the big chiefs, as for instance with my present host Ash Pay, active head of the American Chamber of Commerce in Haiti, who, though in no way connected with the official administration, was a close personal friend of Borno and at that time an ardent advocate of the American-Borno régime.

Ash Pay told me that Ernest Chauvet's father, now dead, founder of the *Nouvelliste*, a distinguished editor and publicist, planning to bequeath the journal to his son, had sent young Ernest first to Paris for university education, and then to New York to get his practical newspaper training on the *Brooklyn Eagle.* Young Chauvet had worked on the *Eagle* for two years, first as a reporter and then as a feature writer. In New York he had never been regarded as a negro, and his wit had made him popular in Bohemian journalistic circles.

Returning to Haiti, on his father's death, he had succeeded to the proprietorship of the *Nouvelliste.* In the first Borno presidential election, conducted under "supervision" of the American Treaty Mission, Chauvet's father-in-law, Stephen Archer, had been the opposing candidate, and young Chauvet, with Latin dramatics and tears, but perhaps with his tongue in his cheek, had proclaimed that it would be his sacred duty for the honor of the family to continue opposing Borno and the Americans forever.

How much his opposition was based on patriotism, how much on family loyalty, how much on sheer cynical devilment, Ash Pay doubted if Chauvet himself could honestly have told.

Meanwhile a car was coming up the driveway. It stopped before the palm-shaded terrace, and out bounced Ernest Chauvet. He was youthful, large, ebullient, and fat. He wore a big wide-brimmed smoke-tan cowboy hat, which he removed and flourished. In his white linen he was like a snow-covered mountain. His clear skin seemed only faintly tanned rather than mulatto, his hair was wavy brown, his eyes pale greenish blue, wide-set in a splendidly shaped large head. He was handsome, decidedly a *beau garçon* despite his fatness.

Ascending the steps, he shouted to Ash Pay, "I bring something for your friend," shook hands with careless cordiality, and handed me a copy of his newspaper. It was an afternoon edition, still wet from the press. On its front page was an editorial leader some quarter of a column long, entitled, with a question mark, "L'Américain, Seabrook?" The tenor of it was that another "friend of the iniquitous military occupation," a writer absurdly claiming to be open-minded, had arrived in Port-au-Prince ostensibly to "write the truth about our unhappy country," and as usual was spending all his time at the American club, sponsored by American officials, and that he was now the house-guest in the home of "the very man whose gigantic schemes to rob the poor Haitian peasants of their lands filled all patriots with horror" (meaning our mutual friend Ash Pay, who was handing him a cocktail).

When I had finished reading this, Chauvet lifted his glass toward mine and said with a gay, expansive grin, "*Gesundheit;* how you like it? And how you like our rum?"

I said, "I like your rum all right—*Gesundheit* to you—but how can you expect a writer to write the truth about Haiti when you mix it up at the start by writing a lot of goddamned lies about him? Ash Pay here was telling me you had your training on the *Brooklyn Eagle*, but I doubt it. I think you must have got your start on the yellow sheets. Furthermore you *are* a liar, as you'd know if you'd been at your own Bellevue club last night. While you were cooking up this tripe, Mrs. Seabrook and I were dancing and drinking champagne with Haitian friends and having the time of our lives—the best since we were last in Paris."

"Sure thing," he agreed, grinning; "I know it. My friend Pradel told me all about it."

"Then why this stuff?"

"Oh," said Chauvet, "I must be faithful to my subscribers. They'd be disappointed. Even the Americans. They all read it. They'd feel cheated if I didn't do my stuff. Besides, news and gossip are scarce just now. Tomorrow I can write something nice about you, and so I'll have two articles instead of one."

"All right, my friend," said I; "but since we are both writers, let's try a little fifty-fifty. It so happens that I am really going to try to write truthfully about Haiti—not any partisan, political, propagandist, or 'devastating' truth, but just to describe your interesting people as they really are, or at least as they seem to me. I am not down here to attack the occupation, and I'm not down here to defend it. I'm not interested in politics. I'm interested in people."

"Fine," said Chauvet; "it's a good idea, if you're not lying. You must let me know any time I can help you."

During the next two hours Ash Pay, Chauvet, and I consumed a good many rum cocktails there on the terrace beneath the palm trees. I doubt, despite Omar Khayyám and the Latin proverb, that any profound philosophic truth has ever leapt from the wine-cup, but I do believe that convivial drinking occasionally promotes the uninhibited expression of opinion. I believe that I may have learned more from Chauvet that afternoon concerning the real feelings of many upper-class Haitians toward the Americans in Haiti than I could have gleaned from a thousand formal reports or more restrained discussions.

"The Americans have taught us a lot of things," Chauvet was saying. "Among other things they have taught us that we are niggers. You see, we really didn't know that before. We thought we were negroes.

"Now I, my friend, *je m'en fiche*, *je m'en fou*, *je m'en foute* that I am a nigger. I laugh and grow fat. For me such things are comedy. But for others, who are more easily hurt than I, these things are not always so comic."

Chauvet paused. His face clouded. For the first time that afternoon he was serious. "You understand French, of course," he said to me. "Perhaps I could explain this matter to you. I can't do it in English because I have lost the psychology of speaking seriously in English. I am always ragging and kidding. *Eh bien*, *alors*."

Chauvet continued in French. There was more than a difference of tongue, however. It was as if a different man were speaking.

"When the Americans landed in Haiti twelve years ago, there existed in our cities a free, proud aristocracy. We regarded ourselves as human beings like any others. We were masters in our own land. And no whites who came to our country could prosper or be happy here without accepting us as such. This condition had existed for more than a century, almost as long as the life of your own republic.

"The homes of our so-called *élite*, our intellectuals and higher bourgeoisie, equaled in refinement those of the best European countries. Our culture was in the French tradition. Our sons, in many cases, had attended the French universities, our daughters the Catholic convent schools in France, and this, my friend, in many families, for a number of successive generations.

"Our homes, our clubs, our social life were like those of any other civilized country. White foreigners who visited or settled in Haiti were received as guests in our homes, frequently married among us.

"If you have read French books like that amusing volume *Au Pays des Généraux*, or books like L'Herisson's *Sena* written by our own native satirists, you may think I am exaggerating this picture. But with these, though they have sometimes made us squirm, it has been like Alphonse Daudet poking his fun at the Meridionals. We have had our Tartarins, also our comic opera generals, our foibles, our ridiculous side, but those Europeans who have exploited them in literature or laughed at them in life have never injected the wholly different element of social-racial contempt.

"No! It remained for the Americans, first the Marine Corps military occupation and then the treaty civilians, to inflict upon us that insult in our own free land. And it has been more than a matter of hurt pride. It has brought something shameful. It has made many of us ashamed in our hearts of our own race, ashamed of our birth and of our families and of the blood that flows in our own veins. For not all are strong enough to laugh and say '*Je m'en fiche*' as I do. . . ."

Chauvet was still enlarging on his theme when Ash

Pay's eighteen-year-old daughter Elsa, blonde, popular débutante of American society in Port-au-Prince, cantered up the driveway and leaped off her pony.

Chauvet had been saying that American women in Haiti were "worse than American men"—that while certain officers and important civilians maintained at least a pretense of politeness, even sometimes cordiality, the wives and daughters of these same men in most cases held themselves contemptuously superior. So Miss Elsa's arrival at that moment seemed to me especially interesting.

The three of us arose as she came smiling up the steps, with a "Hello, everybody," hugged her father, "Hello, Chauvet, I'm just down from Kenscoff. Gee, what a change in the temperature! You ought to ride up there oftener, you wouldn't be so fat." She shook hands with Chauvet, and said, "How do you do" to me more formally—we had met only once before. Would she have a cocktail? No, thanks, what she wanted was a shower. She chatted a moment and was gone.

I looked at Chauvet. It had all been so entirely casual. It had been more casual than if she *had* sat down with us for a cocktail she didn't want. It seemed to me that she had treated Chauvet neither as a negro nor as a white man, but simply as "a human being like any other." In my mind I was quoting Chauvet's own phrase against him, and he knew precisely what I was thinking, though I said nothing.

Chauvet grinned, accurately reading my thoughts, but as if he felt that the joke, if it could be called such, was at my expense rather than his own.

"So! I am a liar again! Do not be deceived, my friend. Elsa is no typical American. She is scarcely an American at all. Madame Davis, her mother, you know, is a lady, most gracious and high-born, from the land of Ibsen and the reindeers. Ash Pay Davis here is an American, a robber of oppressed peoples, a bloody capitalist. He will steal our whole Artibonite valley maybe, but meanwhile he is charming, a civilized gentleman of the world. Now let me tell you a real joke. On this entire island there are perhaps eight or a dozen American women who meet our Haitian *élite* without contempt or patronage, and these same eight or a dozen are perhaps the only American women on the island who, when they return to their native America, are at home in their own high society, Newport, Bar Harbor, Park Avenue, yachts in the Sound, boxes at the opera, snapshots in the rotogravure sections, and prize pups at the Madison Square Garden.

"The biggest joke of all is that one of these ladies is Madame John Henry Russell, wife of the High Commissioner! *Madame la Générale.* She, that lady, she is what you call international society; she is at home in Mayfair, she is at home in the palaces of Chinese mandarins, and she is at home here. *Elle s'en fiche* the color lines drawn by American women whose social experience has been previously limited to Marine Corps posts and their own small towns in Alabama or Nebraska.

"It is said, more often by the Americans than by us, that Madame Russell, because of her high official importance, is being diplomatic, and, of course she is, but that doesn't mean she's hypocritical. Anyway Haitians like her, and despite my own noble patriotic efforts to have General Russell and his whole damned Marine Corps thrown out on their leather necks, I think we'd all be sorry to see Madame Russell go.

"But it is a grand joke, isn't it? The general's wife invites us to tea and finds us charming, but the sergeant's wife, or the captain's, who maybe did her own washing at home, is our social superior and would feel herself disgraced to shake hands with any nigger.

"Do you wonder that I say *je m'en foute de tout ça*, that I find it ironic? Why, many of those white Marine Corps people couldn't have entered my mulatto father's house except by the servants' entrance, and they can't enter my house now by any entrance, except to arrest me once in a while—which reminds me that the last captain who did come to arrest me is a grand *bozo* who had been at my house several times before, and welcome. So now I am a liar after all. He telephoned me first to ask if it would be convenient. I was up at the villa in Petionville where we'd often played bridge together. We had a pint of champagne before we started for the hoosegow. Happy days! There are a few like that in the Marine Corps, mostly Yankees, who had it in their beans before they ever came to Haiti that all negroes were not cornfield coons."

Chauvet had reverted to English again, or rather to the American vernacular he had learned in New York, and I am quoting his literal words here unclouded by translation.

He continued:

"Now if the Americans were all like that, I don't mean if they were all gentlemen—that would be an absurdity—you can't pick an army of occupation from the Social Register or drill them with salad forks—but if they were generally people who regarded us as human beings—well, I'm still against the occupation for lofty patriotic reasons which have nothing to do with racial prejudice, but if they used more tact, more common sense, sent down here only people who were free of this crazy prejudice, there wouldn't be all this added unnecessary mess which has made more mutual dislike, distrust, and trouble than all the senatorial howlings and journalistic rows since the caco revolution.

"By the way, Monsieur the writer, you said something about being in Haiti for human-interest stuff. Maybe this is human interest. But maybe it is too human. You couldn't publish it. Too much under the skin. Lily-white skin, black skin. All the world's kin, Shakespeare . . . Madame Russell . . . and the sergeant's wife, and us niggers . . ."

"Chauvet," said I, "we're getting drunk, but the truth is a beautiful thing. The truth is a beautiful thing even when it's tangled and in doubtful taste."

Chapter IV

"LADIES AND GENTLEMEN, THE PRESIDENT!"

THE chastely engraved card, large as a wedding invitation or a Christmas greeting, said simply: *Le Président de la République d'Haiti.*

On its blank reverse was written in ink—"*Recevra Monsieur W. B. Seabrook au Palais National le jeudi 6 Janvier courant, a 4 h.p.m.*"

There was also an engraved coat-of-arms—parked canon and furled flags beneath a palm tree.

My watch said only half-past three; so I decided to improve the interval by dropping in for a moment at Marine Brigade Headquarters to confirm a guinea-hunting engagement with some of the gentlemen whose armed presence in Haiti, sitting on the lid, is perhaps the reason why the local artillery remains peacefully parked beneath a palm tree.

Of the six presidents who had succeeded each other somewhat rapidly just prior to our intervention, one had been blown up in his palace, one poisoned, one assassinated, another torn into little pieces.

The Brigade was installed precisely in the old Guillaume Sam palace before whose gates, only ten years before, a black woman had been biting chunks out of that defunct president's bleeding heart.

It was only a three-minute walk across the tranquil Champs de Mars with its bandstand, lawns, monuments, drill grounds, and boulevards, to the handsome new presidential palace more permanently and safely inhabited by his Excellency Louis Borno.

Past sentries, up a great white glaring stairway almost

as impressive as that at Washington, escorted then through superb corridors by an aide in glittering uniform, I found myself presently sitting all alone in a vast, bare salon, twiddling my thumbs.

The interior of the palace seemed drowsy, quiet, in the tropical midafternoon. Through a partly opened door, I could see the marble flagging of what seemed to be a wide inner corridor. This angular section of marble floor framed in the half-shut doorway was flooded with sunlight. Presently across it a black shadow passed. At regular intervals this black shadow passed again. It was the head and shoulders of an American soldier, sharp, foreshortened on the sunlit marble floor, the silhouette of a shouldered rifle and fixed bayonet, a wide-brimmed U.S. army hat, a Frederick Remington detail in chiaroscuro. The silhouette was as utterly American as a brass band blaring the "Star-Spangled Banner." I tiptoed to the door and peeped at the man. And it seemed amazing that his face was black. It was illogical, of course, that it seemed so amazing. There had been our own black troops in precisely these accoutrements at San Juan Hill. And I had already seen a thousand black gendarmes similarly uniformed here in Haiti. It was because I had first seen this man as a shadow. Now he seemed to me something which had been masqueraded and projected on a screen. As a barefooted Haitian peasant in overalls, he had been himself. Just what was he now?

As I wondered about him, I began wondering in the same way about President Borno, whom I was presently to meet. Was he too a shadow silhouette projected on a screen? Was he Russell's magic-lantern toy?

It was so easy, I reflected, as I sat there twiddling my thumbs, to find politicians, statesmen, patriots, propagandists, imperialists, anti-imperialists, both in Haiti and Washington, who could answer such questions categorically; our occupation (or mission, if you choose) in Haiti is selfish, it is unselfish, tyrannical, benevolent; the best Haitians like us, the best Haitians hate us, Borno is a patriot, he's a traitor, he's a puppet, he's a smarter man than Russell, he's a monkey on a stick. . . . The only difficulty with these categorical affirmations was that they somewhat contradicted each other.

Monsieur Leys, cabinet secretary, entered briskly, cordially, interrupting my reflections. Monsieur Leys wore a little Napoleon III beard elegantly trimmed, a frock coat with braided edges, the inevitable bit of French colored ribbon in its lapel. He made elegant French gestures and phrases. He was a typical ministry secretary of the Elysée, except that his face was black. If Monsieur Leys was an American-controlled shadow, he was projected by a cardboard stamped *Fabriqué en France.*

Monsieur Leys threw open two sliding doors and ushered me into a richly furnished drawing-room, slightly too ornate, with a gilded boule clock and statuettes in marble and bronze, oriental rugs, two or three vases filled with deep pink roses.

The President of Haiti entered this drawing-room at the same moment from a private door.

Monsieur Borno was smaller of stature than one would guess from his pictures. He was a dapper little man, elderly, almost foppish in his sartorial elegance, but with a fine intellectual head. His brow had dominated his photographs, but his eyes dominated the man; they were serious and rather arresting eyes, behind his pince-nez with its dangling ribbon. He was a pale mulatto; he was clean-shaven except for a small close-trimmed mustache; his features had almost no trace of negroid; his thick iron-gray hair, curly but not kinky, receded from a high forehead.

There was more than a bit of the scholarly dandy in him, a shade too meticulous I thought—professorial; but there was no academic coldness in the man really, I discovered as we talked. He lacked humor, and it seemed to me also, though I somewhat revised the opinion later, that he lacked warmth.

He was outwardly cordial, but formal, on his guard. My letters to him had said I was a writer. So he talked, in precise book English, on the subject in which an American writer no doubt should have been primarily interested—the improvement of conditions in Haiti under the American treaty (which, by the way, Borno's own pen had signed). It was all doubtless important but dry and statistical; for instance, the construction of 1,349 miles, or maybe it was kilometers, of highways. The figures meant nothing to me. I'm probably quoting them inaccurately now. But it gave me a sort of picture when he said:

"You know in 1915, when the Americans landed, there was exactly one automobile in Haiti, an old Ford. Many Haitians were rich enough to own fine cars, but there was no place to drive them. There were no roads outside the cities. Traveling from Port-au-Prince to Cap Haïtien was a matter of days on horseback—weeks if the rivers were in flood. Now there are more than 12,000 motor cars, and we traverse our little country from south to north in a single day. . . ."

By the way, there was to be a presidential *tournée* through the north this same month to dedicate the new bridge, Pont Christophe. Perhaps I might care to be one of the party. If so, arrangements could easily be made, and I should see for myself. . . . I thanked him and accepted. It was the moment to take leave. As I arose he inquired about his nephew, Monsieur Léonce Borno, in New York. I was able to tell his Excellency that Monsieur Léonce had appeared to be in the best of health and spirits, that we had dined together just prior to my departure, and that he had presented Mrs. Seabrook with a copy of the *Haitian Anthology of Poetry*, in which I had had the pleasure of reading some of his Excellency's own verses.

This reminded him that Madame Borno would be pouring tea on Thursday afternoon—quite informal. There would be tennis first in the palace gardens.

When I say that it was like an operetta on a two-acre stage—this tennis party in the palace gardens when Thursday afternoon came round—I do not mean *opéra bouffe* or comic opera; I mean something like Offenbach or Strauss, modernized; it was gayer, more colorful, more kaleidoscopic than anything I was accustomed to connect with official social gatherings.

The tropical setting may have contributed slightly to this theater-like impression—the wide green lawns, trellised summer-houses and pavilions, vine-covered and flaming with bright blossoms, white gravel paths and marble-flagged promenades bordered by flowers, the cycloramic backdrop curtain of the mountains. But it was the crowd itself, really, that was kaleidoscopic, variegated, chromatic, brilliant.

Pretty Haitian girls and women were everywhere, some in ultra-fashionable creations from France; slender, silken legs, tapering to high-heeled slippers; chic hats and parasols, lips scarlet-rouged; others in tennis costume, athletic, flat-shod, with gay sweaters and vividly striped blazers. Their skins were of every tint from seeming pure, creamy white, shading through rose-glowing Spanish brunette to mulatto, café au lait, brown, black; they were like the ladies made of plaster and metal in fashionable gown-shop windows on upper Fifth Avenue, or like Byzantine polychromes; bare arms, necks, and faces mat gold, copper, bronze, even onyx, animated and alive.

Among the men, who composed at least half the gay mingling crowd, there was equal variety of pigmentation and almost equal kaleidoscopic variation in costume, since some were smartly attired for tennis, some in white, some dark frock-coated, many blazing with gold braid and bright-colored military decorations, tall, dusky, handsome, crinkly-haired young native officers of the palace guard.

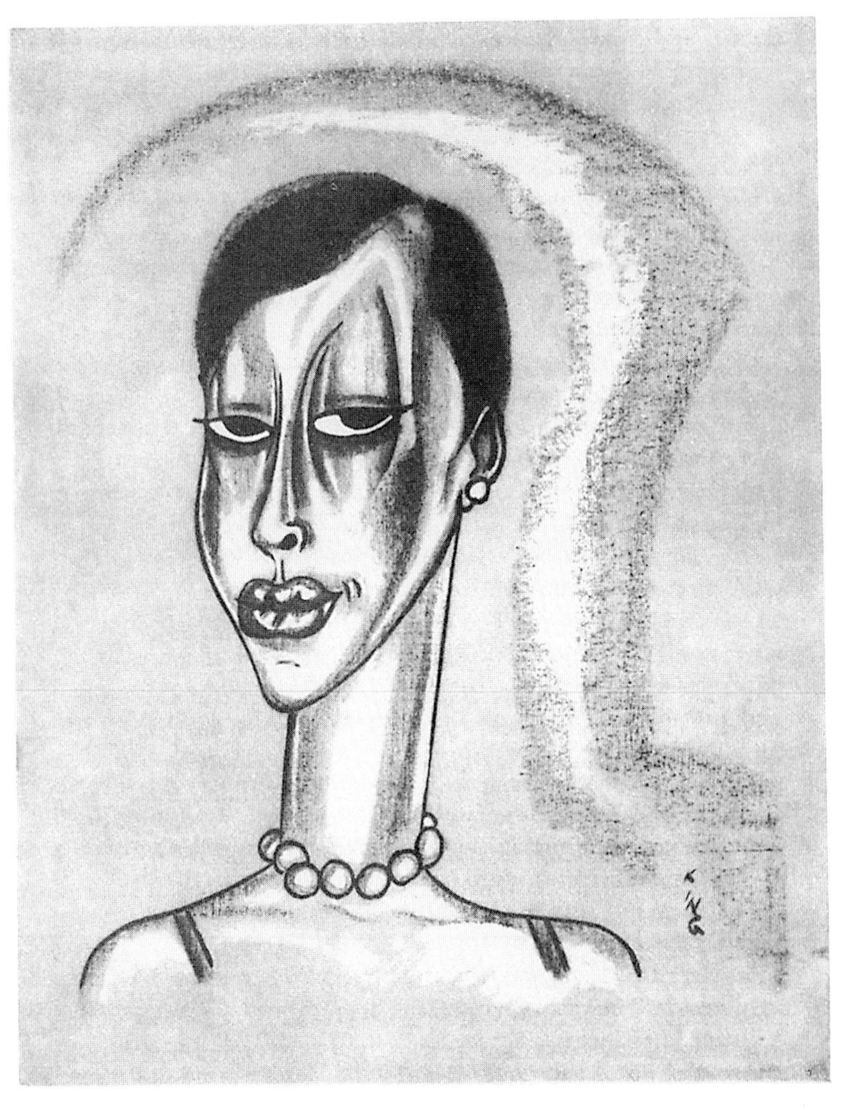

See page 154

"... face mat gold like
a Byzantine polychrome."

It was all very gay, very charming to the eye, very cosmopolitan, I thought. The tennis, it proved, was serious. Six courts were going, mostly mixed doubles; long rows of chairs placed irregularly, comfortably on the lawn were filled with ladies watching the play; men and some of the young girls who were garbed for tennis sat on the grass.

My gray flannel slacks and an old mingled sweater Jack Dempsey had given me in Buffalo, which had been respectable enough, I hope, at Forest Hills, seemed a bit seedy in this fashionable company, especially after I found Mr. Christian Gross immaculate and swanky, but I was eager to play, and he had obligingly arranged for some doubles on a court which would soon be vacated.

My partner was a gingerbread-colored damsel almost as swankily sports-garbed as Mr. Gross. She could hit the ball and had a forehand drive that became finally the deciding element in our match. Mr. Gross's partner was a charming woman, slightly older, who I vaguely imagined would be Haitian, since she seemed graciously at home here and chanced to have dark, wavy hair. She may smile when she reads this, for she turned out to be Mrs. John T. Myers, wife of the brigade commander of the United States Marine Corps, and she was there for no official or policy reason whatsoever. She was there because she enjoyed tennis, had numbers of Haitian friends, and found the Thursday afternoon parties in the palace gardens charming. And it seemed to me that the whole group-social-American attitude in Haiti was a piece of sheer craziness—Alice-in-Wonderland idiocy, without the mad logic which integrates *Alice*. So far as I could gather, no wife of a Marine Corps captain or major had ever attended or wanted to attend a "nigger gathering" socially, even at the presidential palace; and I think 99 per cent. of the sergeants' and corporals' wives would have turned up their noses in honest disgust if they'd been invited. To Judy O'Grady a coon was a coon and that was that, no matter if he'd been a king instead of a president, no matter if he'd been through three universities at Paris and spoke eleven languages instead of four and had sat as a member of a dozen Hague Tribunals. But to the colonel's lady these were just charming people. She came and enjoyed herself. And to pile craziness on top of craziness there was no more highly regarded woman in the lily-white American colony than this same colonel's lady. If she had peculiar tastes, no one dared to criticize them. There were also, for instance, some dozens of naval officers on special permanent duty in Haiti, mostly doctors and engineers, and for perhaps accidental personal reasons a majority of them were on friendly and in some cases intimate social terms with the Haitians. Their Marine Corps friends at the American club had nicknamed the naval officers "kinky-heads," but there was always a discreet limit to such ragging. They ragged me before I left the island; they ragged Katie even more—she happens to come from Georgia and has a marked southern accent—for dancing with coal-black gentlemen. "My God, what would your papa say?" whispered Mrs. Major Davis in horror when she drove into our garden one night, after we had got a house, and found us at dinner with the Baussans. But she didn't let that prevent her from having us to dinner at her own house three nights later. It seemed to me that very little of this transplanted Jim Crow attitude was vicious. It seemed just a form of group insanity for which individuals perhaps should not be blamed.

After we had finished our tennis game I was presently introduced by Haitian friends to an upstanding young American in civilian clothes. His name was Perry. He was a pleasing, clean-cut, impudently debonair chap of the sort one would be likely to remember after a single meeting, but I couldn't recall having met him previously, though in the course of weeks it seemed that I must have inevitably run into him, for the civilian American group in Port-au-Prince was small and highly gregarious. In friendly innocence I asked him if he was a newcomer. It seemed that this was the wrong thing to ask Mr. Perry. He replied sardonically that he was not. Later it was explained to me that Mr. Perry, who had been, I believe, an officer in the Marine Corps, had married a niece of President Borno, and had told the American colony individually and collectively that it could go to hell, before the surprised American colony had had the chance to invite him to do so. He had resigned from the corps, the club, etc., had been found a good job at which it was said he was efficient, had cast his lot with his wife's people. Among his young ranking fellow officers he was generally regarded as a "low-down son of a bitch who had disgraced the service." Among the higher-ups he was regarded, without particular condemnation, as a peculiar phenomenon, who had gone out of their lives. "After all," said Mrs. Deppler, "if he'd merely seduced the president's niece we'd still be inviting him to our houses."

I quite realize that in writing about this social-racial tangle, which I seem to be doing on every other page, just as one encounters it at every other step in Port-au-Prince, I am piling up paradoxes, illogicalities, and non sequiturs. But I refuse to be blamed for the illogicality. The thing itself is essentially tangled, illogical, and insane. It would be the easiest thing in the world to choose selective facts on one side alone and present a consistent picture. But it wouldn't be a true picture.

Meantime the present fact remained that everybody, including some two or three hundred Haitians and some scattering dozens of Americans, were having a thoroughly good time at this Thursday afternoon garden party.

The sun was slanting behind Morne Hôpital, its rays still streaking the green lawn, when a bugle sounded. Tennis and general movement ceased. There was a buzz and hush. At the top of a marble staircase appeared a lone figure with a drawn sword, glittering and grand as the man who rides on the lion wagon in a circus parade. It was Lieutenant Berthol,

American, commander of the palace guard. He had been a top sergeant of Marines (I suppose he still was), but he was wholly unrecognizable as such in his present glory. His uniform gleamed white, glittered with gold *fourragères*, braid, medals, bright-colored decorations. He stood, one lone man on the eminence of the wide white empty staircase, but no brass band blaring could have done him justice. It would have needed a steam calliope. Instead there was a brief moment of impressive silence, in which, with a ceremonial sweep of his drawn sword, he cried, "Ladies and gentlemen, the president!"

Monsieur Borno appeared a moment later, casual but dignified, bareheaded, in a dark blue sack suit. Preceded at some ten paces by Lieutenant Berthol, he strolled down the staircase chatting with two members of his cabinet, one very black, the other mulatto. Some half dozen or more ministers, politicians, bureau functionaries, followed, talking in little groups. The crowd stood formal and quiet, the military men at attention, some of the young women curtsying during the president's progress down the wide pleasance; but arriving on the lawn near the tennis courts, all formality was dropped. He chatted right and left, signed the players to go on with their play. The whole garden was again animated. A quarter of an hour later the scene became again somewhat formal as the crowd followed him in procession up the staircase into the palace.

The huge reception hall held the two or three hundred of us without making a crush. Madame Borno, plump, middle-aged, happy-faced, pale mulatto, rather pretty in a frock of pale brown georgette with pearls, sat beside a large tea table where a bevy of young mademoiselles poured tea for those who came and asked for it, and offered tiny sandwiches, cakes, macaroons. Butlers and servants, liveried in English style, circulated everywhere with trays of champagne. In a far corner there was a buffet, with, among other things, a decanter of twenty-year-old Haitian rum, which I tasted in tiny glasses with Ash Pay Davis and Freddie Cooke.

Perhaps a fourth of the guests were in their tennis clothes, disarrayed after hard playing, dumping their racquets in an anteroom. It lent an agreeable sophisticated informality to the occasion, as if all these people had gathered in pleasant surroundings primarily to enjoy themselves.

It occurred to me as I was being presented to Madame Borno that the society of this small West Indian country, though certainly far behind us in civilization, if civilization is to be measured entirely by material-mechanical-industrial standards, was perhaps a great deal more civilized in some ways than we are. At any rate, it often seemed to me that they lived more agreeably.

I suppose it may have been because I happened at the moment to be thinking of Haitian culture in terms of French tradition—of the fact that Madame Borno herself was more than two-thirds French—that when presented, I bent over and kissed her hand as I might that of any important matronly hostess in France.

Instead, however, of accepting it thus casually—I discovered later she was one of the bluntest and wittiest women I had ever met—she said, "*Eh, voilà! Monsieur l'Américain! Vous avez appris ça pendant la guerre?*"

I ventured to tell her that since the war it was not uncustomary to kiss ladies' hands even in New York. "*Tiens! tiens! C'est la pleine décadence alors.*" She was laughing at me, and at my country, but it was friendly, amiable laughter.

She told me that her young son, now in school at Paris, had been greatly impressed by things he had read and pictures he had seen of *la rude vie d'outdoors* and *le sport* in America. He had clipped a lot of pictures of Lionel Strongfort from the advertising sections of magazines, and had announced that he was going to become a professional strong man. At another time he was going to be a cowboy.

They had compromised by telling him that if he finally objected to becoming a lawyer like his father, they would send him to the Ecole Polytechnique and let him build bridges, and with this he was content after they had taken him to a cinema in which he could see with his own eyes that bridge-building engineers wore high boots and broad-brimmed hats and engaged in epic battles with villainous foremen, sometimes even with red Indians. Madame Emile Vital appeared, and the conversation became general. Among the tea-pouring demoiselles were one or two with whom I had danced at the Club Bellevue. I chatted with them for a moment, then wandered away from the table.

I observed Monsieur Borno with four gentlemen of various colors, standing slightly aloof near a doorway. They were engaged in earnest conversation, which I supposed was political. It was not my intention to approach them, but the president chanced to notice me on the edge of the crowd. One of the group was Granville Auguste, a very black and intensely serious little man connected with the ministry of finance, another the suave mulatto Fombrun, minister of the interior, to whom I took an immediate instinctive and cordially reciprocated dislike. The names of the others I do not recall, but they were ministers and bureau chiefs.

Apparently, however, these gentlemen had other interests than politics. They continued their conversation, which was an animated argument. It concerned the current tendencies and future of Haitian poetry. The dispute involved, as they expressed it, *la muse haïtienne d'expression française*, versus *la muse haïtienne d'expression créole*, but it involved more than a matter of idiom. It was a question whether the genius of Haitian poetry might find its happiest medium in the rich *créole du peuple*, as the poets of the Midi reached their greatest heights in Provençale, or whether pure, academic French were the better vehicle. But actually, as they developed various antitheses, it involved the deeper question whether the Haitian poet should seek his inspiration in the classic French tradition or in African negro emotional tradition; likewise whether cypress trees, marble columns, and weeping-willows had any legitimate place in Haitian poetry, as against the actuality of tropical jungle which was Haiti itself. Monsieur Borno stressed the point that great poetry frequently had no locale, no geography other than the geography of the soul. There was nothing American, for instance, in Poe. He admitted at the same time that Oswald Durand, the one sheer genius Haiti had produced to date, had done his greatest work in creole and that his genius was essentially a negro genius. Granville Auguste was presently quoting something which began:

Plus puissante, O Poète, est ton œuvre idéale
Car le dur métal ou tu sculptes ta chimère . . .

I asked him whom he was quoting. It seemed he was quoting a distinguished Haitian poet whose name was Louis Borno, there present, and who happened to be president of the Republic—a fact which was neither here nor there, apparently, in the literary dispute in which they were absorbed. It seemed that Monsieur Borno was a *poète très sérieux*, no mere dilletante; numbers of his poems were included in the *Anthologie de Poésie Haïtienne* published by Bossard in Paris, with a preface by M. Fortunat Strowski of the Sorbonne. . . .

On my way home from the palace, I reflected how queer it would seem for a group of cabinet ministers and Treasury officials at the White House to be earnestly discussing the poetry of an American anthology which included metaphysical love-lyrics by Calvin Coolidge.

Chapter V

BUT THE TRUTH BECOMES SOMEWHAT TANGLED

I HAVE seen many a triumphal arch, as who has not? including the *papier-mâché* monstrosity under which our own returning heroes marched up Fifth Avenue, an imperial one on the road to Teheran in Persia strung with the bleeding carcasses of sheep, likewise the Arc de Triomphe at a moment when banners and ten thousand gleaming bayonets passed beneath it in the Paris sunshine—but never have I seen any triumphal arch so extraordinary as that erected for Louis Borno, president of Haiti, at the entrance to a nameless village of some half dozen tiny huts in the Valley of Plaisance, deep in the jungle interior of this black Republic.

The four-day presidential motor trip on which I had been included as a guest was primarily for the dedication of a new bridge across the Limbé River in the mountains of the north, but its real significance lay in the fact that for almost the first time in Haitian history, a president, without fear and without elaborate military ostentation, could visit the most remote and formerly most dangerous districts in the interior of his republic without fear of revolution, assassination, or uprising.

This may have been entirely, as his enemies said, because our own armed Marine Corps remained in Haiti, sitting on the lid. Perhaps the doves of peace were really the American airplanes nesting among machine guns, but at any rate the journey had been more like a prolonged picnic party than anything connected with traditional Latin American politics. There were neither *opéra bouffe* troops of the Richard Harding Davis tradition, nor businesslike Marines—

only such personal military aides as might accompany an American president on a motor tour from Washington to New York. The only munition truck that followed our convoy was loaded with provision of cold turkey and beer.

We left Port-au-Prince at dawn of a Saturday in seven touring-cars. The first contained President and Mme. Louis Borno. In the second car rode Brigadier-General John H. Russell, with Mrs. Russell and Mrs. Frederick H. Cooke, wife of the chief engineer of public works. In subsequent cars were American treaty officials and members of the Haitian cabinet.

Port-au-Prince, which we were leaving, rejoices in more daily newspapers than New York before Munsey, and more cynics than Athens in the time of Diogenes.

Free speech and freedom of the press flourish with tropical luxuriousness, despite occasional jailings. When it was learned that I had been invited on the presidential tour, both cynics and the Opposition press urged me not to let myself be deluded by what I was to see.

I was assured all over again that the whole American occupation was for sinister and selfish ends, that all present improvements were but part of a big program of subsequent industrial exploitation, that President Borno was merely a puppet in the hands of greedy Wall Street.

I was equally assured that if it weren't for the gendarmerie and the airplanes, the President would not dare set foot outside his palace.

I was informed that the mass peasantry in the interior cared nothing, benefited nothing, knew nothing of President Borno, in fact had probably never heard his name (which I knew to be true in many remote mountain districts); and that any patriotic demonstrations I saw along the road would be stage set, *claque*.

As a matter of fact a superb *claque* which would have done credit to the late Hammerstein was the first high spot we encountered, two hours out of Port-au-Prince on the road to Saint Marc—a triumphal arch of palm branches surmounted by a big red banner on which was written *Vive son Excellence Président Borno*. All the paid road workers of the vicinity, with their wives, grandparents, babies, and wenches, were lined up on the roadside to shout *Vive le Président!*" as per instructions. That, at any rate, was just as the cynics had predicted. And this, of course, was not the arch which stands out so significantly in my recollection.

Before we came to that other arch I saw many things which were also worth remembering—more than a thousand miles of well-built motor roads where rough trails had existed only ten short years ago, big span bridges and innumerable solid culverts, well-equipped hospitals, rural dispensaries crowded with peasants, dozens of new school buildings both industrial and elementary—efficient native gendarmerie stations and rural constabulary—malarial swamps drained. And against all this improvement which had been paid for out of the public revenues, Dr. Cumberland, treaty financial adviser, in whose car I rode during part of the trip, showed me figures according to which the public Haitian national debt had been decreased from $30,000,000 to $21,000,000.

But not any of this impressed me so much as the arch we saw in the mountain interior on that second day. It was above the clouds and palm trees, on the edge of a high gorge overlooking the Plaisance Valley. One family group of barefoot peasants, with their tiny clustered mud houses clinging to the slope, had built it. They had built it rudely of bamboo stocks and banana leaves, rickety, a bit pathetic, and so low that our cars could scarcely pass under it.

But hanging on it to do honor to their president and proclaim their own prosperity and pride were the cherished and significant possessions of that little family group—a bright new tin coffee pot, a freshly laundered coat and trousers of white cotton, a pair of "store bought" shoes (the ultimate symbol in Haiti of humble prosperity), a gayly colored skirt, a small drum, and a brightly scoured iron skillet.

"See how prosperous and grateful we are!" cried the arch in a symbol language brought by their slave forebears from Africa, which had existed before written speech. *Vive Président!*" cried little black brats bursting with excitement. "*Vive Nord Alexis!*" cried an ancient crone. President Nord Alexis had been dead for a generation, but because his image still appears on current Haitian coins, many peasants of the interior believe that he still rules, helped now by the *blancs.* But if some of the old crones and graybeards didn't know whether the president they were cheering was named Louis Borno or Nord Alexis, they seemed convinced that he was their friend, and that the *blancs* who rode with him were also their friends. And they seemed convinced that there was a definite connection, however vague, between this new régime in which the *blancs* figured and the fact that they had a new coffee pot.

I wanted to get out and talk to the family, but we could stop only for a moment at this arch, to me so memorable. Next day, however, I was able to talk with a peasant of the same sort on a tiny farm near Hinche, in the great central plain behind the mountains, and near the new high road. The old black man with whom I talked wore blue overalls and fiber sandals. He could neither read nor write. He was like three million other peasants, men, women, children, except, I think, that his intelligence topped the average. It seemed to me that he might be speaking, and speaking truly, for a majority of them all—saying what they might have said if they could have been as articulate as he. He said:

"Ten years ago this country was full of *cacos* (bandits) and there were no roads. The *cacos* often robbed and murdered us. Our own government tax-gatherers often robbed and starved us, then gave us nothing in return. It was hardly worth while to plant. It took four days on a *bourrique* (donkey) to go down to the city. And if we weren't killed by *cacos* or drowned fording streams, when we did reach the city we were conscripted to fight for the government, or on one side or the other of some new revolution which was going to make things better and never did. Now the bandits are all gone, there is no more revolution, I live in peace, I plant all I can, I pay a reasonable tax, I go to the city in the motor bus in four hours, and I am not conscripted, and while I am away, my wife, my children, my ears of corn, and my little goats are safe as if they were all in the arms of Jesus. . . ."

It seems perhaps a pity not to end this chapter here, but something forces me to recall the words of another gray-bearded Haitian, also the father of a family—a family which lived in an ancestral villa on Turgeau, a beautiful suburb of Port-au-Prince, with a small secluded public garden, great shade trees, singing birds, springs and fountains. Many Americans also now live there. He said:

"From my own tiniest childhood and in my father's childhood this little secluded garden, public, yet not quite public, has been a place of sacredness and beauty, woven into all our childhood recollections—our own garden, in which to romp and play or lie beneath the trees and dream. Now my little grandson goes no more into that garden. The little American children by the fountain cried, 'Oh, look, see the little nigger all dressed up like a monkey!'

"It took us older ones longer than you would think to understand this thing that the Americans have brought. For us, 'Negro' was a word like 'Aryan,' 'Nordic,' 'Latin,' which connotated differences, not shamefulness. 'Haitian' was a national adjective like Scandinavian, Swiss, English. Around such adjectives cluster patriotic traditions and patriotic prides. Now our children are ashamed to be Negro, ashamed to be Haitian. Some of us older ones, too. It seems to me that we are being poisoned. I am told that the Americans have brought to our country prosperity, peace, security, material improvement. Be it so. Can those things compensate for the destruction of our pride, the poisoning of our souls? . . ."

The truth is at best a tangled thing.

The old peasant in overalls was speaking, I think, for three million peasants who are untouched, unharmed by such social-racial concerns, and who are either constructively helped, or, in their mountain-isolated groups, remain unaffected either for good or bad, by the American political-economic, innovations. Furthermore, the Americans no longer persecute actively or seek to stamp out the mysterious, immemorial religious tradition which is the real soul of this black peasantry.

The old gentleman on Turgeau was speaking, I think, for a small upper class and bourgeois minority of less than one hundred and fifty thousand, many of whom had oppressed and robbed these same three million peasants before the Americans came.

What conclusion emerges from these tangled part-truths? How weigh them? By some evaluations of life, perhaps, the scales tip in one direction, but by a different evaluation of life they upset in a reverse direction. I am not sure of ultimate evaluations where problems of this sort are involved. With Louis and Maman Célie, it was different. Concerning them I have the strength of a profound conviction. But here I think that I, if I am anything, am the onlooker, the reporter—not the solver, surely not the judge. But perhaps others capable of judging (or who deem themselves so) may find in these faithfully recorded observations material for thought.

Part Four: TRAILS WINDING

Chapter I

THE WHITE KING OF LA GONAVE

To hold undisputed sway on some remote tropical island set like a green jewel amid the coral reefs of summer seas —how many boys have dreamed it, and how many grown men, civilization-tired.

It is a strangely potent dream; it has a druglike fascination. It is susceptible of infinite variations. Sometimes the island proves to be inhabited by natives—sometimes not. One man may dream of it in terms of pure adventure—another in terms of refuge, tranquillity, escape—another in terms of despotic power.

It is a dream which for most of us never comes true.

But in Haiti, where the impossible frequently happens—or rather on one of its island dependencies—there is a man, a white man, who has realized that dream, on his own terms. Furthermore, he has been actually and literally crowned a king by the natives of that island.

This is not a fantasy.

On clear days, from any terrace in Port-au-Prince, one may see the blue mountain peaks of an island rising from the sea out yonder across the bay northwestward, thirty or more miles distant. It is called La Gonave. It is an island larger than Martinique or Barbados, dolphin-shaped, some forty miles in length. Despite its proximity to the Haitian mainland and capital, despite the fact that under the Haitian-American treaty of 1915 it is part of the territory over which we exercise a benevolent protectorate, it remains the most primitive and untouched by civilization in the whole West Indies. It has always been so. It is the only part of Haiti on which there were no colonial settlements and on which there are no French colonial ruins. In the pre-colonial Spanish days it was a resort for pirates. When Haiti was owned by France, it was a refuge for runaway slaves. For the past century, under the Haitian black Republic, the government tried sporadically and with slight success to collect taxes from the descendants of these runaway slaves.

A number of years ago, at his own request, the American administration dropped from an airplane on to this island a Pennsylvania farmer boy by the name of Wirkus, who had enlisted in the Marine Corps and risen to be a top sergeant. They commissioned him a lieutenant of gendarmerie and said, "We'll send a plane over every month to see how you are getting along." They said also, "In six months, of course, we'll relieve you." This boy Wirkus who had never set foot on La Gonave, who had only seen it lying distant and mysterious out there across the sea, said, "If you won't let me stay there for at least three years, I don't want to go." It was a queer thing for him to say. They thought it was a queer thing for him to say, but they flew him over and left him. They sent the airplane monthly for his reports, and whenever he cared to, they let him fly back, to spend a monthly week-end in Port-au-Prince. Usually he didn't care to leave his island. Two or three months later a rumor spread around the capital that the ten thousand blacks of the island had convened and crowned Wirkus king of La Gonave. It was supposed to be a sort of harmless joke. Nobody on the mainland took it seriously. And Wirkus himself laughed about it in an embarrassed way when they saw him. He was a husky, efficient, dependable lieutenant of gendarmerie, his reports were always in perfect order, and tax collections on La Gonave had already more than doubled under his administration. If the blacks out there childishly chose to call him a king instead of a lieutenant, what did his superior officers care about that? He was a good man, doing a good job.

And he has been there ever since. He is there today, the sole white ruler, the benevolent despot of an island inhabited by ten thousand blacks. He will be there, he hopes, for another three years. I had a letter from him only a few weeks ago. He is real and his name is Wirkus. If it would amuse you to get a letter from a king, you can write him:

Lieutenant F. E. Wirkus,
Gendarmerie d'Haiti,
Headquarters General,
Port-au-Prince, Haiti.
(Please forward to La Gonave.)

They will take it over to him when the plane goes, on the first of the month, and I have no doubt he will find time to answer.

These are the simple understandable facts, as known to everybody in Haiti, of how Wirkus happens to be king of La Gonave. It chances, however, that I am in possession of some other facts, literal, yet so fantastic in their implication that I hesitate to relate them. Astrologers, numerologists, dabblers in the occult, orthodox fatalist Presbyterians, will be more interested in this phase of the story, than will sensible readers. I feel, however, that it should be included, if only to show what mysterious tricks coincidence will sometimes play in the birth of incredible legends, in the creation by primitive peoples of kings and gods.

In the year 1848, after Haiti had been for thirty years a republic, a negro named Soulouque rose to power. He declared that the Holy Virgin had appeared to him in a vision, angel-winged, perched in the top of a royal palm, and had said:

"You are destined to become a king, to rule over Haiti, Santo Domingo, and the surrounding islands of the sea."

Some months later, Soulouque, amid great pomp and ceremony, invested with scepter, crown, and royal robes, was proclaimed Emperor of Haiti, under the title of

Faustin I. Why he chose the unusual name of Faustin, history does not explain. With his royal armies he sought to invade Santo Domingo. This was exactly eighty years ago. In Bois Noir, among the mountains of La Gonave, there is an old, blind soothsayer, believed by his neighbors to be more than a hundred years old. They say that long, long ago he lived on the mainland, and that he saw the emperor Faustin ride off to war on a white horse, and that he always predicted Faustin would some day miraculously return. You can read about this Faustin I in the encyclopaedias, and if you ever visit Port-au-Prince you can see his jeweled crown and scepter in the vaults of the Banque Nationale. So much for the black Faustin I.

In 1894, in the town of Pittston, Pennsylvania, in the coal mining and farm district near Wilkes-Barre, a baby was born. The father was a German-American who had been a miner and also farmed. The mother, Anna Wirkus, was of Polish-French stock, and a Catholic. When the priest came to baptize this baby, he said to Mrs. Anna Wirkus, "What name have you chosen?" and she said, "We cannot agree; we are going to let you choose the name."

He baptized the baby "Faustin."

Wirkus tells me that up until the time he was twenty, and even after he had run away to enlist in the Marine Corps, Haiti meant nothing to him except a vague name in the geographies which he had studied in public school. He had not the slightest intention or desire to go to Haiti. He just happened to be sent there. He might just as likely have been sent to China or the Philippines, or to have been stationed in Philadelphia.

Only one thing remains to be added to this digression before I bring this story of Wirkus and his island back to solid earth again:

The blacks of that island, when speaking of Wirkus, sometimes refer to him as *Li té pé vini* (he who was to come).

There was no mystical nonsense about Wirkus himself. If he seemed God-sent to his superstitious blacks, born and destined at baptism to rule over them, and if his hard-boiled fellow Marines considered it somewhat strange that a "regular guy" like Wirkus should be content to remain for years at such a lonely post, I am sure that he never thought of himself as being in any way out of the ordinary. Yet he was out of the ordinary, in more ways than one. I learned this before I ever met him. It so happened that I had been in Haiti several months before I heard of Wirkus. Then one of the treaty officials told me about him, suggesting that since I was studying primitive peasant life, his island would be a good place for me to visit. He was sure I'd be welcome, but when he saw how interested I was, he took the trouble to have a message sent over. Wirkus sent back word that I could come any time I pleased, stay a week or a month as it suited me.

On the night before starting I sat in De Reix's bar with Major Davis, Q. M. C., and Captain Pressley of the flying corps, discussing the trip, over a bottle of Haitian rum. They knew Wirkus—had fished with him for barracuda. I was asking what I might take along that would please him.

"Well," said Major Davis ponderously, "you might take him a big box of candy . . . he likes chocolates and bonbons best."

"Is that your poor idea of a joke?" I said. "I thought you told me Wirkus was a hard-boiled sergeant of Marines."

"No," said the major, "I'm not razzing you. He's hard-boiled all right. Look at his jaw. He can outcurse and outfight any tough baby I know in the whole service. But he doesn't drink . . . come to think of it, I don't believe he smokes either . . . and he eats quite a lot of sweet stuff. They tell me alcohol turns to sugar, and I suppose when a fellow doesn't drink he needs more sweets. I might just as well have told you to take him jam. We always take him something of the sort, but I happen to know he's got a whole shelf of it. . . ."

"Don't get off on the wrong foot with Wirkus," Captain Pressley cut in—"this stuff about his not drinking and smoking. He's no Sunday school product by a damned sight. He just happens not to care anything about liquor, and where he is it's a good thing he's that way . . . out there on an island full of rum and nigger wenches and lazy cocoanut groves, he's stayed as hard as nails. He's built himself a rifle range where he practices all by himself . . . rides, hunts, fishes when he's not working. He shaves every morning . . . he's fixed himself a shower better than we've got at the club. A rum-hound or a lazy guy would go crazy out there, but it suits him, and it seems to suit the natives. He's helped them in a lot of ways they were never helped before, and they think he's God Almighty. You've heard, I guess, that they crowned him king or something. That's a hot one."

Next morning it was this same Captain Pressley who flew me out high across the bay toward the smoky-blue mountains of La Gonave, which turned vivid green as we approached. We soared down to land on a saline flat near the shore. As we taxied across it four or five cows loped out from the mangrove tangle, with negroes screaming, running, trying to head them, and Pressley had to swerve sharply, dangerously, to avoid a smash.

As we came safely to a stop and were climbing out, pushing up our goggles and loosening our helmets, disengaging ourselves from the parachutes strapped on our backs, Wirkus came striding across the saline toward us. It was seven-thirty in the morning, and he was bareheaded. This was the first time I had ever seen him. He was wearing grease-smeared khaki overalls, his hands were black with oil and grease, and there were streaks of it on his bare sunburnt arms. But his hair was so straw-blond, his eyes so clear gray-blue, his smooth-shaven face so healthy-ruddy-bronzed, that he looked clean. You could almost smell bath-soap as you looked at him. He was a shade under six feet tall and built like a light heavyweight in training. His jaw was as square as a piece of granite, and he was scowling. He didn't look at us as we came up. He was looking at the wing of the plane, which had tilted and dragged as we swerved, to see if it had been injured. Then he came and shook hands. Pressley had shut off the roaring engine.

Some thirty feet away from us stood four negro gendarmes in uniform, with a handsome mulatto sergeant. They were whispering together and seemed to be pained about something. As Wirkus strode over toward them they snapped smartly to salute, then hung their heads sheepishly.

"Listen," said Pressley, "this is going to be good. They have had strict orders to allow no cows within a mile of this landing-field. We've had trouble before."

Wirkus addressed himself slowly, grimly, in level tones, to the sergeant alone:

"*Ou même responsab' zaffai' là*" (You are to blame for that business).

"*Oui, mon lieutenant*," moaned the sergeant, like a child found at fault, not daring to deny it, and Wirkus, who spoke creole with an appalling colloquial fluency, continued in his same level tones:

"*Ou fait goddam macacq, ou vi goddam macacq, ou mourri goddam macacq; ou p'r aller joiend' rade macacq cinq jou'* " (literally: You made [were born] goddamned monkey, you live goddamned monkey, you will die goddamned monkey; so go join monkey-clothes [prisoner-stripes] five days).

"*Oui, mon lieutenant*," moaned the sergeant, and marched sadly away to put himself under arrest, and take off his handsome uniform, and tote rock for five days barefooted in black-and-white striped monkey-clothes.

As he walked away, Wirkus called after him, still in creole:

"I'm not going to break you, Albert; tell Corporal Dejoie to take over your work for the five days."

"*Merci, empile, lieutenant.*" And that was that. Wirkus felt better. He had tempered justice with mercy. He grinned. Some prisoners appeared, piled my gear on their heads, and disappeared single file up a trail through the mangroves. Wirkus asked Pressley to stay over and fish. He had been tinkering on his old one-cylinder motor boat and had it hitting. But Pressley had to go back.

Wirkus led me up the path through the mangroves to a straw-roofed village overlooking the sea and affording a fine view of the towering mountains of the Haitian mainland over yonder. It was Anse-à-Galets, the capital of his island kingdom. The only buildings not made of mud and straw were his own house, which was a stone-concrete bungalow with a big screened porch, and the gendarmerie headquarters, over which the Haitian flag flew. It looked like a Kiplingesque outpost on the edge of the jungle, which was what it was.

He was comfortably installed. He had some furniture from the States, a plain Grand Rapids dining-room table and two iron cots in separate rooms, Haitian withe-bottom straight chairs and rockers, a cupboard and shelves piled with tinned goods, a rack of earthen water-jugs, a wardrobe closet in his bedroom with books piled on top of it, a washstand with enamel bowl and pitcher, clean white bath towels. On wall-racks in the main room were a shotgun, saddle bags, tarpon rods, and tackle. A gasoline pressure-lamp hung from the ceiling. In the bedrooms there were candles. The floor was clean-swept concrete. It seemed a pleasant place. He had a servant, a boy named Mauvais, who kept things in order, and cooked in a detached kitchen. The shower was in the back yard, a big barrel mounted on poles, surrounded by a screen of woven branches. A ladder went up to the barrel.

From the beginning, Wirkus was hospitable. The feel

of him was friendly. But he was self-contained. He didn't waste words. He was evidently not the sort of man who talked a great deal or gave confidences on first acquaintance. He was waiting, I suppose, to get the feel of what sort of animal I might essentially be inside.

He opened slowly. I think he was somewhat relieved that I was not a highbrow. When he found that I could speak creole, that I had been a good deal in the mountains on the mainland, that I liked to fish and wear old clothes, I could feel that he was beginning to feel it would probably be all right. These things sound like nothing at all, but when two men who have never seen each other are going to live together intimately marooned for weeks, such things take on an importance.

I didn't mention the king business. He could tell me about that, if he would, in his own good time. We fished the first afternoon and killed six barracuda. I had never fished for barracuda, but it was the same thing more or less as fishing for tarpon, the tackle was the same; but once gaffed and in the boat, you had to look out for their wolfish teeth, which could take off a hand at the wrist and had been known to do it. Wirkus and I began slowly to get better acquainted. I asked him about the boat, which was old, but twenty feet long and seaworthy. I asked him if he ever went to Port-au-Prince in it, and what sort of boats the natives of the island had. I had got the impression that his only connecting link with the mainland was by plane. That was a matter of convenience, he said. It was forty-two miles from Anse-à-Galets to Port-au-Prince. The planes made it in less than half an hour. It took him between eight and nine hours to do it in his boat; so he made the boat trip only once or twice a year to have it overhauled. The natives had lots of boats, crude sailboats, in which they fished and occasionally went over to the mainland, but when the winds were wrong it sometimes meant three or four days for the round trip. The gendarmerie had given him his motor boat so that he could make monthly inspections, circumnavigating his island, of his six tiny gendarme stations in its principal coast villages. He would take me along on one of the trips, he said, if I cared to go, but this coming Saturday he thought I might see more, and enjoy it more, if we took a horseback ride up into the hills.

The rapid change in landscape was astonishing. Anse was sun-baked, yellow with its mud walls and straw roofs, rather barren. But not five hundred yards behind the village our trail led beside a stream, into a little green narrow valley that was a paradise, tropical trees, ferns, and flowers, bright-colored birds flitting. Where the stream widened to a shallow basin we came upon a group of girls and women, some naked, some in loin cloths, the streaked sunlight playing through the palm branches on their black, smooth, shiny skins. They were washing clothes, beating them with wooden paddles, singing, and cried out friendly greeting as we passed.

Donkey trains with big panniers occasionally passed us. The women with them, some riding, some afoot, wore cotton dresses; the men and boys, faded blue jeans. All, both men and women, saluted Wirkus respectfully, yet familiarly, as if he were a sort of intimately known superior being. He called many by name, and of some who had come far he inquired about their families, about their crops. A number of times I heard him use the phrase, "*Dis moon bon jou' p'r moins*" (Tell your people good-day for me).

A little higher up in the valley we came to the ruins of a primitive water-mill which had been destroyed by a freshet. In the clearing just up the hillside stood a new building, with cows grazing, poinsettias flaming at the fence-gate, other signs of prosperity. An old woman in white, with a white bandanna, barefoot, gold hoop earrings, and a red coral necklace, who had been sitting in the doorway, spied us. She leaped up. She must have been past seventy, but she was agile as a goat. She called out to us, came hurrying down to the path, seized Wirkus' hand, covered it with kisses, tried to drag him from his horse, and failing in this, began tugging at the reins.

Wirkus was embarrassed, particularly about the hand-kissing. "I guess we'll have to stop for five minutes," he said. So we dismounted and followed the old woman to the house. It was another home-made mill, primitive as the one below, except that it was driven by a shiny little gasoline engine of American make. The old woman gave us coffee and lamented that Jules Narcisse, apparently her son, had missed our visit. When we left, she tried to kiss Wirkus' hand again.

"Are they all like that toward you?" I asked him.

"No, no," said Wirkus, annoyed. "I gave her son a little help once, and she can't seem to forget it. She's getting old."

It was from the son, Jules Narcisse, on a subsequent occasion and Wirkus not present, that I learned the story of the two mills.

Three times, in three successive rainy seasons, torrents had wrecked the mill below, and he was prepared to give up when Wirkus advised him to borrow money, bring an engine over from the mainland, and put his mill up on the hillside. Narcisse had a brother who believed himself to be a mason and who professed complete ability to "set" the engine. But he built the concrete base out of true, and the belt kept flying off. So they went in despair to Wirkus, wailing that the American engine was no good.

And Wirkus went up to take a look. "It was *terrifiant*, Monsieur," Narcisse told me, "it was *terrifiant* what the lieutenant said and did. My brother and I fled from his curses and observed him from the door. He seized a crowbar and we thought he would destroy the engine, but he smashed only its base, and then he went away, telling us nothing, heaping on our heads awful curses. But, Monsieur, he returned! On that selfsame day he returned. And he had taken off his uniform as when he works upon the boat. Behind him came men bearing new bags of cement on their heads. And in his hand there were tools, a trowel. And, Monsieur, with his own hands he set that engine true, as you behold it now."

These details I learned later, but on the trail that morning I suspected that something of the sort was behind the old woman's gratitude, for other illuminating episodes occurred.

After climbing slowly upward, partly through rising jungles and partly along rocky mountain slopes, to an altitude of nearly three thousand feet, we crossed over a range and found ourselves on a wide fertile central plateau, called the Plaine Mapou, with a higher range rising beyond it. It was covered with "gardens" (small farms) and habitations. Across this plain, then turning northward, following its length, we galloped.[1]

[1] Extraordinary as it may seem, no accurate map of the interior of this island has ever been published. None exists or ever has existed except the crude maps made by Wirkus. All the old Spanish maps, and all the French maps, old and modern, show its location and coastline with admirable accuracy, and some of them show its principal coast villages. But the interior appears mountainous, uninhabited, untrailed, its mountains rising to a central backbone range. The fact that there are two parallel ranges instead of one, with this fertile high plateau between them, is neglected by the professional cartographers. On French maps around 1850, in the northwestern interior of the island, the name of a town or village, Dandeville, begins to appear. The part of the island where that town is placed on the maps is a barren, absolutely waterless, thorny desert. No village or habitation has ever existed there within the memory or tradition of the islanders. No village named Dandeville within their memory or tradition has ever existed anywhere. It is as if some whimsical old map-maker, tired of seeing La Gonave blank, had inserted it gratuitously. There are villages in the interior of the island, but Dandeville seems to have been a myth. Concerning water, the geological textbooks on Haiti copy each other, including a recent American one, in asserting that there are only three or four practical springs on the island, and that it has no stream which empties into the sea. Wirkus has listed twenty-six clear-flowing and abundant springs, eighteen of which he eventually showed me, and the very stream up which we had come from Anse empties into the sea at Magazin. The maps made during the last ten years by the American-administered Travaux Publiques are coastally correct for La Gonave, but show most of its interior as still *terra incognita.*

At some of the little farms on the Plaine Mapou we stopped, or rather were stopped. One man insisted on showing Wirkus some baby pigs. I got that tale also later. Wirkus had found scrawny runted razorbacks on the island. He had persuaded the American agricultural station at Jacmel to give him a blooded boar and brood-sow. He had presented them as a gift to a certain dependable *gros nègre* in the mountains, with the understanding that the *gros nègre* must in turn give away all the first litter; after that the pair and its further progeny belonged to the owner. Each person who got one of the litter must in turn cross it with the razorbacks, and give away all of that first brood. So by now, without expense or exchange of money, this new blood was scattering all over the island and everybody benefiting. At another place we stopped, it was the same story over again, this time about melons. Three-fourths of the seeds of the first crop had to be given away. You could give them to your brother or cousins if you wanted to, but you had to give them away. There is much to be said for despotism as a form of government. Wirkus was tyrannical. I began to understand why these peasants looked up to him as a sort of God Almighty.

It was in the Plaine Mapou that we turned aside to see a certain *gros nègre*, a rich, swaggering peasant named Alliance Laurent, who, Wirkus had learned, was infringing on the land of neighbors. With many wives and concubines, he strutted like a proud rooster surrounded by his hens.

Wirkus smiled like a benevolent crocodile on Laurent, took his outstretched hand, fired a string of compliments among his women, and began congratulating Laurent on his handsome breeches and boots.

"You know, Laurent," he said, "why it gives me such pleasure to see you in fine health and fine garments?"

Laurent gaped.

"Because it will add to the joy of the girls and women at Anse-à-Galets when they see you marching barefoot in monkey-clothes (stripes), carrying water all day long on your head for my shower bath."

Not a word had been spoken about the infringement of land-rights, but we weren't a mile along the trail when a terrified and humble Laurent came galloping after us, promising to restore all he had taken.

We saw a woman Wirkus had sent over to the mainland for a double cataract operation. She hadn't wanted to go. She had been afraid. He made her go. He made a boatman down at Pointe-à-Racquette take her. She had come back seeing. She thought he was God Almighty.

And so it went. As we galloped back down to Anse, it was getting plainer and plainer why they feared and admired him. But I was beginning to wonder about the king business. Eventually curiosity got the better of me and I asked him about it, what there was to it, whether it was true. He seemed embarrassed again. He said, well, yes, there was something to it; one of these days he'd tell me all about it, and since I seemed to be interested in the island we'd make another trip up soon, up to the top of Bois Noir, and see the black queen.

This was the first I'd heard of a black queen. I don't think Wirkus realized how startling it sounded.

Chapter II

THE BLACK QUEEN'S COURT

THE night before our projected journey up to Bois Noir to visit the black queen, Ti Meminne, Wirkus told me the story of how he had been crowned king of La Gonave.

Coming to the island four years before, he had set about a thorough exploration of its interior. From peasants who came down to the coast, he had heard that in Bois Noir, in a forest on a mountain top, in the almost exact geographical center of the island, there dwelt an old black woman who had ruled for more than thirty years. In her compound, they said, was a drum "taller than a man," so that the drummers had to stand on a raised platform to boom out the signals for the convocations of her court. She had prime ministers, they told him, a cabinet, and an army.

He hadn't quite believed it, he said, but he had gone up, alone, unarmed, and friendly I gathered, to see what it was all about. The old woman had proudly welcomed him and set the drum booming. In an hour or two, processions of negroes, men and women, blowing conch-shells, beating work-drums, waving flags, armed with machetes, began arriving, until there were several hundred in her compound. She introduced him to an old man who was *ministre l'intérieur*, others who were *ministre l'agriculture*, *ministre la guerre*," etc. Wirkus remained there. He spent almost the entire first day in conference with them. They talked and talked and talked. Also they sent for the old blind soothsayer.

What they really had, he discovered, was a sort of agricultural guild, primitive yet highly organized. In planting-times and harvest, in times for clearing new ground, they went about in little armies, fifty or a hundred to a group, and did the work communistically. They had been organized that way "forever" back in the mountains, one of the old men told him. And the queen with her council and court preserved order among them, settled disputes, dispensed justice. It seemed to me as he told it that he was describing a sort of primitive monarchical communism. The present queen, Ti Meminne, had ruled for a generation. Before her there had been a queen called La Reine Tirhazard, who had reigned from time immemorial. The more Wirkus listened to this, he told me, the more he liked it. It "sounded good to him," he said. "Why bust it up? Let it ride awhile and see how it worked out." So he made a speech to the assembly. He told them he had been sent over "with authority" from the mainland, and confirmed the queen Ti Meminne in power. As for his part, he would stay on the island to supervise everything and help them. When Ti Meminne needed advice, he told her, let her send a messenger down to Anse-à-Galets, and he would ride up for conference. He didn't know how it was going to work out, but he thought he'd give it a trial.

Well, a week later they had sent for him, and when he arrived they waved flags over his head—it seems the old soothsayer had been meanwhile consulted—strewed flowers and palm branches in his path, put a big yellow silk bandanna over his shoulders, set him in a chair, and carried him round and round in a circle, singing, and knelt before him, and laid machetes upon his shoulders, "a lot of stuff like that," he said, and crowned him King of La Gonave.

He had seen a certain humorous element in it naturally —he grinned as he told me the details—but they took it, he said, "damned seriously."

Just how seriously they took it he hadn't realized until some weeks later, when he had started building a stone wharf at Anse; it was in January, and he had estimated that with a dozen men working steadily he ought to get it finished by May. One morning, he said, he was awakened by an ungodly noise, and into Anse poured the Queen Ti Meminne's army, down from the mountains, five hundred of them, beating their drums, blowing their conch-shells, howling, followed by their women, donkeys laden with great panniers of food and iron cook-pots. Flags were planted in the clearing before his house, the old *ministre la guerre* shouted commands, and there they pitched camp. "There were even dogs and chickens," he said, "and pigs." Wirkus stood watching this from his front door, he told me, thinking, "What the hell?" He went back into the house, he said, and put on his belt with his forty-five automatic. He said he also put on his lieutenant's helmet. He had seen his six gendarmes out there, standing off at a distance, gaping like sheep. It was the first, last, and only time he had ever packed a gun, he said, in his whole four years at La Gonave. Wirkus talked well when once he got started. He said he was so surprised at this eruption that the thought of his stone wharf never entered his head. The *ministre la guerre*, escorted by flags, came over to see him and explained. In exactly four days, Wirkus told me, "they had the stone wharf built, completed, finished." They wouldn't take pay from him, they wouldn't take gifts, they wouldn't even take food or permit help from his village. They were "high-handed." And when they had finished they broke camp, came and marched three times around his house, waving their flags and singing a song about him, and went back to the mountain. "Hot damn," said Wirkus, grinning. He grinned in memory over it, of what a fool he'd been to put on his belt, and of how they'd got his stone wharf finished in four days.

He guessed that was about the whole story of how they'd made him a king, except— "well, you know these Haitians, the ones back in the bush . . . they're superstitious, superstitious about everything," and some of the old ones had the notion that he'd been "sent." Well, that was all right, he had been sent, said he—by orders of the U. S. Marine Corps.

We got talking about the peasants. "They're a funny lot," he said. "You think they're simple. They're easy enough to handle. But you think you know everything that's going on in their heads, and then you find out that you don't know a damned thing about them."

We arrived at Queen Ti Meminne's habitation earlier than she had expected us. She was busily engaged in supervising the royal baking for the festivities that would be held in our honor that night. She was a huge, squat negress, past fifty, solid bulk rather than fat, with a big, heavy head, and heavy but not gross features. In physiognomy, except for her blackness and sex, she resembled a certain type of American demagogue politician. She looked capable, but not lovable. When we rode into the compound, she was seated on a low stool under a palm canopy, imperiously shouting orders in a hoarse, deep voice, and munching a stalk of sugar cane.

She was clothed in a checkered Mother Hubbard and a blue bandanna. She wore bracelets and earrings. She was barefooted. She heaved herself up and waddled to greet us as we dismounted. She was very respectful and friendly to Wirkus. But there was no ceremony about it, either on his part or hers. The ceremonies, titles, formalities, and obeisances, I gathered, were confined entirely to the formal convocations and assemblies. She shouted commands about the care of our horses, water and food for them and us. There must have been a dozen people there to serve her, hired servants and relatives, I judged, ranging in age from naked brats to crones. She was a widow and boss of her own household as well as a queen. After seeing that we were comfortable and food spread before us, she returned to her stool under the canopy and resumed direction of the baking.

There was something Alice-in-Wonderland about her

bulk and her baking, her scowling, imperious face; with gingerbread cookies and casava cakes, more than a bushel of them already piled on a blanket before her, and others coming on trays from the oven. There was something decidedly Alice-in-Wonderland about the stalk of sugar cane she was chewing; it was golden in the sunlight and you could half shut your eyes and imagine that the queen was angrily munching her scepter.

Through an open door we could see big flaps of dough being cut up by three girls. On another table, dough was being kneaded, and on another white flour was spread.

Outside, under a smaller *tunnelle*, the casava cakes were being baked by an old man and two boys. A five-foot circular sheet of heavy iron was raised slightly from the ground with hot embers beneath it—a gigantic pancake gridiron. The gingerbread was being carried on trays to an oven cut out of a limestone hillside. The old woman who tended it, pushing the trays far in with a long pole, had built a shelter of banana leaves against the sun.

Wirkus took me to see the big drum which stood upright beneath a tree. It was a monster, as tom-toms go, but nothing of that sort is ever quite as big as you expect it to be—not even a whale or the Woolworth Tower or the *Olympic*. This drum, a cylinder hollowed from a tree-trunk, with a head of bull's hide, was just a few inches taller than a man. I was disappointed. I had thought it was going to be at least ten feet high. It was beaten, Wirkus told me, with the two fists, and the man had to stand on a platform when he beat it. This somewhat assuaged my disappointment. After all, it was a monster.

I hadn't felt drawn toward Queen Ti Meminne. I didn't find her sympathetic. When Wirkus asked her to let me photograph her while there was still plenty of sunlight, I became slightly annoyed with her. She insisted on dressing first, and I wanted her the way she was. She went into one of the houses, yelled for maidservants, and presently emerged with a white muslin "store" dress, stockings, and black patent leather shoes. She had taken off her bandanna and smeared her black cheeks with powder. It took Wirkus five minutes, at my request, to persuade her to wind another turban around her head. When we posed her in a chair, on a mat, with Wirkus in another chair by her side, she yelled to one of the girls to run into the house for the wooden baton which was her scepter. I was beginning to respect her, if I didn't like her. She was a person, and a strong-charactered person. As I was about to press the camera shutter, she felt something still lacking to her dignity and emitted another hoarse yell, this time for the *drapeau*. A young girl came, bubbling with interest but a little afraid of the camera, and knelt with the flag before her. Ti Meminne, who had had some previous experience of being photographed since the advent of Wirkus, considered the matter, and noted that the girl and the flag would obscure the glory of her patent leather shoes. With a well-directed kick in the *bunda*, she toppled the girl over and ordered her to kneel at the left. Then she patted her on the head to show that she wasn't angry, and finally I got the picture. I decided that queens are the way they are. They are not like presidents. They don't have to put on cowboy hats and shake hands and smile sourly and say they owed it all to their mothers. I mentally apologized to her for not liking her. I didn't say anything to Wirkus about it at all. I was wrong anyway. If she had proved to be something like a black tribal queen in an African tom-tom movie, I suppose I should have been enchanted with the theatricality. When, instead of that, she had turned out to be a real and somewhat surly strong-headed person, it had annoyed me. Wirkus and I went down the mountainside to see if we could shoot a few wild pigeons for her.

The events of the evening were sufficiently dramatic. I forgot all about Ti Meminne's patent leather shoes and the powder on her cheeks when that monster drum began to

See page 205

"... he had to whip her once or twice a year."

boom. Toward dusk, up from the narrow, winding footpaths came processions of negroes, headed by women bearing flags, singing, "*Drapeau! Drapeau! Drapeau!*" and men blowing conch-shells. As some of the processions arrived and ceased their noise, we could hear others approaching a half mile distant down the mountainside. The flag-bearers, always women and usually the handsomest wenches, were tall, upstanding, barefooted, their bodies covered only by thin, faded cotton shifts, which molded to their high breasts and powerful buttocks as they moved; they wore barbarically brilliant red, yellow, and sapphire bandanna headcloths, gold earrings, and necklaces of coral and glass beads. All the flags, as the different groups arrived, were stuck horizontally in the thatch roofing of the big peristyle under which the convocation was to take place. The royal orchestra consisted of three drums, a wooden box on which a man rat-a-tatted lustily with two sticks, and a rattle (*cha-cha*) [1] made with pebbles in a canister.

King Wirkus and Queen Ti Meminne sat on a raised platform behind the drums. On his head was a high crown of yellow feathers with little pieces of mirror sewn in, as they are frequently sewn on Hindu tapestries, glittering in the torchlight like rhinestones or diamonds. Wirkus would never let me photograph him with this crown on his head. He felt that if it were published, it might make him seem ridiculous back home. As a matter of fact, it was not ridiculous in that setting, as he sat there, blond, square-jawed, and soberly competent. It wasn't a joke he was lending himself to. These natives took themselves and him seriously.

With some of the groups that arrived were the presidents and *ministres* of various allied Congo Societies, the Belle Etoile, Fleur de Jeunesse, Reservée La Famille, Sainte Trinité. The presidents were old men chiefly. There were

[1] This is a sound-imitative word of African origin. In creole it has several meanings. It means a tin can or gourd with pebbles rattling in it; it means also a woman's clacking tongue; also a kind of locust tree whose dry pods rattle when stirred by the breeze.

also minor queens. Each society had one. Their names were shouted out as they arrived, and some of them were nice names; I remember a venerable old man called Augustin Tranquil, and a woman who was La Reine Masélie. As these special personages arrived, they were escorted into the peristyle with their groups, flag girls holding the flags of their societies crossed over their heads. These flags were of various colors, some cotton and some silk; the flag of the Societé Belle Etoile was of blue silk with white rosettes sewn on it and streamers of orange; the flag of another society was red with three inverted V's in black.

As a queen or president was marched into the peristyle, the drums would beat out the special rhythm of that society as they marched circling three times around, then stopped before the drums. If the personage was a man, he stood to salute, swinging off his hat and holding it straight out at arm's length before him; if a woman, she dropped to one knee, in a sort of kneeling curtsy.

When various of these had arrived and made obeisance, Queen Ti Meminne's own master of ceremonies, armed with a long baton, took charge, assembling before the drums the flag women and officials of Ti Meminne's own court. This is what he shouted, as they assembled:

"*Attention!*

"*Le Roi! Le Roi! Le Roi!*"

("*Helloi! Helloi! Helloi!*" was shouted by the crowd, with a short rat-a-tat salvo on the drums.)

"*Attention!*

"*La Reine! La Reine! La Reine!*"

"*Helloi! Helloi! Helloi!*" (Another drum salvo.)

"*Général La Place!*

"*Adjutant La Place!*

"*Président en chef!*

"*Ministre la guerre!*

"*Ministre l'intérieur!*

"*Ministre agriculture!*"

"*Helloi! Helloi! Helloi!*" (Salvo.)
"*La Reine chanteuse!*
"*La Reine Victoria!*
"*La Reine Drapeau!*
"*Confiance La Reine!*"
"*Helloi! Helloi! Helloi!*" (Final salvo.)

A pale yellow silk bandanna scarf was handed to Queen Ti Meminne, who knotted it around King Wirkus' shoulders. Four big negroes mounted the throne, and lifting up the chair in which King Wirkus was seated, marched with him three times around the peristyle, as the pope is carried in St. Peter's, and then around in circles through the crowd outside it, the people falling in behind, shouting, waving flags, blowing conch-shells. And this ended the formal ceremony.

A *danse Congo* and feasting followed, which lasted through the night.

There is a point scarcely necessary to state, but which I promised Wirkus I would set down in so many plain words so that nobody could misunderstand. Wirkus, though king of the island, is not married to the queen; he is not married to anybody.

Chapter III

A TORN SCRAP OF PAPER

WHEN my city Haitian friends had learned that I was going over to live for a while with Wirkus on La Gonave, they said, "*Tiens! tiens!*" as if I had announced a voyage to the North Pole or the moon. Why La Gonave remains so isolated, although close and in plain sight, requires explaining. There are thousands of fine automobiles in Port-au-Prince, but there is not a single launch, motor boat, or power boat, not a single sailing pleasure craft privately owned, either among the rich natives or in the American colony.[1] When I wanted to go to La Gonave, for instance, there were just two ways to get there: fly by military plane, or knock about in the bay from ten to thirty hours in one of the primitive tubs of some peasant fisherman or some island boatman who had come in with cotton or other produce. Furthermore, there is no reason to go except curiosity. Consequently La Gonave is the subject of fantastic speculation, and around it queer rumors and legends grow. As in the case of the black queen who ruled on a mountain top and the coronation of King Wirkus, these stories sometimes have a basis in fact.

There is the tale of a great cave beneath the mountains; the tale also of a bottomless pool in which dwells a sacred crocodile that no one dares to kill; a tale also that at Picmy is buried a great chest of gold, rubies, and diamonds, hidden

[1] Since writing this I am told that Christian Gross has bought a sloop, and I believe the Marine Corps has acquired a sea-sled, in addition to the High Commissioner's barge.

there by the Indian Queen Anacoana who was hanged by the Spaniards.[2]

A fresh mystery, leading to an unforeseen solution, developed while I was living on the island with Wirkus. One morning as we were at breakfast old Tonton Zo, captain of a fishing-boat which occasionally transported messages to and from the mainland, appeared with a soiled, week-old letter to Wirkus from gendarmerie headquarters. It was official. It said that the newspapers in Port-au-Prince were full of a story to the effect that the tomb of the lost Dauphin of France, the son of Louis XVI, had been discovered near the village of Z'Etroits on La Gonave. The information was specific: ". . . a grotto concealing a small natural basin, having a rock on which is an iron plate on which is written, '*Pour la tranquillité de notre Roi nous l'avons enfermé ici.*' " And, of course it was added, inevitably, in the newspapers, that treasures were buried with him. Clippings from the newspapers were inclosed. Wirkus suspected it was a deliberate hoax, but the letter was an official order demanding an investigation.

We went to Z'Etroits, a God-forsaken mud village three hours up the coast, where he had two black gendarmes permanently stationed. Nobody, of course, had ever heard of any ancient tomb. Wirkus said to the two gendarmes, "I think this is all *blague*, but I want you to keep at it and find out for me if there is, or ever has been, any such thing as an old iron plate with writing on it in this part of the island."

News of the result of that search reached us ahead of the gendarmes. There was great excitement among the natives. A man came riding into Anse, shouting that the tomb had been found. Later in the afternoon one of the

[2] It is a historical fact that Anacoana with her court and dancing girls used to come over from Leogane in long canoes to bathe in the pool beneath the waterfall. People often talk of making a syndicate to go over and dig for the treasure. Treasure-hunting is a favorite occupation of Haitians, high and low. Sometimes it is successful. Treasures were buried by the buccaneers and by fleeing colonial slave-owners.

gendarmes came down by boat, triumphantly excited, with a heavy package wrapped up in gunny-sacking. He had found the plate with writing on it, and had conceived it his duty to rip the thing out of the rock with crowbars, and here it was. We opened it, somewhat sharing his excitement. It was a circular bronze plaque which had been cemented into the rock by the geodetic surveying crew of the United States destroyer *Eagle* in 1919, marked with the altitude, latitude, and longitude, and used as a triangulation point against mountain-tops across the bay. It was a handsome thing. Engraved around these useful scientific data in a circle was the lettering:

"RÉPUBLIQUE D'HAITI. DÉFENSE DE TOUCHER!"

Apparently illiterate peasants coming on the plaque set in the lonely rock had invented a legend that a *roi* was buried there; the legend had spread to the mainland, and the Port-au-Prince journalists had done the rest.

The "sacred crocodile," however, turned out to be no hoax. He was real. His is still alive, I believe. He lives in a pool near Z'Abricots, in the interior, and occasionally drags under and devours a pig or a calf which comes there to drink, but the natives are afraid to let him be shot, and even sometimes provide food for him; he has been there from beyond the memory of man, and perhaps incarnates one of their *mystères*. Wirkus respects their wishes. He is also wisely tolerant in other matters. Wirkus is no reformer. He doesn't trouble himself, for instance, about the almost universal polygamy on the island. He took me to see a tall buck named Charlemonde whom he had made a *police rurale*. Charlemonde had begun as a barefoot vagabond, working in other people's fields. No woman would have him. After he became prosperous, he courted one who had scorned him in the days of his poverty, made her his mistress, and then kicked her out. Charlemonde had a way with women, and now when we went to see him he was surrounded by a harem. They worked in the fields for him and ministered to his comfort. He was like a barnyard cock. Another *gros nègre* named Erté was married to three sisters.

There is also occasional polyandry on the island—that is, real, primitive polyandry, which is different from either promiscuity or variety.

A case of this sort came to our attention in connection with something I have found among my pencil notes of the La Gonave period, at the top of which I seem to have scribbled, "Idyllic Episode Among the Mangroves." Beneath it is a transcription of a short report written in extremely bad French by one of the few of Wirkus' gendarmes who was able to write French at all.[3] Freely translated it reads:

Village of the Big Mangroves, March 29, 1927.

Lieutenant Wirkus,
Commander of the Island of La Gonave.

I send you in the custody of Gendarme André Maurice two good-for-nothings, vagabonds. They amuse themselves all day long with a bamboo flute of the sort called *vaxine;* they dance and sing and that's all they do.

My respects,
Your devoted soldier,
(*signed*) JEAN BAPTISTE.

P. S. Behold also a girl named Lovélia who was with these two vagabonds and who vociferated words prejudicial to the gendarmerie, without cause.

3 Gros Mangles, 29 Mars, 1927

Lieut. Wirkus
Commandant de l'Isle de Gonave

Je vou expédie sous la conduite de Gendarme André Maurice deuz personnes de gens sans aveu. Ils a joué tout la journée avec un bambou, comme sous nom de vaxine; ils fait danser rara et chanter sans rien faire.

Mes respects
votre soldat dévoué
JEAN BAPTISTE

Voici une femme de la nommée Lovélia qui était avec cas deux vagabonds et qui a vociféré de paroles au préjudice de la gendarmerie sans cause.

The gendarme André bearing these dreadful accusations brought his three prisoners down from Gros Mangles on a fishing-boat, and waded ashore with them at Anse, across the coral reefs. The letter sounded more like a page from the Pastorals of Theocritus than it did a criminal accusation. I wondered from what little paradise beneath the cocoanut trees, where two young men and a girl played the flute and sang and danced all day long, the gendarme must have dragged them. None of the three seemed more than twenty or twenty-one. The two youths were scared and sulky; the girl Lovélia, a handsome, slender wench, was still "vociferating." Wirkus fired a string of amusing compliments at her in low creole and told her to shut up or he'd give her ten years in prison. She stuck out her tongue at him, and obeyed. André had confiscated and brought with him as Exhibit A the bamboo flute. It was of noble proportions, several inches in diameter and more than two feet long.

After their names and the charges were inscribed in the register, we took them out under a tree, making André bring the flute. The two young men were at first suspicious and unwilling, but Lovélia, threatening to slap the face of one of them, forced them to acquiesce, and once started, they might have been going still if we hadn't said, "Enough." The flute emitted rich, soulful mooings, the second man tapped with sticks and sang, while Lovélia danced the cancan like a black Salome.

There is a misdemeanor law in Haiti—seldom enforced—against vagabondage, and another against vituperating gendarmes in uniform; so Wirkus sent for the old Anse justice of the peace to sift the matter. André testified against them, saying that the two youths were notorious for never working, had no occupation and no visible means of support, and as for the girl, she had screamed curses at him when he arrested them; so he had arrested her too. But this scarcely made sense. Gendarmes do not arrest people for not working in Haiti—not even on the mainland, much less on La Gonave. The men were frightened still, inarticulate in their defense, but Lovélia was voluble and illuminating. The two weren't vagabonds, she said; she supported them, she provided for them, and they didn't need to work. Was one of them her man? *Bien sur!* They both were. They were *etabli* with her. The whole trouble was, she said, that Jean Baptiste, the other gendarme, was building himself a new house at Gros Mangles, had tried high-handedly to impound her two men to do the *clissage* (withing). It not being needful for them to labor, they had refused. And Jean Baptiste in revenge had them arrested. Why hadn't Jean Baptiste come down? Because he was afraid, said she, sticking out her tongue at André. André, brow-beaten a bit, admitted on cross-questioning that there was some truth in this, but said Jean Baptiste had offered to pay them for their work, so that it was "regular."

"Liar!" shouted Lovélia, "he didn't offer to pay! Who ever heard of a gendarme paying? And if he had, they didn't have to do it for him." Lovélia was asked about cursing the gendarme, about the words she had "vociferated prejudicial to the gendarmerie." Absolutely not! She had not cursed at all, and she had said nothing prejudicial to the gendarmerie, for which she had great respect—only this André oughtn't to be in it. Well, what had she said to André? She would willingly repeat it, for it was the truth: she had said that André was a whoremonger, a robber, a petty thief, he had the yaws as well as a number of other vile diseases, and he wanted to go to bed with her! Those were personal matters, said she, which had nothing to do with the gendarmerie. Lovélia was a smart one. André was beginning to realize that he had made a mistake in adding her to his prisoners. He became confused. He hadn't anticipated all this investigation and cross-questioning over so trivial a matter. He and Jean Baptiste were due for a severe reprimand, if nothing worse.

And presently Lovélia departed triumphantly with her two men, also with the bamboo flute. I hope they are still dancing and singing all day long beneath the palm trees. And I suspect that they probably are. Wirkus is not a missionary.

I felt often on La Gonave as if he and I were a couple of Robinson Crusoes. It had become familiar to him after four years, but we occasionally discovered things that were new even to Wirkus.

The northwestern end of the island is a desert of thorn bushes without springs, almost wholly uninhabited. One day, as Wirkus and I were riding through it, planning to come out at Trou Louis on the coast, where there is a collection of fishing huts, and where we could find water which the inhabitants carried from a brackish well some miles south of the village on the hills, we lost our way and emerged at a point on the barren coast north of Trou Louis. As we followed the coast we saw a man and a donkey wading out into the Atlantic Ocean where there was a flat, low shelving beach. The donkey was laden with a double *sacpaille*. We saw them start briskly, the man leading the donkey, as if they were planning to wade across to Cuba, and out of curiosity we rode down to the beach to see what they were about. Wirkus suddenly shouted at me, "Do you see what I see? Have they gone crazy, or are we crazy?" The man and the donkey were knee-deep in the rippling incoming tide about fifty yards from the shore. The donkey had his nose in the water and was apparently drinking his fill, while the man was scooping water up in his straw hat and drinking it out of the salty ocean. Wirkus shouted to him, "*Ça ou fais la? Ou fou? Ou vlé mouri?*" (What are you doing there? Have you gone coocoo? Do you want to kill yourself?) The man raised himself up, waved his hat, grinned, and called out, "*Bon jou', blanc. Ou gagnin soif? Vini! Li empile douce.*" (Hello, white man. Are you thirsty? Come on! It is sweet.)

Meanwhile we had ridden out through the shallow water to where he was. The donkey was still sucking up long draughts of what seemed to be ocean water, and we got down and scooped up some of it in our hands and tasted it. It was slightly brackish, but good fresh water just the same, bubbling up through the sand over a space that must have been twenty or thirty feet in diameter. It was a big submarine spring of sweet water.

The man said that they had found it from seeing the wild cattle come there to drink and that they had caught or killed dozens of them there until the wild cattle no longer came, but that all the people who crossed that way knew of this spring and preferred it to the water at Trou Louis.

Seeing this negro and his donkey drinking from the salty ocean was one of the memorable experiences I had on La Gonave. Before we learned the explanation it had already crystallized itself as one of the pictures which do not occur except in dreams—like seeing a man with three heads, or like floating in the air, or entering a crowded ballroom naked.

But there was another thing on La Gonave that seemed to me to contain an even stronger element of the fantastic. Its explanation was simple; indeed, it required none; yet it never ceased to affect me with a feeling that some queer influence was at work. I am wondering now if it may not convey a clearer impression of what La Gonave was really like than anything else I have written or will write. Perhaps there will be many readers to whom it will mean nothing at all, who will wonder in their turns why I have so much as mentioned it. It was merely a matter of scraps of old newspaper, some of them several years old, some of them comparatively recent, sometimes rain-soaked and rotting beside a jungle trail where no one had passed for months, sometimes pasted on the mud wall of a thatched hut in the mountains, sometimes yellow and wind-blown in the *bahonde* desert, sometimes wrapped round two cents' worth of dried fish sold by an old woman down at Picmy.

Now, a yellowed scrap of newspaper, particularly when it is years old, and fluttering in the wind or rotting in a forest, *should* be a scrap of any old newspaper. Pick one up at random in Central Park or Central China, and it may be anything. But on this West Indian island, with its five hundred square miles of territory, with its ten thousand inhabitants, every chance scrap of newspaper, when you picked it up and looked at it, turned out as if by a goblin's trick or a crazy man's hallucination to be the Pittston (Pa.) *Gazette.*

For instance, one night when the Congo tom-toms were booming, while hundreds of blacks danced their old African dances and howled and the white king sat beneath a palm canopy decked with flowers, an old woman from Grande Source offered me a casava cake wrapped in a torn bit of paper. There was print on it. Through the grease by flickering torchlight I read how Mrs. Jones and Mrs. Phitty had entertained the Ladies' Aid Society of Pittston with a program of Welsh folk-songs and hymns; how Mrs. Anna Wirkus had been visiting relatives in Wilkes-Barre.

Chapter IV

PORTRAIT OF A "GROS NÈGRE"

THE leading citizen of La Gonave, after Wirkus and the queen, is a *gros nègre* by the name of Constant Polynice.

This big negro, however, is neither big nor black. He is a little, nervous wisp of a man, pale mulatto, scarcely five feet tall, thin, small-boned, with tiny hands and feet. His only obvious virile feature is his long black mustaches. In physiognomy he is a bit like a rice-fed mandarin. He habitually dresses in khaki, with leather leggings which he taps with a bone-handled riding-crop. He is a great deal on horseback.

His plantation, called Dernière Marque, is between the mountains at the head of the Plaine Mapou, overlooking his extensive cotton fields. It is about three miles beyond Bois Noir.

Since I had wanted to remain in the interior of the island for a longer time than Wirkus could spare from his duties, he had asked Polynice to put me up and take care of me. We had hunted together. Constant was an ardent supporter of Wirkus and the Wirkus régime; so I was welcomed and made to feel at home.

Polynice was not a native of La Gonave. He had come over from the mainland a decade ago, and was now chief tax collector for the island.

His habitation is a group of the usual mud-walled, earth-floored, straw-roofed houses, but inside the main house is a big four-poster mahogany bed, brought over years ago from Miragoane. It is the only bed on La Gonave.[1]

[1] All Haitian peasants sleep habitually on thick straw-woven or grass-woven mats which lie all day outdoors in the sun and are taken into the house at night. They are sanitary and comfortable.

Wirkus has iron cots. Natives come from miles around to see Polynice's bed. He also has a dining-room table, a metal washstand with a mirror.

But the proudest of all his possessions is pretty mulatto Julie with her three-year-old baby Marianne. This charming Julie, called Madame Polynice, is in reality his concubine. He would gladly marry her, but he left a church wife over in Port-au-Prince. Julie is a peasant, but she has small, delicately formed wrists and ankles, wavy, glossy hair. He imported Julie, along with the mahogany bed, from the mainland. She wears peasant dress, a single, clean, faded shift with no other garments beneath it, and goes bare-legged in flat leather sandals. But she has also a "store" dress, one pair of silk stockings, and a pair of little French shoes with high heels which hang on a conspicuous peg in the living-room of the *caille* and are admired by visitors. This special finery she dons only for rare descents on donkey-back to Pointe-à-Raquette or Anse. But around the house daily she wears elaborate earrings and flaming, gorgeous headcloths of brilliant sapphire blue, or red. She wears also occasionally a sort of howling purple, one that would kill any white skin but which, with her rich mulatto cheeks, is as effective as something from an Egyptian fresco. And it is difficult to imagine any white baby, naked in the sunshine, half so lovely as is Julie's little golden-skinned Marianne, when an old black woman servant bathes her every morning in a wooden trough.

Marianne's ears are already pierced, and tiny gold rings dangle; her head is tied in a Lilliputian bandanna of soft pastel reds and blues like a scrap of a faded Paisley shawl. She is naked all day long and crawls about the habitation yard. She is beginning to try to walk. She has no fear of donkeys or horses. A pig knocks her over and she laughs. The larger animals are careful not to step on her. But during midday hours servants must watch to make sure she stays in the shade. The place is overrun with old crones who do the cooking and washing, kids who sweep with besoms. Julie takes no part in the household work except to make coffee, which is a ceremony.

Julie regards Polynice as a superior being. He has money and a pearl-handled pistol and sometimes wears a collar and necktie. The peasants who come to pay their taxes say, "*Oui, msieu' le comptrolleur.*" And when they call her Madame la Comptrolleur she beams.

Polynice is an amiable martinet. He is good-natured, sly, often amusing, but he has a fiery quick temper which everybody fears. He sometimes has trouble with peasants who come telling lies about the number of their cultivated acres. Only land under actual cultivation is taxed. It is amusing to see him curse and push and sometimes vigorously kick this or that hulking giant of a black who could break him like a match between two fingers. Once I saw him lay a broom-handle vigorously over Julie's shoulders, and he told me he had to whip her once or twice a year. But usually he is amiable, gentle, charming. Nevertheless all the peasants hold him in wholesome fear.

The truth about this little wisp of a Polynice is that he is a killer—a born killer, and you can read it in his eyes. There are men like that. I do not mean that there is any criminal tendency in Polynice. He is a law-abiding, peace-loving man. I think I can illustrate what I mean. Some years ago Polynice insisted on having a survey made of a certain disputed cultivated tract which he believed the owners had been returning at less than its true acreage. The clan, who were bad negroes in a remote district, sent word that if he persisted they would make away with him or drive him off the island. In the feud which followed, they had killed Constant's own brother, Ludovic. Fifteen of them came one night to Constant's house, this same house where I was now staying. Four of them forced their way in through the door. Three of them had machetes and one had a rifle. Constant remained seated, quiet as a mouse. They told him he'd have to get out, leave the island. The man with the rifle swung it up threateningly to enforce the order. Constant shot him through the head, and killed two of the others in their tracks. The fourth man and the band outside the door fled.

Constant now, at this later time, when I was living with him, had few enemies. He was very popular, for he was considered to be just. But he did have one or two bitter enemies. It was rumored one day when he and I were at a cockfight that one of these enemies was coming to seek a quarrel. Constant, it happened, was unarmed. The man came. He carried a machete, and he was fully twice the weight of Polynice. He swaggered and glared, and edged over toward Polynice. The feud was known. The crowd was hushed, watching. Polynice turned his back, and when he turned again he had in his hand an ordinary penknife, whittling a stick. And the look of the killer—the born, natural killer—was in little Polynice's eyes. The man fidgeted and walked away.

But this was only one side of Polynice. It was latent. It came seldom to the surface. He was in no sense a bully or a quarrel-seeker. He was popular. He was quick-witted, amusing. His nickname was Ti Malice, The Sly One.

He was an excellent mentor, guide, and friend for me in studying the intimate social life of this mountainside. He entered into the peasant life; he was himself a peasant; yet he was also capable of seeing it apart, getting a perspective on it. Constant Polynice was a superior man.

"Polynice was smarter than anybody."

Chapter V

"POLYNICE AND HIS WHITE"

CONSTANT said it was the little snake that had wriggled across our path. Only a couple of fools, he said, would have gone on to the cockfight on that particular Sunday morning. But I think it was the fault of the airplane that dropped bonbons for Julie.

Of course, Constant and I both had it coming to us. He had been giving me lessons for some time past, and I had proven a fairly apt pupil. We had been winning steadily. He was proud of me and I am afraid we had begun to strut and crow as vainly as any of the silly roosters. It hadn't been always merely luck, either. Nor had it always been the superior fighting quality of Constant's birds. It isn't always what's hatched out of an egg that counts in these Haitian cockfights. We had been sitting up nights. There had been the problem, for instance, of a conspicuous little red cock, Le Rouleur (The Roller), so named because he fought in a peculiar way, rolling, or weaving. He was deadly, but he might as well have been dead. Osmann and the crowd only laughed at us when we offered to match him against cocks almost twice his size. It had taken us a good many nights to work that out. It had involved some amateur plastic surgery which completely changed the appearance of Le Rouleur's comb, and it had involved waiting patiently for a small can of floor-stain. We had tried ordinary paint, but it wouldn't work. However, when we finally finished the job, Le Rouleur's own hen mother wouldn't have recognized him. Then we planted him down at Pointe-à-Racquette. On market-day I bought him, for five gourdes.

Some of the Osmann crowd witnessed this transaction, and without suspicion; so it supplied a plausible origin. And we had made a sweet clean-up. Osmann himself had dropped nearly a hundred gourdes on the one fight, and from the crowd we had shaken down a whole hatful of small coins. Of course they had all recognized Le Rouleur thirty seconds after he began to fight, and their pained howls of surprise made bedlam. But it was their own sort of a trick, done to a fine turn, and they pounded me on the back while they cursed me and swore revenge. Constant leaped and danced in a frenzy of pride over "his white"—they used to say always when we appeared, "Here comes Polynice and his white"—he tore off my hat and threw it away and kissed me at least eight times on the top of my head. Osmann sent in for a bottle of rum with three small glasses and said he wished it was poison. The rivalry between Polynice and Osmann was of long years' standing. Polynice tiny and mulatto, Osmann big and black, were the two *gros nègres* and largest landholders of the mountain. Osmann was another one who wore shoes even on weekdays. The cockfights were at Osmann's. They usually lasted all day. Fifty, sixty, sometimes a hundred barefoot, blue-overalled negroes came from up and down the mountain, even from the southern end of the Plaine Mapou, each with a rooster under his arm—and a trick up his sleeve, more often than not. The women came too with their trays of gingerbread, casava cakes, tobacco, dried herring, and raw *clairin*, which they sold at a half cent per dram. It was like a little country fair. As I say, Polynice and I had been doing too much strutting. Constant and "his white" deemed themselves smarter than anybody.

Some weeks after our clean-up with Le Rouleur, a man from Bois Noir came to see us with the whispered news that Osmann had cooked up a trick to take us. Osmann, it seemed, had been across the bay to Saint Marc and had picked up there a little Cuban cock, a veritable *coq gime*, which he was planning to run in on us as an ordinary bird. And it was going to be murder. You see, the Haitian cocks generally, though game enough in a sense and pretty good fighting-birds, are not gamecocks, technically. That is to say, they are not generally pure bred. In Cuba, cockfighting is a sport of the rich as well as the populace, and special strains of cocks are bred there like race horses in England. But in Haiti it is the sport *par excellence* of the peasants, and most of the birds are talented barnyard accidents. They are bush leaguers. To run in a Cuban cock on us, therefore, was like slipping a Yankee pitcher into a prep-school ball game, or a professional prize fighter into an amateur boxing-bout. But fortunately we had been warned. The friend who came to tip us off described the bird minutely. It was a medium-sized *zinga*, which is to say gray speckled, and had a scar beneath the feathers on the low left side of its neck. Polynice and I were setting traps those days, but we weren't falling into any.

The next Saturday when we arrived at the *gaguerre*, there, sure enough, tethered inconspicuously at the foot of a coffee bush near Osmann's other birds, was the new *zinga*. There were several others of his cocks we knew well, a black one he called Diable-en-Deuil (The Devil in Mourning), another big, ungainly, but powerful rooster named Trois Boutons (Three Buttons), and still another called 'Longer Diole (Stick Out Your Beak). Osmann, putting his big gorilla arm around little mulatto Polynice's shoulder as if they were the friendliest brothers—which in a way they were—said, "I've got a new cock; come see what you think of him," and brazenly, since its gaunt leanness couldn't be disguised, "I bought him because he looks as if he might have a streak of game blood in him, paid ten gourdes, haven't seen him fight yet, it's just a chance; so I've named him C'est Peut-être (It Is Perhaps). I thought we might try him out if you've brought something along about his same weight. What do you think of him?"

Polynice picked up the mysterious stranger and examined him critically, verifying, I noticed, the scar on his neck. "He looks pretty good," said Constant, turning his back and winking at me; "you've named him well"—and quickly changing the subject, "I've brought a big rooster along that might make a good match against your Trois Boutons. He's never been in a *gaguerre*—just a barnyard animal, and slow, but he's been picking on our small ones, and Julie says I might as well get him killed or teach him to fight. We might try it for, say, ten gourdes."

Now all this was the simple God's truth, and of no importance. Frequently the fighting for small bets is like that, pure chance, for the fun of it. Osmann didn't press the matter of the *zinga*. He came and looked at Constant's new big one, said, "All right. Trois Boutons will kill him, but that's your funeral."

It wasn't much of a fight. Trois Boutons would have killed him if he hadn't run squawking out of the ring. We didn't care. And the other battles that day were generally of no importance until an ugly fellow named Louira from the Plaine Mapou arrived on horseback with a small gray cock named Queue 'Raché (Torn Tail), which he wanted to fight for big money. Now there are two ways of promoting a match at these *gaguerres*. One way is to run your bird down; to say seriously, for instance, "He's old, he probably won't make an interesting fight, but I don't mind losing a few gourdes for the sake of the sport," or to put the same thing humorously, "I didn't bring him here to fight; I brought him to have him killed, because my woman is too lazy to chop off his head at home." The second way to promote a fight is to brag outrageously, to insult and defy the world. Louira took this latter course. He produced a wad of a hundred gourdes and announced that his cock could whip anything on the island, but that probably nobody here had the guts to match with him and that *sans doute* he'd had his long ride for nothing. And he shook Torn

Tail scornfully in the faces of Osmann and Polynice and Polynice's white. Polynice had given me a small black cock, a vicious little devil which we thought might do the business, but while we were off discussing our chances and whether to risk it or not, we heard shouts, "*Hors la gaguerre!*" (Clear the ring!) and there were Osmann and Louira facing each other defiantly, and the cock in Osmann's arms was the mysterious *zinga*. Apparently Louira had fallen into the trap set for us. We were well satisfied and kept our mouths tight shut, for this Louira was a man neither of us liked. We asked him simply if he cared to place a side bet of fifty gourdes. He said the hundred was all he'd brought and that Osmann had already covered it. Knowing the inside, Constant and I followed that fight with concentrated interest. The *zinga* won, of course, but it was by no means a massacre. It was a good fight, and there were moments when it seemed to us Louira's cock had a chance.

As we walked back up the mountain trail that evening to Constant's habitation, he was unusually silent, but I could tell he was bursting with something. When we came to a big fallen log, he motioned me to sit down with him, and out it came:

"We can beat that cock and we can beat him *net*, without the need of any trick. Osmann is a fool. He doesn't know birds as well as I. Every action, every shifting of that battle just now, I watched very intelligently. That *zinga* is a Cuban cock, but it is an inferior Cuban cock. Osmann has let himself be cheated. That cock is swift and keen, but he is not *méchant* (wicked). A great fighting-cock must have an evil, wicked heart. It is not sufficient to be merely expert and courageous. We can beat that cock without tricks, with a cock that Osmann already knows, and therefore Osmann's discomfiture will be the greater. We can beat him with Tribunal."

Tribunal was the small black cock which Constant had

given me and which we had discussed matching against Louira's on that same day—his name meant Courthouse, because he was black like a judge in robes, and Constant fancied that his frayed black comb resembled a judge's cap.

"Tribunal is perhaps a shade less expert than this *zinga*," Polynice continued, "but he has the wicked heart. He fights to kill or die. In this case, I think he will do both, but I think the *zinga* will fall first. It is a certain risk, yes, but we will triumph."

And so the venture was decided.

It was a week later, on a bright Sunday morning, descending this same mountain trail, that the little green snake wriggled across our path. Constant blamed it all, afterward, on that little green snake, and it *was* a bad omen in Haiti. But we had the wicked little killer under Constant's arm, with a sock pulled over its head to keep it from beaking chunks of skin off his hand—we had nearly seven hundred gourdes in our pockets—we were on our way to "take" Osmann, we were smarter than he was, and we kept right on, in the face of Providence.

Since it was Sunday, there was a mob, and fights were already in progress. Osmann, Constant, and I sat on low stools in a corner of the square ring with its palm-thatched canopy upheld by poles, while the crowd squeezed five deep around the railings. We had the whole day before us. We were in no hurry to start our own dirty work, and it was a lot of fun to watch the other fights, to offer advice, to bet little sums on the side when we liked the looks of a bird. It was even more fun to watch the arguments and antics which led up to the combats. These peasant *gaguerres* in Haiti are highly democratic. The most ragged and poverty-stricken, but hopeful field hand with a dilapidated rooster and a few pennies as his total capital has as much right to his turn in the ring as the *gros nègre*, the landholder, with his string of favorite cocks and his pockets full of money.

But first, of course, he must make his match. To ask for a fight is called *mandér*. This is done in the crowd outside the ring, where men whose cocks are unmatched sit with them tethered. The challenger crouches before the bird he wishes to challenge, and places his own before it, held by a string attached to its foot. If the challenged man is interested, the birds are allowed to fly at each other, but jerked back by the strings. Violent disputes arise. Groups collect, offering suggestions. It is as exciting as a curb market just before closing. "*Filer donc, pour dé gourdes!*" shouts a challenged one finally. ("File, therefore, for two gourdes"—or whatever sum has been agreed on as the bet.) Steel gaffs are unknown in Haiti, but the natural spurs of the bird are pared or filed to needle sharpness just before each combat. Side betting adds to the pandemonium. People rush about, waving small coins or bills, sometimes as little as a single penny—the girls and women too—screaming, "Twenty-five centimes on the red!" "Fifty centimes on the speckled one!" There are no stake-holders. If you wish to accept one of these bets screamed and held aloft, you simply reach up and seize the money. If you win, you keep it; if you lose, you return it double.

Filing finished, the two opponents enter the ring with their birds. Each man takes a piece of ginger root, chews it violently, takes a mouthful of rum, then sprays this mixture through his teeth like a laundering Chinaman all over the cock's body, under its wings, in between the feathers, which he ruffles with his fingers. This heats and excites the bird—gives him Dutch courage. Next, each man tastes the bird of his opponent. Sometimes a tricky fellow, sacrificing the lining of his own mouth, has mixed red pepper with the ginger, which is forbidden, or has smeared his bird with a caustic which will not penetrate its own feathers but may get in the eyes or beak of the other. Usually one does this tasting by simply tapping the bird here and there and tasting one's own fingertips, but if there is reason to be unduly suspicious, you lick him over with your tongue. Each man watches every move of the other, hugging his own bird jealously, reluctantly permitting him to be touched. Even if the best of friends, they are noisy, quarrelsome, and seem angry.

When the combat begins, the two owners remain in the ring. They are permitted to do anything except touch or obstruct the birds. As the battle progresses, they gesticulate, crouch, and leap about, shout, scream, plead, weep, curse, beat their own breasts and Mother Earth. The crowd also shouts and screams while blood and feathers fly. The Haitian cocks usually begin by leaping at and over one another, each seeking to use its spurs in the classic manner, and occasionally a fight ends quickly with a clean spur-thrust, but ordinarily they soon give up these classic gladiatorial tactics and fight it out with their beaks. Battles to the death are therefore unusual. More often one bird finally turns tail and runs, while the other, after pursuing him two or three times around the ring, stops, struts, and crows shrilly in victory. Occasionally there is something grand about this crowing—a thrill in it like brazen bugles. I have seen a cock flap its wings, lift its head to the sky, and shrill its paean of triumph, only to fall dead a moment later in the dust beside its conquered enemy.

So, all in all, it was very exciting and interesting that Sunday morning at Osmann's *gaguerre*, and because of all the noisy shouting, no one heard the distant droning of the airplane. It came roaring down and circled so low that I could recognize Captain Pressley—who is now flight commander of the Marine Corps field at Port-au-Prince—and all of us could recognize Wirkus, waving his arm and grinning. It was evident they were going to drop something for us. Wirkus knew we'd probably be at Osmann's on Sunday; so they'd headed here instead of for Dernière Marque. Sure enough, down rocketed a bag, and after circling again to make sure they hadn't knocked somebody's brains out

See page 214

"When the combat begins the two owners remain in the ring."

with it, they waved and soared away. The bag had a tag on it, addressed to Constant Polynice, and I could see him swell as he opened it, while we all crowded round. There was a letter in it for me, from Colonel Myers, concerning the date on which I should hold myself ready down yonder for flight back to the mainland—but that, to Polynice and all the rest of them, was a trivial detail. The bag was addressed to Polynice. Furthermore it contained a tin box of French bonbons for Julie. Remember that all these people, including prosperous Polynice himself, were mountain peasants. And that an airplane—a great army airplane from Port-au-Prince—which came flying far across the bay to bring a bag for Polynice and a box of candy for his wife, was a tremendous event. Polynice swelled, not only in his own eyes, but in the eyes of all the crowd, to Napoleonic porportions. I have told you that he—and I—were both already thinking highly of ourselves, and now vain pride took complete possession of us like the plague. I somewhat blame what later happened to us on the coming of that airplane, for if Constant hadn't been so totally blinded by vanity and self-assurance, he'd have surely smelt a large rat presently.

And so, that afternoon, we undertook to round out the day by "taking" Osmann and his Cuban *zinga*. "I have been thinking," said Constant to Osmann as one fond, trusting brother to another, "that Tribunal here and your new *zinga* might make an interesting combination. . . ." "They might," said Osmann, "but your Tribunal is a bad bird, and I don't want my *zinga* to be killed. Still, if it went that badly I could take him out of the ring."

"Surely," agreed Polynice, "it would be for the sport; it isn't the sort of thing on which we would want to wager heavily. . . ."

Looking back, it is easy enough to see what a pair of blind bats we were. At the very beginning of it when we squatted outside the ring with the two tethered birds, letting them fly at one another tentatively, verifying them, as the saying is—I saw Constant nonchalantly running his fingertips over the scar on the *zinga's* neck, and Osmann closely examining Tribunal's familiar queer-shaped comb, to make doubly sure there was no trickery of that sort. But we might have noticed, if we had been watching the crowd, that something was in the wind, for instead of pressing close and shouting comments, they hung back, quiet.

When Osmann adroitly pushed up the limit of our initial bet from three hundred gourdes to five hundred, we thought it was as good as in our pockets, and when Louira came to me offering a side bet of another hundred, we figured it was simply because the *zinga* had beaten his own best bird and that it was natural for him to over-estimate its ability.

As we filed the spurs—it is not permitted to withdraw from a match once the filing begins—the crowd came to life, hysterically shouting and waving its side bets, and we heard an insistent chorus of "Two gourdes on the *zinga!*" "Five gourdes on the *zinga!*" with scarcely anywhere a shout for the black. We put it down merely to the crowd's bad judgment, and began taking the little bets ourselves. When they discovered that we were covering the small side bets too, even the women and girls crowded in, laughing, with their pennies. We were busy as a couple of shell-game slickers at a country fair.

The battle began well. Both birds were keen and sailed in with their spurs, attacking, ducking, now over, now under, neither showing much advantage. Barring an accidental spur-thrust, they would presently tire of those spectacular tactics and begin fighting seriously with their beaks. It was thus that this *zinga* had fought a week before, beating Louira's bird which fought in the same way, and we knew that when the slow, vicious beaking began, our little black killer would come into his own. You see, it is practically impossible to kill with a single stroke of the beak. It is a slow, wicked business, at which the most evil and persistent bird almost inevitably wins. And we knew Tribunal from of old. We knew that once settled down to beak fighting, he had one single object, and that what happened to his own bloody head meanwhile was of no consequence.

Presently, just as we had anticipated, Tribunal abandoned the spectacular spur fighting to go after the *zinga* with his beak. And it was here that everything began to go mysteriously wrong. That *zinga*, incredibly, for we had seen it fight before, refused to beak. Contrary to all precedent, and contrary apparently also to the laws of its own nature which Constant had studied so intelligently, it continued fighting with its spurs! Tribunal had definitely ceased hurling himself through the air, and was now dodging about flat-footed, ducking it when he could to administer a vicious peck on the *zinga's* head. But the *zinga* was not standing flat-footed like an honest bird and swapping pecks that day. Contrary to all rules of honor and decency in a Haitian *gaguerre*, it was turning tail and running, but propelling itself in a sort of short half-circle like a fighting plane doing the Immermann, to leap through the air, over and over again, with spurs uplifted for a knockout kill. Apparently the *zinga* didn't know it had a beak or thought that beaks were simply for picking up corn. And instead of being tired, it had just begun to fight!

And now the crowd, which had been nervously intent and more or less silent as if waiting for something, began to howl joyously. It began to howl with joyous conviction, "*Ça y est! Oui! Ça y est!*" which meant, "The thing has arrived! Yes, it has arrived!"

Constant was frantic. He didn't know yet what this precise thing was that had "arrived," and neither of course, did I, but we knew that unless a miracle happened, Osmann had cooked a couple of geese named Polynice and his white. Constant leaped about the ring like a madman, shrieking at Tribunal, kneeling to pound the earth behind Tribunal as if to catapult him into the air by percussion, but it was no use.

We were too excited, watching the fight and hoping against hope, to give any immediate attention to Osmann. I remember vaguely that he had been squatting quiet in a corner of the ring, sardonically stroking his chin, enjoying Polynice's leaps and screams; and then I didn't notice him any more.

The battle ended suddenly, as it was bound to, with a clean spur-thrust that killed Tribunal in his tracks. Polynice, panting and exhausted, stood sadly. Together he and I stood there, looking down at the *zinga*, which crowed lustily and flapped its wings in the middle of the ring. We stood looking down at the triumphant cock and wondering. . . .

Somebody nudged us to turn, and there stood Osmann, and Osmann standing there behind us had the *zinga* in his arms! It hadn't flown over our heads, either. There it was still strutting in the ring, and here it was tucked under Osmann's elbow. Having violated all precedents of a Haitian cockfight, it was now violating the laws of Nature by being in two different places at the same time.

"By the way," said Osmann gently, as one fond, trusting brother to another, "did I mention the fact that I had bought two *zingas* in Saint Marc?"

"*Foutre!*" said Polynice, which is not a pretty word.

Chapter VI

THE "DANSE CONGO"

To please me, since I was interested in such matters, Constant gave a *danse Congo*. He and Julie did not participate in these dances, but once or twice a year he invited the mountainside to a big *bamboche*, and now while I was there visiting him, he said, was a "happy time" to do it.

The Congo dances, African in origin, but without a parallel among the negroes in the United States, are danced to the accompaniment of tom-tom work-drums, rattles, and shrill singing. They are the universal Saturday night diversion of the peasants both in the mountains and the plain. They are lawful, in no way connected with Voodoo, quite easy to see, and nearly all writers visiting Haiti have seen and written about them.

They are, of course, sexual dances. But there is no dancing in couples, no waists encircled by arms, no interlacing. The dancers move their feet in a sort of loose-limbed jigging, but most of the rhythm is with their bodies. It is somewhat like Oriental dancing, but has a special quality of its own. All the phases and variations of the sexual act, including orgasm, are reproduced. With the incessant rhythm of the tom-toms and copious drinking of rum, these festivals often become slightly orgiastic, and travelers have sometimes imagined they were witnessing Voodoo dances. But the Congo is simply a wild frolic. It is the night club of the jungle.

I had seen such dances numbers of times—every one in Haiti has—and they have been described so frequently and so well, as a spectacle, that I should hesitate to include a description here except for a special reason. Always when dancing, they sing, and the words of these songs seem to determine variations of the dance. I had sometimes been able to catch snatches of these words, but unsatisfactorily. And intelligent people, Haitians or long-resident Americans whom I had asked for enlightenment, had said, "Oh, it's nothing, it's just doggerel . . . anything. . . . They make it up as they go." So I asked Polynice to give the *danse Congo*, and help me, if he would, to collect some of these songs with their meaning.

By dark, the crowd was thick round the peristyle, which had been decorated with flowers and torches. *Clairin* and cakes were circulating in abundance. The dancing space was kept clear. The drums began, and a lone male figure leaped into the open space before them. He had been chosen as *mait' la danse*. He was a muscular young buck of medium height, slender-waisted, with broad shoulders, barefooted, in loose cotton trousers, tight-belted, with black negroid features, bullet head, close-cropped. He hurled himself into the air like an amateur Nijinsky, gyrated, came to a statuesque pause, all in rhythm to the tom-toms, then marched thrice around the pole, prancing like a splendid animal, and then standing flat-footed, with no subsequent movement of the feet, began a series of slow, rhythmic motions of the sort usually associated only with female solo dancers. It had seemed to me queer, almost unnatural at first, in Haiti to see a male body exhibiting itself proudly in this peacock sex-strutting and these sexual muscular contortions, but that, I think, was only a limitation of my own, due to fixed-idea associations. There was nothing effeminate or lascivious about it. It was virile and graceful. Men are sexual animals as well as women. But among civilized people there is a curious male shame about it that women do not share. Gilda Gray, for instance, is applauded and respected as an artist by the most refined audiences. Her dances are "aesthetic." And so they are in reality. But if a male dancer attempted to put on a masculine variation of her act the same audience would be disgusted. There is something bred deep in our civilization that causes this. It doesn't make sense, but it's there. I should like, above all things, to have the power of rational detachment in the face of unfamiliar phenomena, and I had seen this sort of dancing before; but as I watched this man it again affected me unpleasantly for a moment. I felt ashamed for him, and ashamed of myself for feeling ashamed. A he-lion or a peacock or a barnyard rooster may strut his sex proudly and publicly before his females. So also do savages. But civilized men mustn't do it. Only females may strut their sex publicly and adorn themselves for sex in the civilized human world. It doesn't make sense, but thus it is.

The mistress of the dance, designated as the *chacha* because of the rattle she carries, was now beckoned into the hollow square, and danced sinuously around the man, undulating and weaving, her face uplifted, her chin held high, her eyes half closed. Then standing before him, she began a dance in rhythm with his, approaching until their bodies almost touched, not quite touching, then retreating.

As these two danced, every one began to sing:

Pitot ou gagnin homme,
Là caille ou;
Passer maman ou.
Oui, ti fi!

(Better that you should have a man in your house than that you should live with your mamma. Yes, young maiden.)

This they repeated for ten minutes or more, others gradually joining the dance until the space was crowded. They stopped for a brief moment, the drums began a new rhythm, and the men, each advancing on the girl who danced before him, and motioning her to go away, to leave him, sang in chorus:

Garder en bas gaillard;
Ou oué iune bout de couteau:
Ou oué iune tête poisson;
Ou oué iune bon borri.
Prends yo—porter—
Bai moins.

(Go and search at the foot of the *gaillard* tree; you will find a knife-blade, a fish's head, and a fine casava cake. Take them—bring them—and give them to me.)

To this the women chanted in counter-chorus:

Oui, moins p'r aller!
Oui, moins bai ou tout!
Moins bai ou manger.

(Yes, I will do your bidding! Everything you ask! Yes, I will provide you food!)

Polynice helped me with the exact wording of these songs, and when they were obscure explained their meaning. I would listen for a while, jotting down notes with a pencil. It was difficult because so many were singing, and after the refrain and new words were well started, many would yell or lilt the tune with mouths wide open, while others would keep repeating perhaps just two words, like "*Oui, moins! Oui, moins! Oui, moins!*"—weaving these variations into the melody. After listening for a while to one of the songs and jotting down what words I could, I would touch Polynice on the arm and we would go into his house, where the noise was less deafening and where we had a lamp and table. Even there he had to shout into my ear the corrections, the meaning of words I didn't know. And this finally became a routine. Each time a new song began, Polynice would cock his head to one side, listening. Then if the words were difficult, he would go over to one man or woman, poke his face within three or four inches of the singer's, and listen attentively to the one voice, at the same time watching the movement of the mouth and lips. Without his help much of it would have escaped me.

There was one song, for instance, in which the men dancing staggered as if ill or wounded, holding their hands in front of their faces while they sang:

Oué yo m' p'r aller,
Fais maladie cinq mois.
Si m' tombé, m' pas levé,
Connais c'est iune madichon femme
Qui tué moins.

(When they see me dragging myself away, sick for five months, if I fall, and do not rise again, they will know that curse of woman has caused my death.)

Madichon femme did not mean the curse or spell of a sorceress; it meant simply the fatal lure of the female.

As the men sang this, pretending to lament in deep-throated chorus, the women sang in shrill, piercing, menacing tones like a band of furies, "*Coiyóu! Coiyóu! Coiyóu!*"

I said, inside the house, "What does it mean, Polynice, this '*Coiyóu*'?" It wasn't French or creole. He replied promptly, "It means if you give yourself up to a woman as much as she wants, she will kill you, wear you out." I said, "How can one word mean all that?" He said, "I don't know, but that's exactly what it means. It means that she will drain you dry, devour you." I subsequently learned that *coiyóu* is an old Guinea word meaning literally the vulva of a female in heat.

The women were taunting the youths, at the same time seeking to inflame and frighten them, proclaiming their elemental, dangerous power as from some old African jungle fertility rite.

Contrasting with that atavistic echo came presently this naïve banality:

Parole Ballon fais moins plaisi';
Nèg la morne pas pé fais
Cou li ac nous.

(The words of Ballon give me pleasure; the negroes of the mountain are not to be trusted like him.)

There had been a man down in the plain by the name of Ballon, now dead, noted for his honesty, and the mountain blacks had made this song in his memory.

The juxtaposition was interesting because it is not easy to understand the Haitian peasants without taking into account this essential duality in their characters.

The various melodies and harmonies to which these words were adapted are difficult to describe, since I am handicapped by lack of technical musical knowledge. Neither the melodies nor the harmony generally had any of the undercurrents of sadness common to the American negro folk songs, spirituals, and blues. These blacks were savage, free, exultant, and their music reflected this. Nor was there any quality in the tempo similar to jazz. The rhythms were frequently tangled, complicated, but the complication was always unsyncopated, against a steady four-four beat. In this respect only it was akin to the Voodoo ceremonial chanting. There were songs in which the counterpoint was woven almost like that of the *Magic Flute* overture; there were also songs in which there was a rapid patter against the heavy choral background, as when one young man in a shrill but musical falsetto, that pierced and rose and soared like the melody on a piccolo, sang *prestissimo:*

Yi . . . yi . . . yi . . . yi! Yi . . . yi . . . Yaá!
Yi . . . yi . . . yi . . . yi! Yi . . . yi . . . Yaá!

It was interesting, meanwhile, to see some girl, off in the shadows, outside the edge of the crowd, unnoticed, un-self-conscious, dancing all alone with scarcely any movement of the feet, in an endless, effortless swaying of the hips and buttocks; it seemed to depersonalize her; it was like the surf or like some cosmic perpetual motion expressing itself through her body.

Another song of the women was:

Au lieu ou bai m' coup na' tout corps moins,
Pitot ou bai m' bon coup na' vent' moins.

(Instead of beating me all over the body with a stick, a well-directed blow in the belly would be preferable.)

This they sang serious and unsmiling, but some of the songs had a humorous implication:

Emanuel, ça ou gagnin ou à pé crier?
'Ti la pas pétit maman ou, ni pétit papa ou.
Emanuel, ça ou gagnin ou à pé crier?

(Emanuel, what need have you for crying? The baby is not your mother's and not your father's. Emanuel, what need have you for crying?)

Polynice explained that it was a joke about a man down at Pointe-à-Racquette named Emanuel Tradeau. He had brought home a girl who gave birth to a baby that was not his. He had made a great fuss about it, and his mother and father, who liked the girl and thought Emanuel was a fool, were taking care of the baby.

They also had a song of Polynice, with words which seemed slightly incongruous, since it was he who was giving the dance and supplying them generously with refreshment:

Polynice comptrolleur!
Li marcher ch'wal blanc la nuit;
Nous bai ou coup de roche;
Malheur river ou.

(Polynice is the tax collector. He comes riding at night on his white horse to rob us; we will drive him away with stones, and a misfortune will happen to him.)

But it was friendly, without malice, and Polynice accepted it without malice, smiling his shrewd, deprecating little smile. Doubtless he would have felt hurt and neglected if they hadn't sung it.

On the Monday following this *bamboche* I bade Polynice farewell, descended to the coast, where I expressed as best I could my gratitude to Wirkus, fished with him for a couple of days, and then the plane came to take me back to the mainland.

Chapter VII

"NO WHITE MAN COULD BE AS DUMB AS THAT"

"No white man," said Cumberland, disgusted yet triumphant, "could be as dumb as that."

He seemed to have the best of the argument.

He had said it to Barker, Barnes, me, and an ass named Mabry as we sat round a campfire wrapped in our blankets like Spaniards, forty-five hundred feet above sea-level, on a mountain-circled plateau behind the Morne Rouis range.

This Cumberland—Dr. W. W. Cumberland—perhaps there is some such degree as Doctor of Decimals—was one of the five American high treaty officials in Haiti. Financial Adviser was his title, and he exercised absolute control over government financial matters. He was as honest as an adding-machine and keenly intelligent, but people said he had no bowels, meaning it in the scriptural rather than slang sense. He was as cold as ice and was obsessed with the conviction that the emotional Haitians, whether high or low, were lazy, undependable as apes, and equally limited in their foresight and mental processes. Yet there was a good deal paradoxically likable in Cumberland. He stood ragging, he was a square shooter, and on a trip like this he always did a little more than his share of the camp work. The fact that he would come along at all on such trips, which meant rough going on muleback and afoot, was a part of his paradoxical likableness. Cumberland is a hard man to depict. He was cold without being selfish or aloof. He was prejudiced, yet full of an active curiosity.

It was he, for instance, who had been the prime mover in this present excursion. Hayne Boyden, flyer, who was making aërial photographic maps for the Marine Corps, had returned one day, greatly excited, from a flight over this mountain plateau, declaring that he had discovered enormous ruins of French châteaux with great paved sunken gardens, circular fountains. He supposed them to be the summer pleasure homes of rich sixteenth-century colonials. There are many such modernly unexplored fastnesses in the Haitian mountains.

When his pictures were developed, he took them to Ash Pay Davis, who is an authority on Haitian archaeology and history. Ash Pay said, "I don't think these are châteaux, but I think they are something just as interesting; I think they are big colonial coffee plantations; I think your immense walls are slave barracks, your sunken gardens drying-floors, your circular fountains decorticators, around which horses revolved, crushing off the hulls. Moreau de Saint Méry (the one source historian on colonial times) mentions that the mountains behind Saint Marc were a great coffee district." But Boyden held out for the château idea; it seemed to him more romantic.

Boyden hadn't been able to land, and aviators are notoriously averse to muleback; so we others had come exploring to see what it was all about. Cumberland had dug up some ancient colonial statistics telling how many thousand sacks of coffee came down from Morne Rouis in 1769. We had motored to Saint Marc, picked up Mabry and our mounts there, and learned what we could about the trails from peasants. Boyden had also given us the general lay of the land. We had found the ruins without much difficulty, had found also a small, straggling peasant settlement, and on its edge we were now encamped.

That afternoon, we had explored a number of the ruins and verified the fact that they were big coffee estates gone to wrack through the centuries, wrecked, burned, partially torn down probably by the revolting slaves. Cumberland had become eloquent, enlarging on his favorite theme. When white men controlled this plateau it had yielded an enormous harvest; now a few straggling peasants, its only population, picked lackadaisically the little coffee that was left growing wild on bushes and carried their few bags down to Saint Marc once a year, just enough to keep them from abject poverty, he said, dead to all ambition and progress. Cumberland, of course, didn't defend slavery, but he thought negroes were never much good except when directed by whites. Barker, who was a field botanist, often following the long trails alone, a bit of a philosopher, and who liked the peasants, had taken up the cudgels for them. He had pointed out that they seemed a singularly happy people, care-free, toil-free, that perhaps they were living more nearly what Bertrand Russell called "the good life" than large groups of white "peasants" he knew, laboring in factories or on intensively cultivated farms, etc., etc. The dispute, like all such disputes, had been inconclusive.

And now, around the campfire, Cumberland had started it again. This time it was about water. Reaching the village—peasants lower down had assured us we would find a spring there—we had asked where the spring was. "It's no longer any good," they told us; "we bring our water up from below." It seemed that an *avalasse*, a little landslide, had choked up their spring two years before, and that instead of bothering to dig it out, they had been toting their water six miles up the mountain ever since.

"And there you are," said Cumberland. "How does that fit into your argument? Good life, bosh! I tell you they are just plain dumb. They trudge six miles and back, because it's easier for the moment. They can't look ahead. *I tell you, no white man could be as dumb as that.*"

Going back next day, we reached Saint Marc around midnight, after having been in the saddle, and part of the time afoot, since before dawn. We were tired, sleepy, and there were engagements that made it imperative to be back in Port-au-Prince by morning. We found the car in Mabry's yard, where we had left it, and climbed wearily in. While we were still in the outskirts of the town, leaving it with Cumberland taking his turn first at the wheel and the rest of us hunching down to sleep, Barker, who was in the back with me, aroused himself sufficiently to say drowsily, "I suppose we've got gas enough, eh, Cumberland?" And Cumberland replied indifferently, "Oh, there must be plenty; it was full when we started." A minute or so later, Barker aroused himself just a bare shade more and said, "There's a garage back there that stays open all night; maybe we'd better stop and make sure." Barnes and I said something, I don't remember what. And on we went. . . .

The car standing stock-still awakened me. I thought we had arrived home, but all around was blackness, except for our headlights streaming down an endless, bare road. The others had already got out. The tank was dry, and we were miles from anywhere. To be more accurate, we were on the edge of a malarial, mosquito-infested swamp, midway between the village of Larcahaie and Source Puante, the Stinking Spring. There was no gas in Larcahaie, but Barker thought he knew a habitation beyond the spring where a man had a gas-driven cane crusher. He remarked that he thought it was just about six miles. He looked at Cumberland when he said six. Barker said he'd go, since he knew the way, and that we could match coins to see which one of us three should accompany him. But Cumberland wouldn't agree to that. It was his car. He would take his medicine. So he and Barker footed it up the road, while Barnes and I spread a blanket in the ditch and covered ourselves, heads and all, with another blanket to keep off the mosquitoes. It was stifling, but we dozed, or at least I did, until, after an infinitely long time, we were aroused by a halloo, and there in the gray dawn, footsore and lagging, down the long road came Barker and Cumberland—Dr. W. W. Cumberland, high treaty official and one of the five wise white rulers of Haiti's destiny—plodding along like any barefoot peasant, toting a five-gallon tin on his shoulder.

We eased it down for him. Barker said, "Yes, I guess it was just about six miles." But he couldn't let it rest there. He had to rub it in. He had to add, with a grin, "*No white man could be as dumb as that*, eh, Cumberland?"

We liked Cumberland, but we had no mercy on him. We all told it the next day at the club; I told it later to Chauvet, who roared with belly-laughter; and it will probably be remembered in Haiti when the millions of dollars a year which Cumberland sweated to save them are forgotten.

All this proved nothing in rebuttal of Cumberland's contention that the Haitians were short-sighted, lazy, and dumb—it was a sort of a *tu quoque*, a sort of "You are wrong, O Socrates, because your own nose is snotty"—but when I related the story to Chauvet, it set him off on a string of anecdotes concerning the guile and resourcefulness of these peasants. The ones I best recall were connected with the rise in the world of a foxy fellow named Theót Brun.

Theót at twenty, ragged, barefoot, and without a copper, wanted a bottle of *clairin*, which is colorless, like moonshine corn whiskey. He found an empty bottle, half filled it with water, and approached a woman who sat retailing her wares, dried herring, little bundles of tobacco leaves, food and drink, beneath a roadside booth. "Replenish my bottle," he ordered, and she filled it, unsuspecting, from her jug. "Thirty cobs" (six cents), she told him.

"Thief! *Criminelle!*" he cried in a passion. "Never!"

"What would you pay?"

"I will not trade with robbers. Take back your *clairin*, pour it out."

And with his bottle still half-filled, but now with rum and water mixed, he played the trick successively at other roadside booths until the pure water he had started with was transformed into pure rum.

At thirty, Theót moved to Port-au-Prince, where he acquired a house and family; but he still had no money and wanted a pair of shoes. He sent a child to a neighborhood merchant, saying, "Theót has rheumatism. Send one shoe, size thus, for Theót to try on, and if it fits, I will return with the money and get the other shoe." There seemed no sense in Theót's trying to cheat him out of one shoe; so the merchant acquiesced. But Theót sent the child with the same tale to another merchant, and Theót rejoiced in a pair of shoes which had cost him nothing.

At forty, Theót, who had risen considerably in the world, had begun to dabble in politics. His shrewdness and trickery made him valuable to men higher up. He decided privately that the time had come for him to go higher up himself. There were some senatorial vacancies to be filled by senatorial ballot. For Theót to aspire to a senatorship was quite absurd, but this is what he did: He went confidentially to one senator and said, "I have a little favor to ask you which can do nobody any harm. On the first balloting for such and such a vacancy, I want you to vote for me, so that when the minutes are published in the newspaper reports, Theót's name will appear written in that honorable company; it will make my wife so proud and happy, and it will increase my prestige with all my neighbors. They will say, 'So, this Theót is getting to be a man of importance!' and it will not do anybody any harm. You can vote afterward for your serious candidate, of course. It is just a little confidential favor you can do me, my vanity perhaps, and no one need ever know who did it. Neither of us need mention it to a soul. But I do want just that one vote." He confided his harmless wish, "in confidence," to other senators, who must have been subsequently somewhat astonished when they discovered that they had elected Theót senator almost without a dissenting vote.

The finest example of peasant shrewdness that ever came within my own personal knowledge in Haiti, though guileful as these tricks of Theót, had a quite different sort of objective.

Dr. Robert Parsons, Lieutenant Commander, U.S.N., detached to Haiti for special medical duty, was the best rural clinic man in the whole outfit. He was chief urologist in the Hôpital Général, but he was never so happy as out on the trails. He had been asked to investigate the rumor that there was an epidemic from which children were dying at Cornillon, in Grand Bois, in the high mountains near the Dominican border. It was a district so difficult of access that the Haitian lieutenant of gendarmerie stationed there reported to Port-au-Prince only four times a year. An old man had come down from the mountains, saying that several children had died the week before, begging the good Americans to send up and help them. Other corroborating rumors had filtered down until Dr. Butler, chief of the service, became convinced that something was wrong up there. He recalled also that the people of Cornillon, some months before, had sent a petition for the establishment of a dispensary in their district, and he blamed himself somewhat for having pigeon-holed it in the press of more urgent matters.

Parsons asked me if I cared to come along. He told me that the district was said to be very wild and beautiful. We motored across the Cul-de-Sac to Thomazeau, which is a gendarme post beyond the big inland salt lake of Saumatre, where the road ended; got ponies there, traversed a flat, thorny desert of *bahonde* and giant cactus to the foot of the mountains, and then began to climb. At first the trail went up barren slopes, but soon it began to thread through magnificent thick primaeval jungle valleys, with palms, giant ferns, and orchids. The huge *mapou* trees, with trunks five and six feet in diameter at the base, which when seen in more open woodland had a smooth gray bark, were here covered, as the *sablier* is, with thick-studded spikes like those on a savage Indian's war-club, to protect themselves from the strangling lianas and vines. Yet many of these jungle giants were being strangled despite their armor, victims of an almost equally gigantic parasitic creature called the *figiér-maudit* (accursed fig tree). The seed of the *figiér-maudit* lodges in a tiny cleft of the *mapou* bark and begins to grow both upward and downward, as a sort of vine. In the course of years its branches, curving like thick serpents, embrace the mighty trunk in a crushing grip. Meantime the *figiér* sends its own roots down into the ground, and presently the *mapou* becomes a dead, rotting trunk, literally strangled to death. Lianas, parasitic vines, cactus trees, monstrous yet beautiful growths, were here murdering each other, like men and animals, for the survival of the fittest.

Through these our trail wound. Late in the afternoon, on bare rocky slopes, this trail, scarcely more than a foot wide, was worn sometimes eighteen inches deep in the solid limestone. It presently passed between high mountains through a sharp divide. This foot-wide trail was the only egress for the Cornillon plateau valley and had been worn deep in the living rock by two centuries of barefoot peasants and the hoofs of their unshod donkeys.

The Cornillon valley, though isolated, was fertile and thickly inhabited. Water abounded, and it was diversely wooded. Hardy banana trees and plantains, palms, too, here some thousands of feet above their normal habitat, grew side by side with northern pines and clover. The top of the divide is more than five thousand feet in altitude, and we judged the valley to lie about four thousand.

The village of Cornillon, which we reached before dark, was pretty, and seemed prosperous. There were perhaps a hundred houses, with vegetable gardens, and a few with little flower gardens. We dismounted at the gendarme post, which seemed deserted. Behind it we found one black corporal playing cards with a private. He was glad to see us, took charge of our horses, brought us water, and asked why we had come. A small crowd had by this time also gathered.

"I am the doctor," said Parsons, who spoke creole familiarly. "I've come to see about the sickness, about the children who are dying."

"Oh," said the corporal—but that was all he said.

"Yes," said Parsons. "Have there been any more deaths?"

"*Pas connais*," said the corporal.

We asked others in the crowd. None of them seemed to know anything about any epidemic. One woman said her child had worms and would the kind doctor look at it tomorrow, another's grandmother had fever, and a third herself was suffering from *biské tombé*, a misery in her tripes—but nobody seemed to know anything about an infant epidemic. Parsons kept insisting. One man remembered hopefully that a child had died in Saint Pierre the month before.

"This is a damned funny business," said Parsons to me. "Do you suppose they're afraid of us?" But they weren't the least bit afraid of us. They were as amiable and friendly as peasants could be. Yet there were side-glances not intended for our eyes, a whisper here and there. They were hiding something just the same. But they were pleased to see us. We were puzzled.

The black lieutenant, we had learned, was off at Saint Pierre. He wouldn't return for two days. Parsons meanwhile had sent some one to find the justice of the peace, the only other official person in the village. The messenger returned, saying that the *juge* was away too, but he'd be back this same night. It was now getting dark, and we were hungry. We also had to arrange about a place for the night. "I guess we'll have to wait until morning to get to the bottom of this," said Parsons.

The corporal got a hatchet and broke open the back door of the lieutenant's house, helped install us, brought water and a bottle of rum, found a woman to cook for us, procured a chicken, eggs, and plantain. "I don't know why we're here," said Parsons, "but this is all right."

The corporal had said they were going to get up a dance in our honor. They had already sent for the fiddler. A fiddle was something new to us. Parsons didn't recollect ever having seen one at a Haitian mountain *bamboche*. We guessed it was the Spanish influence of the near-by Dominican border.

Toward nine o'clock we strolled over to the gendarmerie. The prisoners had come in, some nine of them, in convict stripes, with four guards. They had been laying the cement foundation for a new gendarmerie building. The wooden door of the jail was open, and the gendarmes were inside, fraternizing, gossiping with the prisoners. There was a dispute going on between one of the gendarmes and a prisoner. The gendarme was shouting, "Three!" and the prisoner was shaking his head and repeating, "Two." They glanced from time to time at a sack of cement in a corner. Presently they came to an agreement; the prisoner shouldered the heavy sack and disappeared, unfollowed. He had snitched the cement from the job, and the argument was whether he should pay his friend the gendarme two gourdes or three for the privilege.

When the fiddler arrived, the prisoners came out and danced too. One of them was drummer. We offered to contribute a jug of *clairin*. A gendarme turned over the money to one of the prisoners, who rambled off by himself to get it. The women hadn't come yet. It was like a stage comedy, to see the prisoners in convict stripes doing fandangos and round dances with the uniformed gendarmes. When the girls and women came, they danced with the striped prisoners and khaki gendarmes, and the *clairin* tin cup passed from hand to hand. It was like a vaudeville act. It was also like a millennium. What was a prisoner? What was a gendarme? This was a nice valley. Maybe it was a good thing that only one hard, narrow trail led up to it. Parsons and I were glad we had come. It seemed to us a better place than Port-au-Prince. We had also drunk out of the jug. Maybe they were just playing at being gendarmes and prisoners. This was a nice valley. We assured each other happily that no motor road could ever be built up here—not for years anyway. Parsons was different from Cumberland.

Next morning, while we were having coffee, the old *juge de paix* came to see us. We gave him some. He talked about all sorts of things, entertained us. I thought he seemed to be studying Parsons. Presently Parsons said, "Now about this epidemic? Where are all these dead babies? What's the matter up here? Nobody seems to know anything about it."

The old man lifted his hands as if to say, "Be patient, sir, please." He seemed to have some difficulty in coming to the point.

"I myself was down in Port-au-Prince a year ago," he said. "I was a committee. I left papers, written out in French, at the hospital, in an office. And then in January we had another paper written out for us in your language. And also there were others who were permitted to see and talk with the doctor-chief. But nothing came of it. . . ."

"Nothing came of what?" Dr. Parsons interrupted. "What are you talking about? What's this got to do with an infant epidemic?"

"Well, you see, sir, we are five thousand people up here in this district, and among so many there is bound to be some sickness. There are no doctors, and there isn't any medicine, and it is a hard trail over the mountain, as you know. We are prosperous, there is coffee here, and we would willingly pay the expense of an interne or nurse, Haitian naturally, if once in your goodness a dispensary were established. And then perhaps four times a year would come an American doctor. We thought if you came up to see, you would readily understand the need and wisdom of this—but we were unable to get any one to come and see. But now, in your goodness and thanks to the *bon Dieu*, you have come."

"Do you mean to tell me," said Parsons, "that you deliberately tricked the American Service d'Hygiène into sending me up here—that there isn't any epidemic at all?"

"Oh, no, sir," said the old judge, "not tricked. A child did die at Saint Pierre. . . ."

"Come clean, now. Out with the whole story, and if you tell me the truth, maybe I will help you."

"I am telling you the truth," said the old *juge de paix*. "We regarded the child's death as providential, and agreed that all who went down yonder should tell about it. It became a number of children because a number of people told it, and soon they said in the market, 'Children are dying in Grand Bois,' so that word of it reached the ears of the Americans. . . . We have such faith in your goodness we felt sure that you would come. . . ."

"My God," said Parsons.

I had a letter from him this summer. There was a postscript which read, "Grand Bois has its dispensary."

Chapter VIII

PORTRAIT OF A SCIENTIST

DR. PARSONS and I were at Jacmel, Haiti's southernmost seaport, on the Caribbean. We were in the gardens of the big new American hospital. Parsons had helped build it. It was his baby. He had come back to see how it had grown.

In charge now was a newcomer, Dr. Saundus, over-efficient, with an unflattering opinion of tropical natives and a passion for regulating things.

He came across the garden to us and said, "Look here, Parsons, is it a function of this hospital to harbor beach-combers? I went out on the back terrace a while ago and found a bum there calmly asleep as if he owned the place. I can't make out whether he's German or American. If he's ill, I suppose we ought to take him in, but if he's a plain down-and-outer it seems to me we'd better chuck him out."

Bob said, "All right, we'll go and see."

Curled up in a corner in the shade, sleeping halfway on his belly like a dog, was a lean, unshaven, sandy-haired nondescript fellow with Haitian rope-soled shoes, no socks, clothes stained and shabby; tossed beside him was a bundle that seemed to contain old newspapers, a greasy cap, an old machete. The man was turning bald, had a little ragged, bristling mustache, and a week or ten days' growth of scraggly yellow-gray beard.

Parsons winked at me solemnly and said, "He does look all in, doesn't he? I hate to wake him up."

"Well, I'll wake him up," said Dr. Saundus and prodded him with his foot. The man grunted and turned over. He finally opened his eyes, observed Dr. Saundus and me with a total lack of interest, and then spied Dr. Parsons, who had stepped back.

"Vell, vell, vell!" he shouted and scrambled to his feet. "Vat you do here, Parsons? This is goood! I thought you in the north."

"And I thought you were in Santo Domingo," said Parsons—"but," turning to Dr. Saundus and me, "I want you to meet my friend Dr. Eckman of the Royal Swedish Scientific Society, Fellow of the Smithsonian Institute. He happens to be the world's leading authority on West Indian flora."

This was pie to Eckman, whose childish vanities and eccentricities proved to be even more remarkable than his attire. He beamed and strutted. I found him, when I got to know him better, the vainest and most cantankerous and at times most exasperating chap whose heels I have ever dogged. Each time I took the trail with him, I swore I'd never go again, and each new time he invited me, I gladly went.

I had heard of Eckman before. He was one of the people Parsons had wanted me to meet. But he spent nearly all his time in the bush and among the mountains, cutting his way through jungles where neither black nor white had ever gone before. He had a room in Port-au-Prince, rent-free, which was like a littered dog-kennel, upstairs above the pharmacy of Dr. Bouc—a Haitian druggist who knew that Eckman was a great man—but he occupied it only the few weeks in the year when he was sorting out his specimens.

He was totally indifferent to money—some of these things Parsons told me, and others I learned later for myself—he had no means except a nominal fifty dollars a month from the Swedish Scientific Society. They had offered him more, but he had refused it impatiently, saying he couldn't be bothered. He cared nothing for dressing decently; his aggressive vanity compensated itself in other directions. He loved insulting people.

Dr. Paul Wilson, big chief of the Hôpital Général, who liked Eckman and gave him as good as he sent, tells how once, returning in his car from Trouin, he observed Eckman on the back of a borrowed donkey, ambling along, mildly spanking it with the flat of a huge machete. Eckman habitually scorned any means of locomotion except his own two feet, and Wilson hailed him: "Hello, Eckman, what's this? You're getting old."

"Bah," said Eckman, "I sprained my ankle."

"Well, since you have to ride, why don't you cut a switch?"

This enraged Eckman, who spat out: "You and your svitch! You vould ruin me if you could, joost like that! You tell me today to get a svitch, ven any fool can see that this machete is joost as goood. Ten years I carry only my machete and a knapsack for my specimens, and they suffice me. Today I should get down and cut a little svitch to please you because you are a fool. And then vat? Tomorrow you vill tell me about microbes and make me load my shoulders vith tin cans of boiled vater vorse than a donkey and vith stinking potted meat, and then you vill have me in shiny leather leggings to make varicose my veins and vith a helmet maybe to make ache my head, and soon I vill be traveling vith pack animals and thermos bottles and arriving novhere, like the rest of you!"

"Balls," said Dr. Wilson. . . . "If your sprained ankle bothers you, phone me."

"Yah," snorted Eckman, smiting his donkey, "and you vill cut it off!"

The fashionable high-up American ladies, I am told, tried to be nice to Eckman, when they first came to Haiti. Eccentric scientists are sometimes interesting. They invited him to a tea. First he refused, then bought a celluloid collar, got himself shaved, and came.

"Do tell us all about the wonderful tropical flowers! How fascinating it must be to be a botanist!"

"Yah," said Eckman, and then just sat and glared uncomfortably.

Then an individual charmer who fancied herself intellectual tried to draw him out. "You know, I studied botany at Bryn Mawr, and I am so awfully interested in flowers. I wonder, Dr. Eckman, if you would be so kind as to give me the names of some books concerning plant-life here."

"But, my dear voman," said Eckman, "botany is a science. How vith your silly mind could you hope to understand vat is in those books? It is impossible."

The tea was not a success, and Eckman was let alone thereafter.

Eckman had no use for women. Parsons once asked him why he had never married. "Vell," said Eckman, "I could only marry a botanist, and there are only six vimen botanists in the vorld. I have met them all, and they vere too ugly. There vas a Polish voman not so bad, but she is dead."

But Eckman sometimes liked men's company, occasionally came to Parsons' house and stayed talking long after midnight when Mrs. Parsons was away, and it was there that he agreed to take me along on the first trip I ever made with him. He promised to show me a manchineel tree, deadliest of all tropical poisons. It looked, he told me, like a stunted apple tree and had little red fruits like small crab-apples. Their juice was a violent caustic poison so deadly that a piece of the fruit no bigger than a small pea produced certain and painful death. Its resin was almost equally poisonous. When the colonial French first came to Haiti they had made every effort to stamp out this tree and partially succeeded. It was a dangerous weapon in the hands of the slaves. Eckman told us that he had personal knowledge of only about fifty trees left on the whole island, and that of these he didn't believe more than a dozen could be known or accessible to the present witch-doctors and sorcerers. It sounded to me more than enough. Parsons recalled to us that this tree was the famous *manzinillo* of Meyerbeer's opera, *L'Africaine*. The two lovers fleeing through the jungle go to sleep in each other's arms beneath a *manzinillo* tree. The dew falls through the branches, and in the morning they are found dead. "And that," sniffed Eckman, "like every poetry, is a lie." Then, disappointed when neither of us contradicted him, he said, "But it is not so much a lie as you ignorantly might think." He told us of once cutting his way, tired and perspiring, through thick jungle growth. His shirt was open at the throat and torn. Suddenly he thought that stinging gnats had swarmed on his face and arms and shoulders. He had slashed the branches of a small manchineel tree, and tiny particles of the sap had touched his skin. It made little white burns, he said, like sulphuric acid, and left tiny sores which were days in healing.

The first trip on which he let me accompany him was a three-day exploration up the Rivière Fourche, a little tributary of the Grande Rivière de Léogane. It came out of a jungle canyon which he believed was passable. He thought we might reach its unknown source. It was one of many mountain streams in Haiti which maps both old and new merely indicated with tadpole tails. After we had made some eight miles up the winding canyon, swimming a number of pools between sheer cliffs and clambering up slippery cascades, we came to an impassable waterfall tight-closed between sheer walls. But even the eight miles was something, and we brought back with us that small accurate material which was duly filed in the cartographic folios of Captain Freddie Cook's Travaux Publiques.

Along the trail reaching the canyon, Eckman had scolded and instructed me. He had insisted on my bringing nothing but a blanket roll and a quart canteen. He had promised to bring along what supplies we needed. It turned out they consisted of a box of matches and a small baking-powder box of tea and sugar mixed, which he boiled together. I was a tenderfoot, or so he regarded me, and he was breaking me in. Sometimes he was pretty exasperating. He didn't offer to pay the peasants, not even for the bread which we took from them and carried up the river. But that was his own affair, and theirs. They knew him of old. He treated them with a sort of scornful friendliness which they didn't resent, realizing him queer. They respected him, perhaps feared him slightly, always seemed well enough pleased to see him. Whatever they had in their pots they gave us, usually millet or plantain with dried fish or a bit of goat-meat. It was a new way of trailing for me. I had traversed hundreds of miles of these trails, but always with a horse or pony and filled saddle bags, always willing to pay for hospitality, though in the mountains pay was frequently not accepted. But this was their affair and Eckman's. On the question of water, I was more dubious. High up it flowed clear and there were springs, but we traversed also thickly inhabited valleys, and Eckman drank like a dog in any ditch. He had a "scientific" theory that flowing water purifies itself in the course of a hundred yards. If he couldn't see peasants washing clothes, an old crone cooling her withered flanks, pigs defecating, he drank, and it was all the same to him if all these things and worse revealed themselves when we turned the next bend. I watched him, thirsty, and finally succumbed. "Ten years I have done it, and see me! I never catch anything. I am stronger still than you. I go farther than those who drink boiled water." Some time after I had succumbed completely to his example, drinking wherever he did, I said, wanting to be reassured, "Eckman, you tell me that drinking this filthy water has really never hurt you —you have never had anything?"

"No, my friend, nothing . . . sometimes in ten years I catch a little dysentery . . . once typhoid . . . once or twice black-water fever. But it did not hurt me. I vas soon out. It vas nothing. It cannot hurt you."

This was one of the many times when I should have enjoyed killing Eckman.

I had two little revenges on him during that first trip, and they both got under his skin, the first metaphorically, and the second literally. He had been telling me all sorts of interesting things about his own subject, illustrated by the growths along the trail. He always knew everything, and nobody else knew anything; but in this case there was some justification for his vanity. It was all interesting, and a lot of it was not dry technicality. On a bush were things that looked like big brown caterpillars. Eckman said, "Don't touch it! It vill drive you crazy." I have forgotten the Latin name he gave them. The negroes, he said, called them *pois gratter* (scratch-peas). When they got into the big cane fields below, the peasants would burn the fields rather than be sent in to cut the cane. Then they would blame it on the fire-hags, which are supernatural. A planter has maybe a hundred acres of fine cane, almost ready to cut. Some day when he is sitting on his porch counting up the profit, fire breaks out in an isolated spot. Not a soul near it. No negroes in there. You rush about the edges with dogs and shotguns. You never find anybody or anything. The negroes all have unbreakable alibis. But the night before, they had gone in there and lighted two or three candles with dried leaves piled at their bases. The fire started many hours afterward. All you could ever get out of any of the blacks was that the fire-hags did it. Yet curiously enough, some of them believed in fire-hags too. What fools the peasants were, said Eckman—what silly names they gave the plants and flowers, for instance. Some of the names had a silly sort of colloquial aptness, he granted, like this *pois gratter*, like that thing over there which they called *matta-caval* (horse-killer), a shrub with little red and yellow flowers, a milky sap; it was one of the queer plants, because it would kill horses and cows but not hurt humans; then there was the *maman guêpe* (wasp), a thorny rod with rose-red flowers and stinging leaves like thistles. But some of the names, he said, were stupid and meaningless; for instance, this plant here they call *corban*, which makes no sense at all. . . . It seemed to me Eckman was ranting a bit, that his point was poorly taken anyway. The names seemed to me nice names, showing a good deal of primitive imagination. I suggested that *corban* probably meant something equally apt of which he was ignorant. It always annoyed him to be told there was anything he didn't know. I annoyed him further by plucking some of the leaves from this plant—it bore no flowers—and by stopping peasants along the trail to ask why they called it *corban*. Several shook their heads, but finally one knew. It was absurdly simple. He put his finger on the leaf, "*Ou capab' oué li, li cou cuire*" (You can see, it is like leather). It was true. The leaves were heavy, dark, smooth, with curious deep grooved markings, exactly like hand-tooled leather—like the crude tooling on the leather scabbard of the machete this very man was carrying. And *corban* was simply "cordovan." I pointed this out to Eckman. I said, "These peasants have more imagination than you."

"Vell," he snapped, "how could you have me to know that? I am a botanist, not a philologue."

It got under his skin.

My second petty revenge, in which Providence aided me, came in connection with Eckman's sleeping habits. Whenever there was a *caille* or even a hut available, he insisted on sleeping indoors. This was possibly because he had to sleep so often without shelter. I preferred sleeping under a tree, and he tried to bully me into sleeping inside just because he preferred it. One morning about two o'clock, as I lay peacefully sleeping, he exploded out of a hut, howling that the ants were all over him, and biting him to death. I didn't offer to help him. I said, "You swine, if you'd bathe as often as these negroes do, the ants would let you alone."

I liked him better after that episode.

See page 221

"... she began a dance in rhythm with his."

Chapter IX

MORNE LA SELLE ADVENTURE

It was a clear, crisp, starry night, with no moon. One got an impression of total darkness; yet shadow-like objects loomed. Eckman was somewhere up ahead of us, doubtless quarreling and mumbling to himself—shouting back impatiently from time to time because we couldn't keep pace with him.

I could dimly see ahead the receding white rump of Aubrey's mare. It became my pole-star guide. I followed it as the Children of Israel followed the cloud of smoke and the pillar of fire. I seemed to follow that white rump for hours as it floated ahead in the path like a receding ghost. So long as I followed it, I wasn't completely lost. I couldn't have had more solace in the white flanks of the Callipygian Venus. I reflected that had Aubrey elected to ride a bay or black I should have been irrevocably lost. We had climbed more than five thousand feet that day from tropical sea-level, and the rarefied air made me flighty.

Polyglot Aubrey, ahead of the white mare, leading it, and therefore with nothing to guide him, was moaning, "*Dio mio*, *Gott in Himmel*, *sacré nom de bon Dieu*," and I called out to him, "I think your *bon Dieu* has abandoned us, and I've lost faith in Eckman; suppose we offer prayers and promise candles to Christophe, the patron saint of travelers."

"Five, six—a dozen candles—a basket of candles—as many as you like," he called back to me. "My feet are blistered and I am *cassé dans les reins*."

So, winded though we were, we shouted supplications

to Saint Christophe, promising him a dozen candles, with gilded fluting, finer than any which burned before the Blessed Virgin, exceptional and expensive candles, for his shrine in the cathedral at Port-au-Prince, if he would lead us to a habitation that night.

We were on our way—or hoped we were—to climb Morne La Selle, the highest and most inaccessible mountain in Haiti. It was the peak of a great central broken ridge, its summit visible from far out in the Atlantic and the Caribbean when it wasn't covered with clouds; but when one approached near to the coast by ship, whether from north or south, it usually disappeared behind closer high, guarding ranges. From Port-au-Prince, for instance, it couldn't be seen at all, though its summit was almost ten thousand feet high. There is no other mountain in North America so high between it and the Rockies. In Santo Domingo, which lies eastward, there is one slightly higher range. No man now living in Haiti except Eckman had ever climbed it. The United States Geodetic Survey had reached its summit in 1919, by taking a mule train up the Jacmel side and establishing a base at six thousand feet, but no members of that expedition were now in Haiti. Dr. Paul Wilson had tried three times in as many years, and failed. It was not a problem of technical mountaineering, scaling sheer Alpine cliffs. It was mainly a problem of not getting lost.

Apparently we were lost now, with the added temporary complication of darkness. We had come up from the Cul-de-Sac by a long trail over many high ranges. In the morning there had been three points on the trail from which the Morne La Selle salient was visible, its summit lost among the clouds, but since noon other ranges had inclosed us. We would not see it again, Eckman told us, until we got on the top of the La Selle ridge itself. We were trying to reach this night a place called Camp Franc, at an altitude of fifty-five hundred feet, where there were colonial ruins, immense chestnut trees, and some native huts which were the last human habitation Eckman had seen on his former ascent. From that point onward he was going to lead us by a new route which he had worked out theoretically, as being more practical for the last stage than the one he had previously taken.

There were five of us beside Eckman: Dr. Wilson, Dr. Parsons, Barker, American botanist of the Service Technique, and M. Aubrey, a middle-aged, handsome, bronze-colored Haitian who had learned mountain-climbing in Germany and Switzerland.

And now apparently we were all lost together, Eckman included, straggling along behind each other but still within shouting distance, leading our horses, Aubrey and I begging Saint Christophe to aid the weary travelers.

It was doubtless fortuitous rather than miraculous that twenty minutes later, Eckman shouted back that he had found the chestnut trees. Aubrey and I gave him no credit for it.

They were gigantic European chestnut trees, an avenue of them planted two centuries ago by some rich colonial whose name is forever lost, leading to the ruins of what must once have been a superb estate, which we examined later by daylight.

Had we arrived here a hundred and fifty years ago, a marquis might have welcomed us, slaves would have tended our horses, wines of old France would have been brought from the cellar for our refreshment, and we would have slept in a château amid gardens of roses.

The giant chestnut trees, planted in a double row at intervals of some fifty yards, guided us in the darkness along the top of a ridge, and when we came to the last of them, no longer in any footpath, Aubrey began shouting to Eckman, but there was no reply. We sat down, holding our horses' bridles, while Parsons, Barker, and Wilson straggled up and joined us. We shouted now in concert, and when still no answer came, began to wonder if Eckman had slid off a cliff. "Not that goddammed mountain goat," said Wilson.

There was nothing to do but wait.

After a while, from somewhere forward and down the slope toward the left, came the mocking voice of Eckman, so close that he scarcely needed to shout,

"Vell, you lazy fellows, vy don't you come on?"

Forward and down we stumbled, until we came to plantains and knew we were on the edge of a habitation, then saw a dull glow, and arrived, missing the footpath, at Maman Lucie's *caille*. Beside a fire, in the little compound, sat Eckman, brewing tea. By the other side of the fire, crouched Maman Lucie, an old crone with her head swathed in cloths, apparently half asleep. Eckman said to her in creole, "These are the other doctors; call some of your little world to give a hand with the horses." It seemed the "big world"—the old man—was away. Maman Lucie, half aroused from her torpor, called, "*Amelisse, Ti Sôn, vin icit bai coup.*"

By the red glow of the fire, we saw in the doorway of the mud hovel a wench of fourteen or fifteen years, apparently stark naked, who stared at us dumbly. High lights on her white eyeballs and her black, pointed breasts made her like a figure on a Rembrandt canvas. Hiding behind her, huddling against her, was a still littler "world," a boy of eight or ten.

"*Vini donc*," said Maman Lucie, and "No need to gain fear," said Eckman, and they came out reluctantly to help us with our saddle gear. The girl, who had a necklace of bones and beads and the inevitable *ouanga* strung round her neck on a cord, totally unconscious of her nudity, was more timidly curious than fearful. The boy, clad in a raggedy-tailed old shirt, was breathless with terror. His hands trembled as he helped unbridle and halter the horses, and when Parsons patted him on the back and asked if he was Ti Sôn, he replied "*Oui*," in a shrill falsetto treble like the squeaking of an animal. I do not mean it as a figure of speech that he was breathless; I mean he was so frightened he actually couldn't get his breath to utter normal sounds. It turned out that except for Eckman, he had never seen a white face before. When Aubrey snapped on his flash-light, Ti Sôn darted back screaming; the girl too leaped as if shot, but stood her ground.

They helped pile up our gear, and showed us where we could tether our horses for the night, among the plantains.

The five of us who had ridden at least half the long road were too tired to care much about eating, but Eckman, who had walked the whole distance with a heavy knapsack, was devouring a warmed-over mess of millet from the old woman's iron pot. So long as he could get native food, he scorned the elaborate canned stuff we had lugged along in our packs. We squatted in a wide outer circle around the fire and had some of his tea in our canteen tins with a bit of bread; then we smoked and talked. Close by the fire, inside our circle, sat Eckman and Maman Lucie. Presently Amelisse, drawn by her curiosity, came and crouched beside the fire to watch us.

Eckman, with his belly full of millet, was becoming amiable.

"Vell," he said expansively, "it is all right, yes?"

But when all of us, even including Wilson, agreed that it was quite all right, he couldn't bear the harmony, and added, "Joost the same, you vere fools to go on; it vas better ve should stop by the chapel."

And then he tried to brow-beat us all into huddling inside the *caille* to sleep, because he preferred it to lying beneath the stars. We told him to go to hell, and disposed our blankets among the plantains, near where the horses were tethered.

As Wilson bunked down, he groaned, "What a swine Eckman is! You'll never get me on another trip with him."

Aubrey protested, "No, Eckman is good; it is just his way," and Barker's voice, out of the darkness, interrupted,

"You're a liar, Wilson—you'd go with him again next week."

"Well, if I would," retorted Wilson sleepily, "it just shows what a fool I am."

Dawn awakened us, refreshed but sore. We routed out Eckman, who was still snoring, Maman Lucie made coffee, and we were off.

Maman Lucie's habitation was the highest and last Eckman had touched on his former Morne La Selle adventure. He had taken to the woods, avoiding human contact, because it was said in Port-au-Prince that one obstacle in climbing the peak was that superstitious peasants, believing it a sort of savage Olympus, home of gods and demons, refused to let explorers and travelers pass.

However, rumor said that a village existed on the Merion ridge, across a deep gorge from Camp Franc, and perhaps a thousand feet higher up. No such village was shown even on the large-scale detail maps—not even the trails were charted any higher than Camp Franc—but if it did exist, Eckman believed we could find it.

Scattered around Camp Franc there were a half dozen habitations like Maman Lucie's. None of the dwellers on this ridge had ever crossed the gorge, but they assured us that people of some sort lived above, because at night they sometimes heard the sound of drums.

We were as much interested in this—and in putting the rumored barrier of superstition to a test—as we were in climbing the mountain. Parsons had brought medicines in his saddle bag—the best of all passports—and Eckman, with his unwieldy folio of botanical specimens, was generally considered to be a *docteur feuille* (leaf-doctoring sorcerer).

We descended the gorge by a clearly marked footpath, single file, forced most of the time to lead our horses. When it became certain that this path merely wound down the ravine to emerge in a lower valley, we turned back, and

Eckman presently discovered a fainter trail—he said it was a trail, though we could see nothing—which promised to take us up Merion; and it did.

On a small plateau at six thousand feet we saw smoke and came to cleared fields, planted in congo peas and millet—even a few plantains, rare at that elevation—with a number of scattered habitations.

"Oy, oy!" cried Eckman—one of his favorite ejaculations, though there wasn't a trace of Hebrew in him—"maybe they vill be surprised to see us."

As we rode toward the largest of the habitations, men and boys, all with machetes, came running from the fields until a group of twenty or thirty were gathered close round us. They gave us no greeting—which was strange—and refused to respond to our questions, whispering among themselves. They seemed puzzled and worried rather than hostile. Women came to the doors, even out toward the path, and stared at us silently, wide-eyed, but not afraid.

Here for the first and only time in Haiti I saw tattooed faces of men and women. The markings were thus, diversely, on cheeks or forehead:

The first two symbols, I believe, had both a sexual and a serpent significance; the heart-shaped one I cannot guess unless it was intended to represent a heart; the fourth and fifth symbols represented perhaps the triple paths and triple circles through which the voodoo *mystères* move.[1]

[1] Fred Baker, who spent many years in the hills and is now engaged in rubber experimentation for the U.S. Department of Agriculture, says these tattoo marks, which are really burns, seen only in the most remote and isolated communities, are made with a caustic from the shell of the cashew nut (Anacardium occidentale), and that the heart-shaped mark is the natural outline of the split shell pasted against the cheek.

Except that their clothes were home-made rather than store-bought, they were all dressed like any Haitian peasants, and seemed prosperous. At the point where the path passed in front of the largest habitation, the men crowded across it, not barring our progress in a threatening way, but as if it were taken for granted that we must stop there. Still they stared dumbly, refusing to parley. We had all dismounted. Ordinarily, rural etiquette required them to take our bridles. Aubrey, to establish contact, offered his bridle to a youth, who hesitated and turned toward an older man, who shook his head. Eckman, impatient, said he had *grand soif* and demanded water—a request which it was difficult to deny, and which somewhat broke their reserve. There were hurried whispers, and then one said, "*Besoin 'tend gros moon.*"

Ten minutes later, the *gros moon*, chief of the village, arrived, a tall old man, barefoot, in overalls and blouse, head swathed in a bandanna, sparse, white, pointed beard.

We had been prepared to meet suspicion and obstacles, but not for the surprise he gave us.

"Where are your papers?" he demanded, and it was our turn to gape and stare.

Aubrey asked him to please explain what he meant.

"I," said the old man, "am Authority. I am General Telemon, chief of section, and in the name of Nord Alexis, president, I demand to see your papers."

"My friend," said Aubrey, "I also am a general, and I salute your authority, but President Nord Alexis, alas, has been dead these twenty years. Our president now is Louis Borno, there is peace in the plains, and a *laisser-passer* is no longer required of travelers."

The old man seemed in doubt whether to believe Aubrey or not, and puzzled what he ought to do. "It may well be," he said, "that Nord Alexis is dead. There have been no travelers here in many years, and we do not go down from the mountain; but who are these white men, and why do you come to my village?"

Aubrey explained that we were doctors, looking for herbs which grew still higher in the mountains, and that we came asking his friendly hospitality, water, forage, and care for our horses, while we went farther on foot.

We showed him Eckman's specimens, which carried conviction, the bottles and boxes in Parsons' saddle bag, and offered to treat any sickness in the village.

Their suspicion melted, and now they disputed for the privilege of taking our horses and gear, three or four seizing the same bridle, fighting and tugging over our saddle bags and rolls, so that an untitled cinema flash, had one been taken, would have carried the impression we were being roundly pillaged. Old Authority restored peace, designated individuals to take our horses to water and pasture, ordered all our gear piled up against the wall of his own house, and set his women-folk to pounding coffee for our refreshment.

Then came an episode that increased their friendliness. A cousin of Old Authority lay on a pallet with a dislocated shoulder, badly swollen. Fastened to his arm was a wooden cross, and around his neck a *ouanga* bag of greasy black cloth, the size of a goose-egg, filled with *merde-diable* (their name for assafoetida), dried pig-tree leaves, and snake bones. It was an excellent, high-smelling *ouanga*, but it hadn't worked.

Wilson and Parsons prodded him over, and said, "Papa, we are going to throw your shoulder back in place, but it's going to hurt, and you're going to howl."

They did, by main force, to the accompaniment of yells that Maman Lucie might have heard 'way over on the other ridge. Then they gave him a light shot of morphine, and when he went peacefully to sleep, the entire village knew that we were mighty doctors.

We had been discussing in English, among ourselves,

the advisability of confiding to Old Authority our real objective, the ascent of Morne La Selle, whose black, forbidding slopes rose over yonder behind Merion, disappearing as if they went on up forever among the clouds.

Barker, who had been turned back some months before by superstitious peasants who became angry and threatening when he had tried to climb Morne au Diable in the north, was in favor of saying simply that we sought plants on the higher slopes of Merion, but the rest of us—now that Old Authority and his people were friendly—felt it would be more interesting to tell him, and if he raised objections, argue it out.

So we did tell him, more keen on his reactions than his help, which at a pinch we could get along without. He shook his head vigorously. It was forbidden, he told us, but not by his or any other human authority; on Morne La Selle, as everybody knew, were *loup-garous* and demons. We couldn't go, not because he forbade it, but because we would be killed. There was an old trail, he said, which skirted Morne La Selle some thousand feet higher, crossing the Merion ridge, and leading down to Sal Trou; that far we could go, though even there it was dangerous after dark, and that far he would gladly give us guides and carriers; beyond that there were no trails—at least none made by human feet.

Now there was no use whatever to argue with Old Authority that demons and *loup-garous* did not exist; rather, we pointed out that Dr. Eckman was not merely a *docteur feuille* but a *bocor* (sorcerer) under the protection of his gods, and that no demon of any sort had power to harm him or those under his protection.

At this point Aubrey had an inspiration. He broke in on the old chief's dubious objections by saying, "Papa, one reads in your face that you have courage, and this is a great adventure. I am a black man like yourself, and I am going because I know that no harm can come to me with this white *bocor*. Why not yourself come with us? It will increase your power."

It was a splendid idea of Aubrey's. It flattered the old man; it made him as one of us; it made him an ally. His eyes glowed with excitement, and then the excitement died and he said, "Ten years ago, I believe I would have done it; now I am too old; but I will provide boys, if any can be found who will dare it."

"Vell, dat is fine!" said Eckman, and patted him on the back. "In vun hour ve vill start, yes?"

"Masilia," shouted Old Authority to one of his wives, "call the major and make sound the drum!"

A work-drum boomed the village assembly call, and thirty or forty men and boys gathered in Old Authority's compound, where he explained that Eckman was a great *bocor*, that we were going to the top of the Morne, where no human being had ever been before, that we guaranteed protection and wanted carriers.

Such a whispering and buzzing and wide-opening of eyes and general chatter and excitement hadn't been known in the village for a generation. "No, no, no," came at first from all sides, the women protesting loudest and dragging at the arms of their men and boys. Then one boy, not over thirteen, stepped out. He was pop-eyed with fright, but he blurted, "*Moin pr'allér!*" (I am for going!)

You could see the quick, elementary emotional psychology leap through the crowd, at that. "Who's he any more than we are—if he's not afraid, we're not—if he goes, we want to go too!" Despite superstition, they were a crowd of half-grown children.

It was like a game of Follow the Leader. Here was this village of Badeaux, probably the highest and most isolated group-habitation in the entire West Indies, whose people had believed for generations that the black, forbidding, gorge-broken mountain which towered above them and lost itself in the clouds was the abode of demons and sure death

—so that never had the most venturesome, young or old, ever dared set foot on its slopes. And now all of a sudden, because one kinky-headed, pop-eyed, scared kid, with his heart in his mouth, said, "I am for going," we could have had them all. At that moment, if not later, we could have marched off with the entire youth of the village trailing after us as the rats followed the piper.

Each of us chose one—boys ranging from thirteen to sixteen—and we planned to make our start immediately from the village spring, at the head of an adjacent ravine on Merion. Men, women, babies, dogs, and Old Authority himself followed us there to see the start. This was the last water, and our boys, in addition to carrying our blankets, canteens, tinned food, etc., were each to tote a calabash.

At the spring, we sat around for a short time, ate a cold snack, filled ourselves and the containers with water, and imagined that we were ready to start.

But Eckman, usually in a hurry, sat like a sore toad on a rock.

"Well, let's get going," said Wilson briskly, at which Eckman swelled up and sat tighter.

"What's the matter?" Wilson asked him, as it became plain that something was.

"I am vaiting," snapped Eckman, "for the elephants and cannons."

Parsons caught his meaning instantly and howled with laughter. Eckman, at his cantankerous worst, was a hateful but gifted master of sarcasm. And he couldn't bear tranquillity for an entire day. Back in the village he had apparently acquiesced in the scheme of taking a gang of carriers along; now he revolted:

"Am I Hannibal, that you expect me to lead this army to the top of a mountain! Am I Moses that I must be followed by tribes! All over these mountains, all over Cuba, I go alone with a machete and a piece of bread—but you, for vun little trip, must have an army of carriers and servants who vill only hinder us and hold us back! Vith this straggling mob ve never get there. So let us end this foolishness and send back these boys and start."

In our several ways, some of us angry and some amused, we told him to go to hell—that if he wanted to lug his own pack, like a donkey, he could do it and be damned—but that as for us, we were going to keep our carriers.

Off he started, finally, still grumbling, and carrying his own stuff, we single file after him, followed by our boys, with our gear on their heads, so that we looked a bit like Stanley starting into darkest Africa.

An hour later, around noon, Eckman, loaded with thirty pounds and cutting through lianas and thorn-bushes to open our upward trail, was making better time than we were, unloaded and not having to stop and cut; even the boys behind us were complaining.

Every quarter of a mile or so, he would draw away from us by a hundred yards, and then we would climb puffing up to find him seated on a rock as if he had been there for weeks, sucking an orange, or examining some leaves. And the conversation at these stops was eloquent.

Eckman, now in his element, was amiable again, but still pretended to grumble, and when Wilson muttered that he thought he could keep up an ordinary decent pace as well as any man but had never claimed to be able to follow "a stinking mountain goat," Eckman beamed on him and offered him the quarter of an orange.

He was gay because we were suffering, and because he had a final dirty trick up his sleeve that we did not then suspect. Toward four o'clock, marching on easier ground, through enormous pine trees, on the Merion ridge, we came, at the point where it joined the salient of Morne La Selle, to an old, faintly marked trail, crossing our path at right angles. It was the highest trail on the Caribbean islands; Eckman guessed that our boys would know of lower, roundabout connecting trails that would take them back eventually to Badeaux. And waiting there until they all came up, he tried deliberately to shake them, to discourage them from going further—he talked to us in rapid creole, solely for their benefit, describing vague dangers and saying that we had no right to lead them into them.

It was another of the moments when I thoroughly hated Eckman and would have really enjoyed killing him. He'd have got away with it except for one thing; the boys were caught because the sun would set soon now behind high ridges; they were afraid to come on, but they were even more afraid to go back with the certainty of being overtaken by black night before they could get out of the shadow of La Selle and its demons. So they came on, miserable, with us.

Crossing this trail, we were on Morne La Selle itself. Our plan was to go up its slope as far as we could before dark, make camp, then start at earliest dawn next day for the final climb of some three thousand feet, hoping to reach the summit by nine o'clock, spend only an hour there in observation, and get back to Badeaux the same night.

We tried to keep to ridges, but sometimes, in order to hold our general direction, had to lose altitude, descending into gorges and ravines. Toward twilight, we descended into a rocky one, and clambering up its opposite side, came to Eckman, who called, "Look at this, Barker. Here is something strange." We were climbing up an eroded limestone escarpment, bare of vegetation, at an angle sharper than forty-five degrees, and there, worn in the rock, he had found an unmistakable footpath, not leading in the direction we were trying to climb, but clinging and winding along the side of the salient, leading up toward the cliffs at the head of the gorge.

There was something eerie about it, for there was no rhyme or reason in its being there.

"Vould it be vild goats then?" said Eckman. "I do not think so. Vat you think, Barker?"

"No, it's a human foot-path all right," said Barker, "and it's been here a long time, and I believe it is still used; but what for?"

Our boys had come up and had seen the path, and their eyes were all but popping out of their heads; if we were puzzled, they were not; it was all too simple to them—no natural feet or hoofs had made that trail, but demons, *loup-garous*, *sans-proels*. I felt genuinely sorry for them; their terror was pitiful.

The direction of the path indicated that it went up to the head of the gorge, hemmed in by sheer cliffs from which there was no egress. To have followed and explored it, which we discussed (for even Eckman was keenly puzzled), would probably have meant abandoning reaching the summit. Parsons and I voted to do it, but the others, more reasonably perhaps, said we had left Port-au-Prince for a definite purpose, and that we should go on. Meantime, Barker had walked along it a short distance alone, and was out of sight behind rocks. Eckman shouted to him that we had decided to go on; he hallooed back and presently returned, saying, "I believe I've found out where it goes; I wish we had time to see. There's a higher ledge up there. It goes up the face of the cliff, and there seems to be a cave—"

"Yah," jeered Eckman, "and an old man with a white beard in it, sitting looking at a skull."

"Well, there might be, at that," said Barker. "Somebody still goes up there, and I'd like to know what for."

"We can't do it," said Eckman—and I believe he regretted it too. "We've got to go on and make camp." So on we went, climbing out of the ravine, emerging on a plateau where there were huge pine trees, an open forest in rocky soil—trees here and there fallen, with rotting trunks and branches.

It was almost dark. We were at some seven thousand feet, and even in the tropics it was getting shiveringly cold; at the same altitude in the temperate zone, we'd have been above the snow-line.

Wood from the fallen trees, some of which had lain there rotting for generations, was plentiful and easy; branches as thick as a man's thigh, great hunks of stumps, came loose with a little tugging; and working in pairs, we built three huge bonfires, forming a forty-foot triangle in the center of which we camped, warm and comfortable, and stuffed ourselves to repletion with tea, bread, and tinned meat. The boys, huddled together as close as they could get to us, were worthless from fear; so, Eckman beginning, we took watches of an hour each, feeding the bonfires and keeping a lookout that they didn't spread, while the others slept.

Eckman and Wilson had mutually depended on each other to bring a thermometer; so we had none, but walking outside the triangle of bonfires was like emerging from a kitchen door on a cold November night in New England. We guessed the temperature to be just above freezing.

I was awakened in the middle of the night by something alive moving against my feet; it was my boy Diner who lay there, pressing against them, curled up like a ball, shivering, more from terror, I imagine, than from cold. I pushed the bottom of the blanket down over his shoulders, and he squirmed under it against my feet, whimpering his gratitude.

Barker, who had the last watch, awakened us an hour before dawn. Night and the mysterious trail on the cliff at twilight had so increased the fear of our boys that they concluded anything was better than following us farther, and announced that as soon as it got light, they were going back down. They decently agreed, however, to carry back our blankets and other gear we had no further use for.

We made breakfast of bacon, biscuit, and tea, drank what little water remained, except four reserve canteens containing each a pint and a half. One of these, with a big hunk of *biscuit* and the remains of our cheese and sausage, we tied in a bandanna and slung from the limb of a tree, to be picked up on our return; we were to take three canteens to the summit, drink them there, and come back down thirsty; Eckman had wisely figured that we were safe in using all our water for the climb; he believed that on the descent, we could make Badeaux before dark. If we got lost, it was his plan to waste no time wandering, but simply keep descending, with the certainty that even if we missed our objective, we should arrive, by following ravines, at a spring of some sort.

The first part of the climb was easy going along an open, rocky ridge among enormous pines; but we were forced to lose nearly all the altitude we gained the first hour, scrambling down and up the further side of a barren ravine; the only really dangerous point came as we traversed the stony razor-back edge of another ridge, which dropped on one side some two thousand feet down a sheer cliff, and from which, for the first time, we saw, through a break in the clouds which were both above and below, the slope of what Eckman said was the Morne La Selle peak.

The final hour was hard, but not dangerous, clambering among rocks, with the big pine trees left behind, no vegetation but occasional stunted pines, moss, and clumps of ilex.

On the last slope of the summit itself, we came to another, old, faint footpath, and followed it because it wound upward. We began to believe it was going to lead us to the top, but within a few hundred yards of the summit, it slid off to the left, so that we abandoned it and kept climbing.

The summit itself was undramatic, a round knoll or cone of soft, eroded limestone, on which were half a dozen small pine trees, three or four century plants and some ilex scrub.

Cemented in a rock was the bronze tablet put there by the Geodetic Survey six years before. The plaque said, "République d'Haiti, Travaux Publiques," "Défense d'Abîmer," etc., but the spaces left for the date and the elevation to be chiseled in had for some reason been left blank. There, close by, lay the rotting tin can containing the hardened remains of the Portland cement which had been used to affix the plaque, and beside it a proportionately rotted sardine tin, with partly legible lettering which we guessed was Seacoast Canning Company, Eastport, Maine, plainly a relic of the same expedition. The clouds were all about us. There was no view. We occupied ourselves by looking for possible traces of other visitors, but found nothing; and clambering about, skirting the cone, we assured ourselves that the mysterious path we had seen a bit below did not lead here.

Our aneroids, allowing for compensation, checked 9,780 feet.[2] It was chilly, but not bitter cold. Toward nine-thirty, after we had been there for half an hour and dared to stay only about a quarter of an hour more, the clouds suddenly began to lift—and what we saw was magnificent. We had come up so gradually from one higher range to another that the little cone on which we stood had seemed nothing more at the last than a casual knoll, and it was startling, when the clouds opened, to find ourselves standing on the top of the world. Great blue ranges and jagged peaks lay far below us; beyond them, southward, shimmered the Caribbean, and far northwest the misty expanse of the Atlantic Ocean; northeastward in the green Dominican plains was set, like a small inland sea, the salt lake of Enriquillo, and beyond it, facing us, massed in the sky, the great interior Cordillera range of the Dominican republic.

Less than a quarter of a mile away, and connected with

[2] We inscribed the date, our names, the altitude as registered by the aneroids, inclosed the writing in a metal tube and buried it under a pile of stones beside the Geodetic plaque, leaving also a heavy staff protruding from the top of the stone mound. On my return to Haiti in February, 1928, Captain Pressley and I flew over Morne La Selle, and circling close within fifty feet of the summit, observed the staff and stone mound undisturbed, as we had left them. The figures I give from memory; probably wrong.

us by a dipping ridge, was an eminence, only about a hundred yards lower than the summit on which we stood, and which looked as if it would afford an even better view of the Haitian plain below.

We decided to leave the summit immediately and use the remainder of our scant time exploring that other eminence. Barker said, "I bet that's where the path led; I bet we find it there." And so we did. We found the path, narrow, faint, yet clearly worn as if it had been used intermittently for many years. It led up straight to the brow, where we found a table-rock overhanging a cliff, dominating the whole plain of the Cul-de-Sac, indeed the whole of Haiti northward.

"My God, what a spot, what a view!" cried Parsons.

"Yes, and look here," called Barker. "I guess this settles it."

On a great flat stone at our right, on the cliff's edge, were the black, unmistakable traces of a huge bonfire, and in near-by crevices we found charred sticks which Barker examined and cut into with his knife; some, he estimated, were two and three years old; at last he found some which he declared were only about four months old, perhaps less. This would have dated the last fire there around Christmas, the time of the great annual Voodoo sacrifices and ceremonials.

Time was pressing. We left the cliff, and shortly before noon arrived at our camp, where we divided the *biscuit* and cheese, stuffed them in our pockets, drank the last of the water, not more than a gill for each, and began our hurried descent.

Going up, it had seemed to me that those of us who lagged most had a doubly hard time of it, for Eckman, pushing ahead and then sitting down for us to catch up, had longer rests; also he instinctively chose the best going, and we, out of sight, only in shouting-distance behind, and guided by reluctant replies to our shouts, sometimes floundered about and needlessly wasted our energies pushing through bushes, clambering over rocks. So I made up my mind, as an act of will, to cling to Eckman's heels like a dog until I dropped, and I persuaded Parsons to try to do the same. At first he grudgingly praised us for it, but finally it injured his pride, and I think he deliberately tried to shake us off. I do not mean that he tried to abandon us, but once or twice, up slopes or down, where the footing was good, he broke into the slouching trot of the peasants. We were hot, thirsty, and miserably tired. Wilson suffered most, and Barker least—Eckman apparently didn't suffer at all. In the afternoon we picked up the Sal Trou trail, and used it for an hour or so, then leaving it to follow the Merion ridge. Toward five o'clock it became clear that we had side-slipped down a wrong ravine and were lost, as we had expected we might be. We had also begun to lag and lose time. I was still dogging Eckman's heels, but Parsons had torn the side of his shoe on a rock and developed an abrasion that must have hurt him cruelly; for he limped, and the side of his sock was clotted with blood. Wilson, the heaviest of us, not fat, but sanguine, florid, suffered most from lack of water. His face was congested, and he became feverish from dehydration.

We abandoned hope of finding Badeaux that night, and followed the ravine, sure that sooner or later we would come to water or a habitation. And at twilight we reached a cool, deep spring, bubbling among the rocks, from which a little stream flowed downward, and beside it great clusters of mint were growing. We drank, we thrust our arms, our heads and shoulders into it. We absorbed it. We shouted to Wilson and Parsons. Courage came back to us, and a sort of elation. We laughed and joked, and congratulated ourselves, and even Eckman was gay. Aubrey produced rum in a little leather-covered flask; we put handfuls of mint in the cup-bottoms which fitted over our army canteens, poured a bit of the rum in each, and filled them up with the cold spring-water. After drinking, I carried a refilled cup of this mixture fifty yards back to Parsons, who was limping up; he looked at me with dazed eyes as he drank. He gave Wilson half. Wilson wallowed in the stream, absorbing water through all his pores; and drying our hands, we lighted the last of Barker's cigarettes. We were hungry, but it didn't seem to matter. Trails came up to this spring, but it wouldn't be much use following them in the dark, and we knew that in the morning people would come who could take us to food. We decided to lie the night there and sleep if we could, though Eckman feared it would be too cold for sleep. And then from the westward, apparently just over a ridge, less than a mile distant, a drum suddenly began to beat. We supposed it was for a Congo dance or perhaps a religious ceremony—but as I listened to the rhythm, I was soon convinced that it was neither Congo nor Voodoo, but a village signal call. Further down the ridge presently came the identical call from another drum, and then, more faintly, the same call from drums farther and farther distant.

I ventured a guess, which proved correct, that Old Authority at Badeaux, fearing we might be lost, had sent out his drummers, along the slopes of Merion, to guide us.

We went over toward the ridge, shouted, there was an answering shout, which we followed, and presently we found the man, by himself, with a drum, sent indeed from Badeaux. He thumped out a rhythm telling that we had been found; a drummer across another ridge took it up; and thus Old Authority back in Badeaux, six miles away, learned that we were safe.

As we followed the drummer, who now acted as our guide, we presently heard the Congo drums going at a great rate in Badeaux; they were starting a jubilation to celebrate our return.

It was pitch-dark when we straggled in. Home-made tin lamps and pine torches illumined the yard of Old Authority's habitation. A dance was in full swing beneath the *tunnelle*, which stopped as they all thronged around to welcome us. The old man kissed us all. A big pot of chicken and another of millet were steaming, awaiting us, and a bowl of water, big as a tub, covered with leaves, brought fresh from the spring. Somebody tugged at my sleeve; it was my boy Diner, who patted me shyly, and then pressed into my hand secretly two small tomatoes. I wondered why he was so secret about it, whether, perhaps, he had stolen them.

We stuffed ourselves with food, spread out our blankets there on the edge of the yard, and lay down to sleep, if sleep we could with the whole village crowded there dancing, the drums going wildly. It was evidently going to be an all-night affair, and since, in a way, it was in our honor, we could scarcely protest. Aubrey and I, meanwhile, had got quietly, philosophically drunk on *clairin*, and except for once or twice in the course of the night when dancers stumbled over me or stepped in my face, I slept like a dead man.

Next morning we bestowed largesse, bade good-bys (Eckman remained, to be gone weeks, looking for new plants behind Merion), and set off on our fattened, rested horses, stopping across the gorge to give Maman Lucie news of the neighbors she had never seen but whose dogs and drums she heard at night, and to look at the relics of the old French colonial habitation at Camp Franc.

Here once, in a spot as isolated then as it is now, had dwelt slave-owning luxury—that was clear in daylight—but no oral traditions lingered; whether the owner, like Count Kenscoff on the lower ridge, had been a monster who amused himself by having his yellow mistresses torn by bloodhounds, or a kindly marquis whose slaves had helped him down to Jacmel when the bloody revolution came, to kiss his hand and see him with his family safe aboard a frigate for Port Royal—no one will ever know.

All Maman Lucie knew was that they called the ruins Magasin, for no reason she could assign. We guessed it was because the only walls still standing were a circular stronghold on a slope behind the gardens, which might have been the powder magazine of a fort, but in all probability it had been a storehouse. There were foundations, still traceable, of an extensive villa, overlooking what had been a terraced rose garden, with scattered bushes still blooming there, a plum orchard, and the avenue of huge chestnut trees which led to it along the ridge. There were ruins also of a big circular cistern.

Two nights later—covered with mud and dried perspiration, unshaved and unwashed for five days—we sat on the beer terrace of the "German Ambassador's," tired but well content.

Chapter X

THE SOUL OF HAITI

On the last bright Easter morning which I spent in Port-au-Prince—this was only a year ago—the Champs de Mars, a fashionable park adjacent to the presidential palace and new government buildings, resembled an untidied battle-field on which scenes of wholesale carnage had been recently enacted.

It was impossible to drive through it without swerving to avoid mangled torsos; it was impossible to stroll through it without stepping aside to avoid arms, legs, heads, and other detached fragments of human anatomies.

It was impossible also to refrain from smiling, for these mangled remains were not gory; they exuded nothing more dreadful than sawdust, straw and cotton batting. They were, in fact, life-sized effigies of Judas and Pontius Pilate's soldiers—done to death annually by naïve mobs bent on avenging at this somewhat late day an event which occurred in Palestine during the reign of Tiberius.

My black yard-boy, Louis—sweet, gentle soul—had come to me on Saturday and begged in his soft creole accents the loan of our garden machete in order that he might be suitably armed to participate in the pious slaughter. A Judas, he told me, was hiding somewhere in the jungle ravine just behind the house of Colonel Myers, one of our near neighbors; if I listened, he said, I could already hear the crowd howling and beating drums to drive him from cover. "Go, Louis," said I, "and God go with you." It seemed a sort of neighborhood duty as well as a devout one. I suggested that he might take also an old *caco* sword which Général Télémaque Jumelle had given me, but he thought the machete would suffice, and departed, filled, it seemed to me, more with glee than pious zeal.

Through Louis' previous kindness—he had taken me earlier in Holy Week to call on an aunt who lived near Bizoton—I had made the acquaintance, so to speak, of one Judas before he had betrayed our Lord and fled to the woods. All the little community had contributed toward his construction. He sat propped in a chair outside the doorway. They had stuffed an old coat, a shirt, and a long pair of trousers with straw, fastened old shoes and cotton gloves, also stuffed, to the legs and arms, and had made ingeniously a head of cloth, stuffed with rags, with the face painted on it and a pipe stuck in its mouth. They introduced me to this creature very politely. They were rather proud of him. He was Monsieur Judas, and I was expected to shake hands with him. You see—or perhaps you will not see unless you can recall the transcendental logic which controlled the make-believe games you used to play in childhood—that Judas had *not yet* betrayed Jesus. He was, therefore, an honored guest in their house, as Peter or Paul might have been.

And so their righteous wrath will be all the more justified when they learn on Saturday morning that Judas has turned traitor. Then it is that all the neighbors, armed and shouting, the men with machetes and *cocomacaque* bludgeons, the women with knives, even more bloodthirsty in their vociferations, invade the habitation where Judas has been a guest, demanding, "*Qui bo' li?*" (Where is the traitor hiding?)

Under the bed they peer, if there is a bed; behind doors, in closets—I happened to witness this ceremony in city suburbs, where they do have beds and closets—while members of the household aid in the search and make excited suggestions. But nowhere can Judas be found. It seems that he has fled. (What really has occurred is that the head of the house has carried him off during the night and hidden him, usually in some jungle ravine or thicket close on the city's edge. Judas usually takes to the forest as any man would, fleeing for his life. But this is not always predictable. A Judas has been known to hide in a boat, in a public garage yard, even under the bandstand in that Champs de Mars whither so many of them, wherever found, are dragged for execution.)

So tracking Judas becomes a really exciting game. A group collects, shouting, beating drums, marching in the streets, racing up side-alleys; meeting other groups, each intent on finding the Judas planted by its own neighborhood, but nothing loath to find some other Judas and rend him to pieces *en passant*. Crowds may be heard also crashing and beating through the jungle hillsides. It is rather like an Easter-egg hunt on a huge and somewhat mad scale.

Saturday morning, after lending Louis the machete and wishing him good hunting, I got into my little car and drove out slowly toward the suburb of Bizoton. I had been told that I should see many Judases dragged along this road. I am sorry now that I didn't go along with Louis instead, for as it turned out I had the bad luck not to see a single Judas at the moment of actual capture. I did see numbers of them, however, being stabbed, hacked, and torn to pieces along the roadside, others being dragged into the city at the ends of ropes. It seemed to me that the women were more savage than the men and entered more frenziedly into the mimicry, but this may have been my own illusion, or merely that female voices are naturally more shrill.

As a matter of fact, I think it was all somewhat less savage, less gruesome, more good-humored, than this description might indicate. There were jokes and laughter, comic episodes; there was a conscious element of carnival foolery in it, if you please. There were moments, indeed, when this carnival foolery seemed dominant, particularly back in the Champs de Mars, where I stopped as many other amused sight-seers did, both Americans and upper-class

Haitians, watching the ludicrous straw-stuffed effigies, some with cocoanut heads, being ludicrously ripped and buffeted about. . . .

When a memory of Gilbert K. Chesterton's mythical president of a mythical Nicaragua popped suddenly into my mind, as I sat there in the car, I was not immediately conscious precisely why it had popped into my mind. This mythical character occurs in the prologue to *The Napoleon of Notting Hill.* He is an old gentleman who strolls down the Strand in a top hat and gaiters, but with his body draped in cheesecloth, green and white. From passers-by he inquires where he may buy a strip of red cheesecloth, and they find him comic. But when he gashes his breast with a penknife, dyes a part of the white cheesecloth with his blood, and marches onward, they find him no longer comic but rather a figure which inspires awe.

It was, however, only because I was slow-thinking that I did not realize immediately the precise reason why this had popped into my mind. There in the sunshine before me stood the palace of the late Guillaume Sam; beside it stood the French legation in its walled garden; and there also in the sunshine, howling and dancing and brandishing their machetes, now ludicrous and harmless, was the same identical crowd, the populace of Port-au-Prince, which only in 1915 had invaded those buildings, shouting, "*Qui bo' li?* Where is he hiding?" just as they had shouted in search of these comic effigies of Judas, looking under beds, in closets, just as they had looked this morning for a straw-stuffed dummy; and finding President Guillaume Sam, the man of flesh and blood, had tossed him over the wall, torn him limb from limb, and dragged his mangled torso at the end of a rope through this same Champs de Mars, just as they were dragging the comic effigies of Judas now.

And it seemed to me that during this last generation at least, perhaps even in the older days when more gigantic figures loomed, that the Haitian people, so far as their politics and revolution were concerned, were somewhat comparable to Chesterton's mythical symbolic figure.

The whole Guillaume Sam episode, for instance, which ended in blood, anarchy, and American intervention, began as *opéra bouffe* comedy and for months ran its normal comic-opera course.

In the late fall of 1914 Davilmar Théodore made himself president in Port-au-Prince and made also the mistake of sending one of his generals, Guillaume Sam, north to the Cape. In less than three months, Sam, after private consultations with the notables of the north, announced that Théodore's election was illegal, proclaimed himself Protector of the Liberties of the People, sent out to Fort Liberté, which is a seaside jungle village east of the city of Cap Haïtien, and there organized a revolutionary army consisting of some thousand generals and two hundred privates.

I recently visited Fort Liberté with a man named Pettigrew, who is clearing the jungle thereabouts to plant sisal. While rambling along the desolate shore to see the old Spanish fortifications, we came upon a brass cannon, still upright on its ancient worm-eaten wooden carriage, and Pettigrew, who knows something about guns, said, "Look here, somebody has been firing this piece; look at the powder stains. How the devil could that be?"

With us was one of Pettigrew's barefoot black overseers, who explained proudly, "I myself am the man who shot it. I was Guillaume Sam's commander of artillery." He patted the green-rusted antiquity which pointed immovably askew out to sea in the general direction of New York or Labrador, and continued, "Yes, with this I fought valiantly for the revolution; with this great cannon which you see I shot nine rounds."

Pettigrew said, "What in the name of God were you shooting at?"

"But, oh," the pained late commander of Guillaume Sam's artillery replied, "you do not understand these matters! It was not to shoot at anything. It was for the capture of the town of Terrière Rouge; you see, they could hear the noise there."

And it was more or less thus, for the several hundredth time, that the revolutionary army moved on, and the city of Cap Haïtien fell. The government troops fired three musket volleys over the heads of the triumphantly entering army of the Protector of the Liberties of the People, fell back without casualties, sent a telegram to Théodore's minister of war down in Port-au-Prince, announcing that they had suffered a bloody defeat—and joined the army of the Protector.

From this point onward these Haitian revolutions proceed habitually by fixed rules, somewhat like a game of checkers. The Protector of the Liberties of the People, with an increasingly augmented rag-tag and bobtail army, marches southward, liberating various villages, and camping presently before the important commercial city of Gonaives, generally defended by a government army. The German and Syrian merchants of the town come out and beg the besiegers not to burn it. Once or twice, purely through mutual misunderstanding, a part of the city has been burned, but usually the matter is arranged without arson or bloodshed in a manner profitable to the new Protector of Liberties, and his troops receive their first pay.

Thence they march upon Saint Marc, which is connected with Port-au-Prince, the capital, by a railroad line. As they approach the Saint Marc railroad head, predictable events are also happening in Port-au-Prince. The minister of war calls on the president and says, "Excellency, this is awful."

"How awful?" asks His Excellency. "Well, perhaps with one hundred thousand dollars . . ." replies the minister of war. The minister of finance is called in. When they learn from him what government funds they can grab in a hurry, they vote it in a lump "to maintain the government." It may be as much as two hundred thousand dollars.

Most of this they put aside privately for emergencies. A little of it is given to the army, which entrains northward. The generals of this defensive army, having received their pay in advance, put up a harmless demonstration, and retire on Port-au-Prince, announcing that all is lost.

At this point, as the liberators are clambering aboard trains at Saint Marc, it is customary for the president, the minister of war, and the minister of finance, taking with them the emergency funds, to sail for Jamaica.

When the Liberator of the People arrives, therefore, in Port-au-Prince, there is no argument. He finds the palace empty, swept, ready and waiting for his occupancy, and a few days later he is elected president. It is an almost iron-clad rule of the game that he mustn't loot or burn in Port-au-Prince. That wouldn't do at all.

And this, more or less, is the manner in which Guillaume Sam made himself president in March, 1915. And he also, in the normal course of events, might have ended his rôle in the oft-repeated comedy by sailing in his turn for Jamaica.

But on certain occasions—occasions much rarer, by the way than detractors of Haiti have led the world to believe—these comic-opera revolutions have got out of hand and turned to bloody tragedy. This is inevitable in a land where the mass of the populace, possessing childlike traits often naïve and lovable as well as laughable, have also a powerful underlying streak of primitive, atavistic savagery; and Guillaume Sam himself was a black negro of the people. Only six presidents in the entire republican history of Haiti have been assassinated, a record proportionately not much worse than our own, but distinguished from our methods by a certain hearty largeness of gesture somewhat shocking to the Anglo-Saxon mind, as when in 1912 they blew up President Leconte with dynamite, including his palace, his little grandson, and most of his bodyguard.

What happened in the case of Guillaume Sam, reduced

"... dark mother of mysteries."

to its essentials, is current history. I should scarcely be including it in this narrative, which pretends no concern with either politics or history, except that it seems to help picture so adequately the emotions and psychology of the Haitians, which I am concerned in presenting, for good or bad, as honestly and truly as I may. And I do believe that there is basic truth—not a mere trick of perhaps picturesque analogy—in this comparison I have been trying to establish between Chesterton's mythical-symbolic gentleman on the Strand and the Haitian people; they are habitually a little comic, a little childish, a little ludicrous, they are easily vulnerable to a certain sort of caricature, like Tartarin and the French Meridionals; then suddenly from time to time something that is essential in the color and texture of their souls—essential perhaps too in the color and texture of their skins—something more than atavistic savagery, but which may trace none the less to their ancestral Africa, dark mother of mysteries—some quality surges to the surface of group or individual; and when this happens, we others are in the presence of a thing shorn of all that can provoke superior smiles or scorn, a thing which strikes terror and sometimes awe.

In March, 1915, President Guillaume Sam was installed ephemerally in the palace, and by early summer another self-constituted Protector of the Liberties of the People was already organizing a revolution in the north, just as Sam himself had plotted the overthrow of his predecessor. The situation contained similar comic elements. It should normally have ended with the *envoi* so repeatedly written after the names of ephemeral Haitian presidents that the Haitians themselves have come to realize the humor of the phrase as a political epitaph: "He sailed for Jamaica." But now comedy turned to bloody earnest. There were numerous tangled contributory causes. The real break came, however, when President Sam learned that a group of politicians allied with the socially important aristocracy of Port-au-

Prince were plotting to betray him. Encamped outside the city were numerous bands of *cacos*. *Caco* is an old Spanish word, meaning a bird of prey that swoops suddenly and flies away.[1] In Haiti it has come to mean the roving guerilla bands which fight or loot for profit; sometimes they are revolutionists, sometimes patriots, sometimes plain bandits. They will defend a president or aid in his overthrow, as the case may be. President Sam learned that certain frock-coated gentlemen in his capital were secretly treating with these armed bands encamped in the near-by hills. Immediately he made two daring, risky, and potentially savage counter-moves. First he sent his own soldiers through the city, arresting representative members of the aristocracy and throwing them into prison. Next he sent messengers out into the hills to summon secretly the leader of the largest *caco* band, a "general" named Matelius. And on the following night this *caco* chief, by President Sam's own invitation, marched into the capital with his ragamuffin, rum-drinking, machete-waving horde, to build their campfires in the very shadow of the palace walls. It was a sight that must have struck immediate terror to the hearts of the fashionable mulatto ladies whose fathers and husbands had already been dragged away to prison, and who from the luxurious galleries of their richly furnished villas could now see those *caco* campfires burning so close to the palace that they could be there only by Sam's own orders.

Nearly two hundred leading citizens of Port-au-Prince had been herded into the prison. They were all fathers, husbands, brothers, chosen from the rich, the socially *élite*, chosen regardless of whether as individuals they were suspected of participating in the plots against Guillaume Sam. He believed that people of their group were about to betray him; so he seized the group as hostage for his own safety. And on that selfsame night, Sam wrote a letter to Charles Oscar, commandant at the prison. The letter was ambig-

[1] Derivation doubtful, and quite possibly wrong. W. B. S.

uous. Sam was an ignorant peasant who wrote French badly, but it seemed to mean, and apparently Oscar took it to mean, that if Sam were attacked in the palace, he should kill the hostages. Sam was so fearful of treachery that he meanwhile disarmed all but a few of his own palace guards, some of whom were former household servants of the men he had thrown into prison, and intrusted his safety entirely to the *cacos*. At four o'clock that morning, inevitably, hell broke loose in Port-au-Prince. Charles Dalvar—who survived the subsequent events and happens at this present writing to be mayor—crept down a deep ravine behind the palace with some twenty or thirty friends who had escaped Sam's dragnet. They were armed as such men would be, with fancy shotguns and sporting rifles; Dalvar himself had the silver-chased Le Fèvre, hammerless, which to this day remains the finest light fowling-piece in Haiti. These gentlemen, so singularly armed for such a desperate business, appeared suddenly at the palace gates and began firing. The *cacos*, who could easily have repelled and slaughtered them, offered no resistance, but hot-footed it back to the hills, apparently under the impression that the whole city had arisen. The capital has never been a healthy place for *cacos*.

As Dalvar and his men entered the palace yard, President Sam darted from the palace and leapt like an ape, clambering over the high stone garden wall to seek refuge in the French legation immediately adjacent. He was shot in the buttock as he rolled over the top, and dropped, not badly wounded, in the French legation grounds, whither Dalvar and his men, aware of international law, made no effort to pursue him.

But meanwhile, a thing which Dalvar did not then know, Commandant Oscar, hearing gunfire from the direction of the palace, had carried out complete and bloody reprisal in the prison. The massacre was started with rifles . . . but it was finished with machetes. Later the next day, when the wives and mothers of the Haitian capital went to the prison in their fine carriages to claim their dead, they had to carry the remains away in baskets.

At dawn, when news of the prison massacre ran through Port-au-Prince, the entire city really rose, and there were no social distinctions in the rising. Aristocracy and populace demanded the heart's blood of Guillaume Sam. A great mob, on the following morning, gathered in the Champs de Mars before the gates of the French legation, and by some curious psychology that mob was for the moment patient as a bloodthirsty tiger.

The mob squatted like a patient monster licking its chops in anticipation while four gentlemen of Port-au-Prince, whose names have been by common consent forgotten, appeared before the tall grilled gate of the legation, meticulously garbed as if for a formal morning call, and discreetly sounded the little bell which tinkled in the far interior. Perhaps Guillaume Sam, guest of the legation, heard that faint, discreet sound of the little tinkling bell.

The French minister answered in person. I am told that he recognized the four callers and that he immediately opened the grilled gate. It would scarcely be polite to parley with such courteous visitors through a grating; it would perhaps also indicate that there was something to conceal. I am told that his young daughter stood beside him. I am told that he said, "Gentlemen, will you come in?" I am told that they doffed their hats to Mademoiselle and thanked him gravely, but remained standing just outside the gate while they explained their errand. I am told that the French minister lied like a gentleman and said, "He is no longer here." I am told that they also lied like gentlemen, saying, "Sir, we believe you; your word is enough for us, but unfortunately it will not suffice for the populace. It is better that we should enter discreetly and verify the fact than that they should enter to search."

"I must warn you," said the minister, "that either course

would be equally a violation, which I am compelled by law and duty to forbid."

"We regret it," said the four gentlemen.

"Unfortunately," replied the minister, "I have not the armed force at my command to prevent you."

Guillaume Sam had been well hidden. But one thing had been overlooked. His wound had been dressed with iodoform, and they nosed him out as the Danish soldiers in *Hamlet* did the body of Polonius hidden behind the arras at Elsinore. He offered no resistance until they were descending the staircase, and then his bodily courage snapped. One of those four gentlemen, with whom I have talked many times, tells me he believes that Sam never lost his moral courage or his mental intent to march bravely down that stairway to his certain death. But he could not control his automatic muscular reactions. His thick peasant hands gripped the heavy wooden balustrade, and offering resistance of no other sort, he clung to it for dear life. Sam was a powerful black negro of the people, a brute in physical strength. It would have been impossible for those four men to dislodge him without a regrettable and undignified struggle, and above all things they wished no struggle, no disorder, inside the legation. They whispered for a moment. One finally lifted his hands, palm outward, in a shrugging hopeless Latin gesture of acquiescence, and nodded to a second who raised his heavy, gold-headed cane and broke Sam's arms above the wrists.

Arriving in the garden, they did a strange thing. They avoided the gate, over which hung the French consular coat-of-arms. It may have been Latin-negroid theatricalism. It may have been something finer. But at any rate they avoided the gate. They lifted the president in their arms and threw him over the wall to the mob outside.

The mob, of course, simply tore him into pieces. Mostly they used their hands. But one woman cut off his head with a machete and marched with it. Another woman, they say, ripped out his heart and marched, tearing it to shreds with her teeth. Ropes were fastened to the torso, and it was dragged through the streets. . . .

Meanwhile, Charles Oscar, commandant of the prison, had sought refuge in the Dominican legation. He had apparently been forgotten by the mob, but he had not been forgotten by a certain gray-haired, quiet, dapper little colored gentleman whose three grown sons had been among the victims of the prison massacre. This little gentleman donned his long-tailed coat with its tiny red ribbon of the French Légion d'Honneur and his lemon-yellow gloves of the old *boulevardier* (some Americans now in Haiti find material for derisive amusement in old gentlemen of his sort) and called upon the Dominican legation. I am told that he sent in his card. I am told that Charles Oscar, who was a cruel man but not a coward, entered the drawing-room with a nervous smile. Be those things as they may, the little old gentleman shot him carefully three times through the heart, one bullet for each of his dead sons. . . .

At the precise hour when these events were occurring, the American battleship *Washington* was steaming into the harbor. More than twelve years have passed, and the Americans have been in Haiti continuously ever since. The presence of the Americans has put an end to many things. It has put an end to revolution, mob violence, and many other deplorable conditions which the entire reasonable world agrees should be put an end to. It has also put an end, or if not an end, a period, to more than a century of national freedom of a peculiar sort, which has existed nowhere else on earth save in Liberia—the freedom of a negro people to govern or misgovern themselves, to stand forth as human beings like any others without cringing or asking leave of any white man. I do not understand these things. But I think I understand something that was in the soul of the little gentleman who called at the Dominican legation, and I hope we haven't put an end to that too.

From the Author's Notebook

From the Author's Notebook

NOTES ON PART ONE

CHAPTER I

1. Haitian creole is a language based on French, simplified, corrupted, and elided—also occasionally enriched—into which are incorporated scattering words of African, Spanish, and English origin.

It has no standardized orthography. The written language of Haiti is French. Haitian writers, including Georges Sylvaine, Oswald Durand, and Frédéric Doret, have invented divers highly varied systems of creole phonetic spelling which are more or less intelligible to the French reader but puzzling to the English eye and ear.

Endeavoring to patch together a phonetic system that might convey some notion to American and English readers of how creole is actually spoken, I have succeeded, I fear, in employing a mixture of French and English phonetic spellings which will be approximately satisfactory only to the reader who already has some knowledge of French. In cases where words or phrases are closely parallel with French, I have used French spelling so that there might not be too grotesque distortion, but when the creole word is materially changed from its original French form, I have substituted where it seemed necessary English vowel and consonant sounds. For instance, the creole expression which means "children" is a corruption of the French *petit monde*. It is pronounced, to use purely mechanical English phonetics, *tee moon*. Durand and Sylvaine both write it *'ti moun*. *'Ti* seemed to me intelligible to the American eye and ear so that it would be an unnecessary distortion to spell it *tee*, thereby losing all connection with the original French word. But *moun* I was afraid of because it has a less obvious connection with French and seemed to risk being pronounced by American readers as in "paramount" and "mountain." So I have compromised and written it *'ti moon*. Similar instances will be found in my spelling, indefensible philologically, but forgivable, I hope, for practical simplification.

There are certain elemental rules of creole grammar and syntax which should also be explained.

In pronouns, there is neither declension nor gender. *Moin* (also *moi* and *m'*) means interchangeably I or me. *Ou* (corruption of *vous*) means you. *Li* (corruption of *lui*) means he, she, it. *Yo* (probable corruption of *eux*) means they, them, those.

Nouns and particles likewise have a tendency to remain unchanged, whether masculine or feminine, singular or plural. In creole it is equally *iune homme* and *iune femme*, and similarly with qualifying adjectives; if a thing is beautiful it is always *belle*, never *beau*. Another peculiarity of creole nouns is that if the original French noun begins with a vowel, it frequently has grafted on it an initial "z" consonant-sound, from the French form, *des oranges*, *des herbes*, etc., so that a Haitian will say *iune zorange* instead of *une orange*.

In the case of verbs, each verb root has one simple form which never changes. This form is likely to be the French infinitive or a close variation of it, if the infinitive of the given verb happens to be its simplest form, as in the case of *aller*, *marcher*, *marier*, *tuer*, etc. But in cases where the infinitive is not the verb's simplest form, as for instance *vouloir*, *connaître*, etc., the creole root becomes *vlai* or *vlé* from *voulez*, and *connai* from *connaissez* or *connais*. In the case of *donner* the second person singular *donnes* becomes the root form and is corrupted almost out of recognition into *bom* or *bai*. Certain other verbs are given specialized meaning: *gagner* corrupted to *gagnin* means to have; *joiend'* from the French *joindre* means to find or to get.

The verb *être*, to be, as a modifying verb in conjugations, has almost completely disappeared in the processes of natural elimination and simplification.

The future tense is formed with the prefix *pour*, usually contracted to *p'r*. The past tense is formed with the prefix *té*, an abbreviation of *était*. Sometimes, however, an even simpler final form of the past tense is implied by the use of what may be the past participle, but has in spoken language exactly the same sound as the infinitive. For instance, when a peasant says *li marcher*, meaning "he walks," or *li marché*, meaning "he walked," the sound is identical. And when he uses the prefix *té* to establish the past tense, the root sound is still the same and can be phonetically written either *marcher* or *marché*.

Combining these above elements, a verb in creole is conjugated as follows:

PRESENT

I go	*Moi aller*
You go	*Ou aller*
He (she, it) goes	*Li aller*
We go	*Nous aller*
You go	*Ou aller*
They go	*Yo aller*

PAST

I went	*Moin té aller* (or *allé*)
You went	*Ou té aller*

etc.

FUTURE

I shall (will) go	*Moin p'r aller*
You will go	*Ou p'r aller*

etc.

The language is much richer and also much more complicated than these few crude rules indicate, but they may serve to make easier an understanding of the creole phrases, sentences, songs, etc., which occur in this book.

2. Dr. J. C. Dorsainvil of Port-au-Prince, Haitian philologist and historian, has made a long study of this subject, seeking also to trace back the Haitian Voodoo gods to their African origins. I quote from a paper read by him before the Haitian Geographic Institute in 1924 and subsequently embodied in one of its bulletins. I have made no effort to coördinate orthography, for all the spellings, both his and mine, are necessarily phonetic. In the few cases where attributes academically ascribed by him to various daimons and deities differ from those ascribed to the same daimons and deities by my peasant friends in actual worship, I beg to point out that similar variations between historic orthodoxy and current practice occur in all religions, and the more so in a religion like Voodoo which has no written tradition. Dr. Dorsainvil says:

The word Voodoo, whose origin has been sought in a thousand ways, even in the words *veau d'or* (golden calf), *vaudois*, etc., is simply a generic term of the African *fongbé* dialect—the greatest word of that dialect, since it embraces nearly the entire moral and religious life of the *Fons* (an African racial group in Dahomey) and is the original root of a whole great family of words.

What is the exact sense of this word in *fongbé?*

It designates the genii, good or bad, inferior to Mawu, and by extension the statue of one of these genii or any other object symbolizing their cult or their protective or malevolent power.

From the root word *vôdu* comes immediately the word *vôdunu.* It is the vocable designating the religion of Voodoo in its entirety. The pontiff or priest of Voodoo is called *vôduno. . . .*

The statue incarnating the spirit of a *vôdu* is a *vodū-wutū* (*wutu,* body).

Let us follow the considerable part played by this word in *fongbé.*

The Dahomean's Sunday is called *vôdugbé*, literally, the day of the *vôdu*.

From this term and utilizing the word *azà*, which as *gbe* means day, the Dahomean priests designate all the days of the week *azatewe* (*aza*, day, *tewe*, seven), as follows:

Vodugbé, day of the *vôdu*. . . .
Vodugbé sayihû, day of the games. . . .
Vodugbé sazàto, third day after *vodugbé*.
Vodugbé si azene, fourth day after *vodugbé*.
Vodugbé si azato, fifth day after *vodugbé*.
Vodugbé si azaize, sixth day after *vodugbé*.
Vodugbé si azatewe, seventh day after *vodugbé*.
NOTE: *Âtô*, third; *ene*, fourth; *ato*, fifth; *aize*, sixth; *tewe*, seventh.
Âtô and *atô* are distinguished by their pronunciation, about like *antô* and *atô*.

It is seldom that you find, even in French, a root word comprising so many other meanings in its extension. And we are still far from having exhausted all the Dahomean vocables deriving from *vôdu*.

The most notable primitive form of the Voodoo religion in Africa was the cult of the snake or adder, Dâ, pronounced Dan, incarnating the genius Dâgbé, pronounced Dangbé.

The two principal sanctuaries of this cult were in the sacred forests of Somorné near Allada and at Ouida. Here, by contraction, the Dahomean expression Dangbé Allada became the name of the god or *loa* (a Congo word) Damballah, for whom the symbol is still the adder (Damballah-Ouédo *cé coulève*). As for the term Ouédo attached to the name of the *loa*, it comes from the connection which Haitian Voodooists believe exists between Dangbé and Ayida-Ouédo, or better, Wedo, the goddess of the rainbow, a sort of Dahomean Juno.

The temples of Dangbé were served by priestesses called by the name of *dangbesi;* thence the song, certainly modified, heard here very often under the *tunnelle:* "*Damballah dangbesi Ouida,*" etc., which may be translated: "The women of Dangbé at Allada and at Ouida," etc. Furthermore, the cult of Dangbé was secret, with degrees of initiation. Certain words pronounced by the priestesses were passwords like *Bohsi*, *Bohla*, incomprehensible to the layman.

Another great *vôdu* of Dahomey is Legba. He is the Priapus of Dahomey, the god of generation and fecundity.

Before the French conquered Dahomey, the statue of Legba stood on all great highroads, at all corners, in all the obscenity of a primitive art to mark well the particular attributes of this god. You will understand then why here Legba is called master of the crossroads and highways. Thence the well-known chant: "*Papa Legba ouvri barriè pour moin ago-é; papa Legba ouvri chemin pour li ago-é*," etc. (Translation: "Papa Legba, open the barrier for me, pay heed; papa Legba, open the road for him, pay heed.") To this *vôdu*, they liked to sacrifice sheep—in *fongbé*, *legbo*, Legba's animal. . . .

Ayida-Wedo is the goddess of the rainbow, as Ayiza, pronounced Ayizan, is the guardian goddess of the paths. Ayida is also servant of the genius of the thunder. In *fongbé*, rainbow is called Ayido-Wedo, sun of the earth. Ayida had her principal temples in Dahomey and at Ouida. The doors and walls of these sanctuaries were covered with hieroglyphs, which Captain Fonssagrives, aided by some natives brought up at the French school, deciphered.

Alivodu, or tree-genius, is the protector of the house, the lar. He has as his symbol trees planted in the yards of dwellings. He is invoked in case of sickness. You find here the origin of the Haitian custom of consecrated trees. Aguasu is another great *vôdu* of Dahomey; he is the guardian of customs and traditions. His cult is served by the *aguâsuno* or priests of Aguâsu.

Hû is the Neptune of Dahomey. In Haiti he is confused with Agbéto (likewise Agoué), another genius of the sea.

Héviyoso is the Jupiter of Dahomey, the thunder god. He corresponds to Piè Jupitè-Tonnè of the Haitian Voodooists. Nevertheless one sometimes hears the name of this *vôdu* under the *tunnelle* in Haiti.

We would never end if we had to give a detailed study of all the Dahomeyan *vôdus*. The Voodoo Pantheon is as rich as that of Greece or Rome. Let us mention rapidly certain other deities:

Gbo is the Dahomeyan Mars; he is the protector of the braves as he is the enemy of the cowards. Gbeji-nibu, a country genius, somewhat like a guardian of herds; *nibù* means steer. Zo, the god of fire; Tokpodû, protecting genius of Dahomey, *Avlekété* and

Agheto, two genii of the sea. Honéli, another lar. *Asé*, the Hogoù Féraille of the Haitian Voodooists, patron of the blacksmiths. Azilahi, Hoho, protector of twins or *marassa*. Lisa, genius of the moon. Kpo, protector of the royal family of Dahomey. Akwaji, Deje, Gù, Gbociyo, Josusu, Mate, etc. As for Loko, he is a genius which the *Fons* thought was incarnated in a very poisonous tree of their country, the *loko*. This entire cult, fundamentally animistic, rested on the belief in the possibility of incarnation of all these *vôdus* in the body of their servants. . . .

What has, according to all probability, been preserved without alteration among us, is the Voodoo rhythm, the music peculiar to this cult.

It is a solemn rhythm, in the mood of prayer or invocation contrary to the Congo dance music which is petulant, hacking, hysterical. The expressions *ago-é*, *ago-yé!* which recur as a *Leitmotif* in Voodoo song, are nearly equivalent to the "grant us" of the Catholic litanies, *ago* meaning "pay attention" and *é*, *yé*, being two personal pronouns corresponding to the English pronoun, they.

This Voodoo rhythm is so persistent that it is maintained when the ritual songs are composed with exclusively creole words or when they proceed in a series of unintelligible sounds. . . .

By comparison with the other African tribes, *Arada*, *Congo*, *Nago*, etc., the *Fons* have been infinitely less numerous in Haiti. How, then, explain the strong religious imprint by which they have marked the people?

It is here that all the importance of the Voodoo cult in Haiti appears. Whether you like it or not, Voodoo is a great social fact in our history. The colonists tolerated all the noisy dances of the slaves, but feared the Voodoo ceremonies. They instinctively feared this cult with its mysterious air and felt confusedly that it might be a powerful element of cohesion for the slaves. They were not mistaken, for it was from the bosom of a Voodoo ceremony that the great revolt of the Santo Domingo slaves sprang. Toussaint himself knew this so well that, having become the first power of the colony, he, too, no longer tolerated this cult.

The *Fons*, to come back to them, formed a warlike and conquering tribe, remarkably intelligent.

They represented among the warlike tribes of Dahomey what the

Bambara Negro, praised by the French general staff for bravery, represents among the Senegalese tribes. . . .

A religion so hierarchic, so clouded in mystery, necessarily exercised, it is understood, a powerful attraction for the other African tribes represented in Dahomey. It offered them a body of religious doctrines which were founded in no degree on the superstitions practiced by them. As it grew, Voodoo divested itself of some of its original characteristics and absorbed those of other beliefs: *aradaennes*, *congolese*, *mines*, *nagos*, *caplaous*, *moudongues*.

Nevertheless, one may find in Haiti the essential lines of Voodoo, simply masked now by the newer, superimposed Catholic faith.

CHAPTER II

1. Labat, a Catholic writer of colonial times, complains:

> Les nègres font sans scrupule ce que faissient les Philistins; ils joignent l'arche avec Dagon et conservent en secret toutes les superstitions de leur ancien culte idolâtre, avec les cérémonies de la religion chrétienne.

The Catholic priests of Haiti today are still confronted by this same paradoxical problem. On a number of occasions since the American occupation, when they have participated with the Marines in raiding and burning Voodoo temples, they have been somewhat embarrassed to find among the articles, consigned by their own hands to the flames, holy crucifixes, lithographs of the saints, and statuettes of the Blessed Virgin.

Recently a plaque of St. James the Greater carved in high relief was presented to a little country church in the north. The saint was depicted with a bag and a pilgrim's staff. A local priest, not long from France, was overjoyed when his parishioners began to throng the chapel of St. James, bringing pennies and candles in abundance, but when they began to bring also gourd dishes piled with food, fruit and cooked rice, he smelled a mouse and reported the circumstance to his vicar, who investigated and finally in despair removed the plaque. What had happened was that the peasants had joyfully recognized in St. James their old African celestial friend Ogoun.

Another episode was told me in gentle humorous despair by a tolerant old Breton priest who has lived in Haiti for twenty years and loves his peasants despite the fact that he knows he has never been able to wean them completely from their ancient gods. One of his rural chapels was by the seashore, and parishioners from neighboring little islands came to monthly mass in their crude-sailed fishing-boats. One morning as the bell was ringing, with the church already half filled, he saw outside the coral reefs a boat crammed with negroes coming to worship. What good Catholics he seemed to have made of them! But a few hundred yards from the shore, outside the reefs, they became completely becalmed. A few moments later on the boat there was a mighty blowing of conch shells, the thumping of a drum; a shrill chant arose. They were making Voodoo incantations to Papa Agoué, begging him to send a wind that would blow them in to Christian communion.

Conversely I witnessed one night an episode in which the Christian gods were invoked to aid in a Voodoo ceremonial which was going badly. The sacrifices had taken place, the ritual whirling had begun, with chants invoking the descent of the *lois*, but for some reason the *lois* had not descended. Finally, however, a girl shrieked and fell. Aided by the *mamaloi*, she got to her feet, still in a trance, and tried to dance, as a space was cleared for her, but tottered, stumbled, and fell again. Suddenly she arose unaided, stood straight, erect, and made the full Catholic sign of the cross with sweeping gestures, touching her forehead, the lower center of her breast and the two sides of her breast, saying, "In the name of the Father, the Son, and the Holy Ghost," and then praying, "Help me, blessed Virgin Mary." Her strength came upon her in her trance and she danced for a long time.

2. The Legba invocation:

I am indebted to the West Indian composer, Justin Élie, for this and other melodic transcriptions which appear in this book.

3. The prohibition against Voodoo in Haiti is contained in Article 409 of the criminal code (Code Pénal):

Tous faiseurs de ouangas, caprelatas, vaudoux dompedres, macandals et autres sortilèges seront punis de trois à six mois d'emprisonnement par le tribunal de simple police; et en cas de récidive, d'un emprisonnement de six mois à deux ans par le tribunal correctional, sans préjudice des peines plus fortes qui'ils encourrant à raison des délits ou crimes par eux commis pour préparer ou accomplir leurs maléfices.

Toutes danses et autres pratiques quelconques qui sont de nature à entretenir dans la population l'esprit de fétichisme et de superstition seront considérées comme sortilèges et puniées des mêmes peines.

(All makers of ouangas, caprelatas, vaudaux dompedres, macandals [bags, packets, talismans, Voodoo objects of various sorts for whose names there is no English equivalent], shall be punished by from three to six months' imprisonment by the police court, and for repetition of the offense by an imprisonment of six months to two years imposed by the criminal court. Such convictions shall not prevent the infliction of additional severer penalties for more serious crimes committed in this connection.

(All dances and other practices of whatsoever sort which are of a nature to foster the spirit of fetichism and superstition among the people shall be considered as sorcery and punished by the same penalties.)

In actual practice, however, the application of this law is comparable to that of the Volstead law in the United States. Great piles of drums and other sacred objects were confiscated and either burned or sent home as souvenirs by the Marine Corps during the early years of the occupation, and a number of temples were burned. But today Voodoo temples stand unmolested by the main public motor highways, and on any quiet night, even from the stairway of the national palace in Port-au-Prince, one may hear Rada drums booming in the hills.

CHAPTER III

2. Petro or Service Petro is the name given to the blood-sacrificial Voodoo ceremony. It derives from the name of a slave who was a famous *papaloi* in colonial times. There are numerous other Voodoo ceremonies in Haiti in which no blood is shed. In March, 1927, in company with Dr. Robert Parsons, U.S.N., then chief urologist of the General Hospital at Port-au-Prince, Katie Seabrook, and two Haitian friends, we saw a typical Legba service, without blood sacrifice, on a farm in the hills east of Jacmel. I have not included a description of it in the main text because casual readers might find it repetitious. I quote here from notes made on the following day:

Leaving our car off the road, we followed a footpath southward, and arrived on a hillside at Auguste's habitation, a group of three thatched houses in a clearing; hard-pounded earth.

No one was there but Auguste, his wives and children—no signs of special activity, nothing mysterious. They were peasants, Auguste himself a gray-haired, dignified old negro in blue overalls, barefooted, a straw hat with a wide, torn brim.

He remembered well our appointment, but had waited, uncertain of our coming. But he had "notified" the Haitian gendarme who patrolled that road, and there would be no interference.

All of us, including Katie, were taken into the mystery house, a simple hut with whitewashed walls, and shown the altar, a low cement platform, on which was spread a white cloth; calabash bowls containing millet, corn meal, white flour, fruits, vegetables, and bouquets of flowers.

Beside the altar were three drums, tall, pegged, painted, of unequal size, and the *açons*, gourd rattles. As old Auguste talked quietly, explaining the meaning of the ceremonial which was to follow, a drummer arrived, fetched from a neighboring habitation. He took out the Maman drum, the largest, with cowhide head, a chair was brought him, he seated himself with the drum between his knees outside the *houmfort* door, tightened the pegs by pounding them with a stone, and began booming out the Legba assembly call with the two hard heels of the palms of his hands. Homemade rush chairs were brought for us, and we sat beside him. Auguste's family had gone inside their house, from which only a dim light came. The compound was dark, deserted.

Presently, singly, in twos and threes, men and women, children too, appeared and stood or squatted, waiting in the compound. Among them arrived the second and third drummers, and soon all three drums were being beaten, but there was no dancing, no movement; the crowd was quiet as if in church.

After some fifty or sixty people had assembled, the drum-call ceased. Auguste, now in his rôle of *papaloi*, accompanied only by the *mamaloi* (his wife), entered the mystery house and knelt before the altar. Neither had any special vestments or symbol of office. The crowd remained outside, some kneeling, the drums began a new measure, and this invocation was chanted:

Legba, me gleau, me manger;
Famille ramassé famille yo;
Legba, me gleau, me manger.

(Legba, food and drink are provided;
Family is gathered together with family;
Legba, food and drink are provided.)

As the chant continued, endlessly repeated, the crowd fell back on all sides, leaving a clear space before the *houmfort*, with the drummers sitting beside the door. In this open space two men began digging holes in the hard earth with their machetes; others came bringing long poles, which were set upright in the holes, and cross pieces were lashed to them, running to the *houmfort* roof; there was a sound of chopping outside the compound. A palm tree and another fell crashing in the bush. Boys and girls came bearing great armfuls of palm-fronds, singing in the moonlight.

With the palm-fronds was built a canopy, laid awning-wise, making a roof for the bare pole structure. We were watching the building of a primitive temple, which took form before our eyes, built of palm-leaves, in the tropical moonlight. Next morning, I was told, all trace of it would have disappeared.

When the *tunelle*-temple was finished, like an open roofed portico before the mystery house, the people crowded around it, making a hollow square.

The *papaloi* emerged from the mystery house, ringing a little tinkling bell, and bearing a lighted candle; behind him came the *mamaloi*, bearing in her uplifted hands a calabash bowl. Boys and girls followed with bowls, china cups, other receptacles. Libations of water, wine, rum, brought consecrated from the altar, were poured on the earth, before the drums, and at the four corners of the *tunelle;* corn meal and white flour were then sprinkled.

The drums ceased, the singing stopped, there was a whispering argument. It evidently concerned us, seated in the shadow a little away from the drums, keeping ourselves out of the way as much as possible. We guessed it concerned us because faces were turned in our direction, disputing something, but amiable and friendly. An old man whispered with the *papaloi.* The *papaloi* acquiesced in whatever they were talking about. He laid aside his bell. Somebody handed him a machete, and the *mamaloi* a short, heavy *cocomacaque* stick.

In silence they came over to us. The *papaloi,* holding the machete in his right hand, gripped my right hand with his left; then reversed the machete to his left, and gripped my left hand with his right one; then he dropped the machete, and gripped both hands at once, reversed, so that my arms were crossed and his arms were crossed. He did this with each of us, including Katie; the *mamaloi* followed him, doing the same thing, except that she had the *cocomacaque* club instead of the knife, and that after she had finished, she kissed each of us on the forehead.

I took it to be the survival of a primitive ceremonial toward stranger-guests, meaning, "We could kill you, but we refrain, establishing instead mutual obligation of friendship." I was interested that some of the younger ones crowded around and craned their necks and whispered as if they had not seen it before.

Then the ceremonial proceeded, with no more attention paid to us.

The invocation hymn, "*Papa Legba ouvri barrière pour moins,*" was intoned loudly at first by the *papaloi* alone, afterward taken up by the whole crowd.

The *barrière* is the gate through which they hope to enter

the trance-ecstatic world, transported, leaving their common everyday world and life behind.

Seldom does Papa Legba open the gates for all, but usually for a chosen few, and no one ever knows which of the company they may be. They chant this choral for an indefinite period—as a certain hymn may be sung at a revival, or in a New York spiritualistic séance—until "something" happens. They help it along now, men, women, and children, by drinking raw rum, and dancing, not the Congo sex dancing, but rocking, rolling, shivering.

An old woman shrieks, leaps, and falls senseless. A space is quickly cleared around her and then we see her as she lies twitching; presently another shriek, this time a girl, and soon an old man.

The gate has been opened, the *lois* have come. Those into whom the spirits have entered are the center of all attention. The drum-beat changes and the chant becomes simply: "*Les lois! Les lois! Les lois!*"

Hail and welcome to the gods who are present and manifest.

Then comparative silence, broken only by two of the ecstatics who have got to their feet, whirling, leaping, and speaking "in strange tongues."

Then begins a litany—the *papaloi* shouting a line, and the people chanting it for many moments, until he makes a sign and a new line is given. Among them, which I took down then, scribbling as best I could on the back of an envelope, and Parsons afterward correcting, and remembering one or two which I had forgotten, were:

Pas lacher plui sou nous. ("Do not deluge us with rain"—bad at that moment for the crops. At another season the plea might be the reverse.)

Pas lacher avalasse. (In creole *avalasse* is not always avalanche but often swollen mountain streams.)

Pas bruler caille moin. ("Do not burn my house.")

Pas tuer chwal moin. ("Don't kill my horse.")

A strange one was *Pas virer sable* (Do not send the sandstorm). There are no sandstorms in Haiti. I wondered if it was the creolized version of an older line in the Litany, brought over from Africa, and repeated now traditionally. Other prayers included sparing of crops and protection of homes, beasts, crops, and land from various natural misfortunes. Because Papa Legba is not a slayer or devourer of humans, his litany includes no prayer to spare human lives.

3. The Voodoo drums are always three in number, of unequal sizes, called *maman*, *papa*, and (baby) *boula* (sometimes also called *cata*). Each is long, bulging, cylindrical, made in a solid piece from a length of tree trunk, hollowed and shaped by gouging and burning. The head of the *maman* drum is usually made of cowhide, sometimes with a fringe of hair left on its edges. The heads of the *papa* and *boula* are usually of goat skin. The average height of the drums is about three feet for the *maman* drum, two more or less for the *papa*, and eighteen inches for the *boula*. I have seen drums, however, five and six feet tall. The head is held in place by pegs wound around with rope or cord. The drums are usually painted, sometimes in mottled colors, perhaps to imitate the body of a snake; sometimes in solid colors, usually red, blue, or yellow.

Newly made drums, before being used in a ceremony, undergo a consecration and baptism in which they are given personal names. Three drums afterward presented to me were thus baptized. They were ranged in a row before the *houmfort* altar, the large *maman* drum in the center, flanked by the *papa* drum and the *boula*. A flat wooden platter was placed before the central drum, with a bottle of rum, sweet cakes, and white bread crumbled. There was also a small cup containing coffee, and a single candle burning. A little boy stood before the drums with a cup of water in his left hand and a piece of rock salt in his right. With the rock salt he made the sign of the cross on his own forehead, and afterward dropped the lump of salt in the cup and placed it beside the candle. The *papaloi* then stood before the drums, holding a leafy twig, and called forward an old man and an old woman who had been chosen godfather and godmother for the drums. The *papaloi* asked what name they had selected for the *maman* drum and they replied Sainte Rose. The godmother and godfather placed their hands on the head of the drum, while the *papaloi* immersed the twig in the salt water and sprinkled the drum three times, saying, "I baptize you Sainte Rose in the name of the Father, the Son, and the Holy Ghost; I dedicate you to the Service Petro." The two other drums were baptized similarly, the *papa* drum as Saint Isador and the *boula* as Saint Antoine.

These drums are of the type called tom-tom in English, but this name for a drum does not exist in Haitian creole. The only generic word they have for drum is the corrupted French word *tambor* (*tambour*). Their common non-ritual drum, used for Congo dances and working in the fields, shaped also cylindrically, but frequently made of several joined pieces like a barrel, and never pegged, but with the head fastened by cords, is commonly called *tambor-travaille*, work drum, as distinguished generically from the Voodoo drum, which is *tambor-Rada*. There is a Haitian word *tom-tom*, but it means a dish prepared with *plantains*, *patates*, and *malanga*.

In a *houmfort* near the main auto road between Gonaives and Ennery, I was shown a curious set of *Rada* drums, or rather a substitute therefor, made simply of three unequal lengths of a big bamboo, tubes about four inches in diameter without heads, on the sides of which the drummers tapped with soft wooden sticks. These had been used, I was told, in 1919 when the Marines were more active in suppressing Voodoo ceremonies.

4. Another processional chant to Damballa is:

CHAPTER IV

1. A *ouanga* bag confiscated by Marines in 1921 near Gonaives is described as follows:

> It was a hide bag, and in it were these objects: luck stones, snake bones, lizard jaws, squirrel teeth, bat bones, frog bones, black hen feathers and bones, black lamb wool, dove hearts, mole skins, images of wax and clay, candy made of brown sugar mixed with liver, mud, sulphur, salt, and alum, and vegetable poisons.

2. Called to a neighboring habitation to treat a young woman said to be dying of brain fever, Maman Célie permitted me to witness the treatment. The girl lay on a pallet in a room, on the earthen floor. She was burning with fever. I had no thermometer but guessed it to be 104 or more degrees. Her family said that for three days she had been alternately delirious or unconscious. Maman Célie sent members of the household out to pick leaves of the *bois cochon* tree, of which they brought back nearly a peck in a basket. Meanwhile she demanded soap, and they gave her a piece of yellow bar stuff, store-bought, the same commonly

called kitchen soap in the United States. She boiled water in an iron kettle, cut the soap up into small pieces, made a mess of soap suds into which she dumped the leaves, and stirred them into a sort of stew. She borrowed a pocketknife from the girl's father, held it in the fire, made small gashes, not deep, all over the girl's scalp. A thick poultice was made from the mess in the kettle, allowed to cool a little, applied to the girl's head, and tied on like a big unwieldy turban. While engaged in these operations Maman Célie made prayers to Papa Loco and Papa Legba, traced a cross with her finger tips on the girl's forehead, and murmured incantations. When we went away she left instructions that the mess in the iron pot be kept warm and the poultice changed every few hours. Next day the girl's fever broke, and she subsequently recovered. I asked Maman Célie if she did not believe the treatment might have been just as effective without the prayers and incantations. She was hurt with me, and I asked her pardon. She was sincere.

I do not mean to imply that there are not charlatans and even criminals among the herb doctors, witch-doctors, and *papalois* of Haiti. I knew personally a wily *bocor* near Kenscoff who brought a negro with a glass eye from Jamaica to astonish his adherents, and who also through a Syrian dealer in Port-au-Prince bought a chest of "stage magic" paraphernalia made in Germany; he also understood the almanac, and predicted eclipses, claiming to control them.

An engineer named Smythe, connected with the Public Works, told me of seeing a *bocor* at a ceremony near Bassin Général pick up a bar of red-hot iron which he took between his teeth and capered violently around. Smythe himself picked up the bar after the old man had dropped it, and burned his hand badly. He suspected trickery but was unable to suggest an explanation.

Major Best, U.S.M.C., chief of police in Port-au-rince, told me of a more sinister case which had occurred in Petite Rivière. A child fell ill, and the local *docteur feuille* (leaf doctor) was called. He cured the child and demanded a pig in fee. The child relapsed; he cured it again and was paid a goat. In a few weeks the child again fell mysteriously ill, and the parents became suspicious. They learned that the herb doctor had been paying a servant to poison the child with a sickening weed for which he possessed an antidote.

I think, however, that the majority of the *bocors* and sorcerers believe as sincerely in their own powers as did Maman Célie. I want to quote as an example of extraordinary candor a conversation with Ti Cousin, the famous Léogane *papaloi*. He said to me: "There are many things my father [who was one of the great *hougans* of the past generation] could do which I cannot do. He could make thunder. He left me all his thunder stones. You saw them there on the altar; there are no finer in Haiti. He instructed me throughout his lifetime. I have all the secret words. I do it exactly as he did, and I have never been able to make anything happen. He was able to change the course of storms. I have seen him drive them back across this mountain and into the sea. I have succeeded in controlling them a little only a few times. Usually I fail, but in the matter of making certain *ouangas* I am stronger than he was."

Whites long resident in Haiti, particularly those who have lived in the interior, frequently appeal for treatment to friendly witch-doctors when orthodox medical aid is unavailable. When Fred Baker, an American expert now engaged in rubber experimentation for the U.S. Department of Agriculture, was working in the St. Michel plain, one of his white foremen sprained his ankle badly. Baker sent for the local *docteur feuille*, who first pulled the foot hard, wiggled the toes, killed a cock, and marked the ankle with crosses and circles in blood, meanwhile chanting; then made a plaster of *sureau* and *barrachin* leaves which he bound on beneath a poultice of hot cornmeal, and bandaged tightly, with excellent eventual results. Père Plombé, a Catholic priest at Furcy, lay ill of dysentery, and his servant, fearing for his life, brought in a leaf doctor who successfully dosed the priest with a concoction of juice from the leaves of the *liane sorossi*, juice of sour oranges, and stump-water drawn from the base of a dead plantain. Daniel Vital, Jacmel coffee exporter, told me of a case on one of his plantations in which a sorceress cured or seemed to cure, with herb teas whose formula she refused to reveal, the wife of a prosperous planter who was suffering from loss of blood and anemia after childbirth and whose recovery had been despaired of by the white doctors.

When my yard-boy, Louis, was cut one night in a fight and I took him to the hospital to have the small wound dressed, we found, on unwrapping his own bandages, that he had plastered it with leaves of the *écorce*—also called *bois soie* in creole. Among negroes who come to the American rural clinics for treatment of wounds, it is frequent to find pieces of sheet copper, usually hacked with a machete from some old engine, bound tightly against the wound and turned green, put there at the recommendation of some witch-doctor. The natives believe that any antisepsis or relief they obtain from this is pure magic, but I am told that copper sulphate has an actual therapeutic value.

Among the leaves and herbs used for remedies are *immortelle*, *bois lait*, *medicinier beni*, *feuille patience*, *racine seguine*, *gayac*, *feuilles corailles*, *manioc*.

The *mirliton*, one kind of squash, is supposed to be cooling to the blood; the *beregine*, another kind, heating. I suspect this is imitative magic in its most senseless form, for the *mirliton* is pale, cool green in color, while the *beregine* is a rich ox-blood red. I am not sure whether the same imitative principle is at work in the case of the *lambie*, which is a large salt-water conch, whose meat is highly esteemed as an aphrodisiac. The shell, like the conch shells seen on old-fashioned mantelpieces and hearths, is obvious for its primary sexual symbolism both in form and color. I made a meal of stewed *lambies* out of curiosity, and found them palatable, but as to their potency, imagination, I think, plays so strong a part that opinion would be valueless. Another aphrodisiac, sold in bottles by sorceresses, is made from a small octopus like the squid, dried and powdered and dissolved in rum. It is called *chat rouge* (*red cat*). Herb doctoring in Haiti is usually connected with Voodoo and sorcery, but not necessarily always. Sometimes the remedies are applied without mumbo-jumbo, with a simple belief in their natural remedial virtues.

3. Maman Célie was sent for to help discover who the thief was who had stolen a jug of money from a habitation across the gorge. There were only about six persons including members of the family who could have known where the jug was hidden or have had access to it. There was reason to suspect that some member of the actual household had taken the money, though all protested their innocence, but they were rounded up by the old man and forced to be present at the test which took place in broad daylight in the compound. Having asked for a bucket of ashes, Maman Célie took handfuls of it and traced a circle about five feet in diameter. Inside the circle, she traced four small crosses, then sprinkled sand and corn meal at the foot of each cross. She cut from a bush two switches that were covered with twigs, placed a chair in the center of the circle, and sat in it holding the two switches. She then got the old man to recite slowly in sing-song the names of the five or six suspects there present. As each name was called, she crossed the two switches behind the leg of the chair, and then drew them forward, pressed against the leg of the chair and against each other, muttering meanwhile. I was told that when the name of the thief was called, the twigs of the two switches drawn across each

other would become tightly entangled. Three or four times the process was repeated while all the names were run through. Finally the twigs tangled and caught solidly at the name of a fifteen-year-old boy called Ti Pierre, there present, a nephew who lived in a neighboring *caille* on the habitation. He first protested his innocence, but under a whipping confessed and returned part of the money.

4. John W. Vandercook returned from the Surinam jungle convinced that black magic can kill. In an article entitled "White Magic and Black: The Jungle Science of Dutch Guiana," published in *Harper's Monthly Magazine* in 1927, he wrote:

Magic is the great reality of the jungle. We northern races, when we think of magic, see a vaudeville performer with a pack of marked cards. Magic is trickery, sleight of hand, legerdemain. It is serio-comic foolery. Magic to us is the thinnest stuff in the world—the semblance of empty illusion.

We must forget all that in the tropic forests. There magic is the vital craft of survival. In a land where a locomotive turns to dust, where all the science of Europe is empty and will avail nothing against the powers of the jungle, magic, developed through a thousand, thousand years has taught the Negro how to live, how to meet the terrors of the manifold deaths that lurk always amid the immutable silence of the trees. It is the most serious, most important thing in the black man's world. . . .

Jungle magic is never for effect. It is purposeful, studied. When famines, pestilences, and evils come upon the forest people, it is magic that wards them off. It deals with things—with medicines, potions, and ideas—which, in the forest, are more real than steel and far more dangerous. Magic saves. Then it is white. Magic kills. Then it is black. It is the science of the jungle.

The way of an enemy is never direct. The mysterious ways of jungle death are the only ways down which death comes. Sometimes a Bushnegro, out of jealousy, anger, or fear, wishes another dead. So he sets his fetishes against his enemy, invokes the *winti* of the bush to set upon and destroy him. It is dangerous business, for the murderer knows that in time he will himself be almost inevitably destroyed. But there are stronger passions even than fear.

The spirits of evil are set in action. The one against whom they are working learns of his mortal danger. He attempts propitiation, seeks to make his protective fetishes stronger than the destructive fetishes of his enemy. But almost surely, soon or late, he dies, and his family know that he has been murdered. That is the forest way.

5. Here is another Haitian formula for the concoction of a protective *ouanga:*

A small piece of gold, a small piece of silver, a small piece of lead, a small piece of iron, a small piece of bronze, a small piece of thunder-stone, a small piece of river sandstone, a small piece of logwood gum, a small amount of fire ashes, a small amount of fire smoke, an eye without an eye, a tail without a tail, conducted by St. John Baptist, accompanied by St. Monton and the Holy Spirit. Take a cross from a cemetery, one leaf of Congo peas, a brand-new thimble, a set of needles and a bunch of hairs taken from the center of the head. Leave the *ouanga* during seven Fridays on your window.

6. The following, literally translated, is one of the formulas pronounced by the sorcerer over a death *ouanga* before hiding it in the secret place where it is to lie rotting:

Old master, now is the time to keep the promise you made. Curse him as I curse him and spoil him as I spoil him. By the fire at night, by the dead black hen, by the bloody throat, by the goat, by the rum on the ground, this *ouanga* be upon him. May he have no peace in bed, nor at his food, nor can he go and hide. Waste him and wear him and tear him and rot him as these rot.

Patron saints as well as the old daimons are also occasionally invoked to aid in wreaking vengeance on an enemy. Sometimes these curses are written or printed, wadded into pellets, enclosed then in the *ouanga* bag or cunningly hidden in a chink in the wall of the victim's house or in his saddle or sleeping-pallet. Here is a characteristic one:

Prière à St Bouleversé

Saint Bouleversé! vous qui avez le pouvoir de bouleverser la la terre, vous êtes un saint et moi je suis un pécheur, je vous invoque et vous prends pour mon patron dès aujourd'hui. Je vous envoie chercher un tel. bouleversez sa tête, bouleversez sa mémoire, bouleversez sa pensée, bouleversez sa maison, bouleversez pour moi tous mes ennemis visibles et invisibles; faites éclater sur eux la foudre et la tempête, en l'honneur de Saint Bouleversé. 3 pater.

(Prayer to Saint Bouleversé [the Overturner]. Saint Bouleversé, you who have the power to overturn the earth, you are a saint and I am a sinner. I invoke you and take you as my patron saint from this day. I send you now to search out a certain one. Overturn his head, overturn his memory, overturn his thoughts, overturn his house; overturn for me all my enemies, visible and invisible; bring down upon them the lightning and the tempest. In honor of Saint Bouleversé, three Pater Nosters.)

Here is another method of putting a *ouanga* on an enemy: Contrive first to become in his debt for a sum of money. Then take the money, go to a cemetery, open a grave and lay the money next to the flesh of a corpse, repeating certain formulas. Go back in three nights, dig up the money and pay it to your enemy who will fall sick and die.

Life-sized images of human heads, sometimes carved of wood, sometimes cast in lead, also play a part in Voodoo death magic. I was shown one of these leaden heads on a so-called caco altar and was given a partial explanation of its uses. The effigy is named for the man who is to be slain, and remains on the altar under a sort of death sentence until the death occurs, when the leaden head is replaced by the real head if it can be obtained. At variance with this, however, is an episode which occurred when Henry Morales, nephew of a former president of San Domingo, was barricaded on a St. Michel farm during the caco uprising; a wooden head, carved and painted, was hurled through a window of the farmhouse. This head is in the collection of Mr. H. P. Davis, who permitted me to photograph it.

CHAPTER V

1. The worship of the serpent in Haiti has been generally misrepresented, as have many other phases of Voodoo beliefs and practices. The *Museum Journal* of the University of Pennsylvania, Philadelphia, March, 1917, page 125, says:

> In Hayti the basis of Voodooism is the frank worship of a sacred green snake that must be propitiated to keep off the evil spirits. The meetings of the cult are held at night about bonfires in secret places in the forests. The presiding official is an old man "papaloi," or woman "mamaloi" who has gained renown as a Voodoo sorcerer. After assembling, all present take an oath of secrecy and then the priest exhorts them to remember the sacred green snake, and to hate the whites. Prayer is offered to the divine serpent that is supposed to be present in a box placed near the fire. Then follows the sacrifice of a cock which the "papaloi" kills by biting off its head. With a great deal of drumming and incantation the blood is smeared over the faces of the worshipers and drunk by the officiating priest. A goat may be sacrificed with similar ceremony. After the goat there might be a human sacrifice, as was reported by a French priest. He said that it was the wish of some of the devotees that "a goat without horns," that is a child, be sacrificed. This was done and the flesh, raw or partly cooked, was eaten by the members of the cult.

Above: Maman Célie, Voodoo Priestess, Seated Behind the Ritual Drums. *Below:* The Sacrificial Goat.

White-robed Chorus of the Voodoo Blood Rite. Note the Central Figures with Flags, Sword, and Gourd Rattles Wound with Snake Vertebrae.

Above: Voodoo *Houmfort* (Mystery-House, or Temple). *Below:* Altar Inside the *Houmfort.* Note the Serpent Symbols on the Wall, the Serpent on a Staff, and the Crucifix.

Anthropomorphic Figures Painted on Voodoo Temple Walls. *Left:* The God Legba and the Goddess Ayida Oueddo. *Right:* The Bloody Ogoun Badagris.

Above: A Voodoo Warning. *Below: Caco* Altar, with a Head Molded of Lead, for Which the Severed Human Head of the Victim Is Substituted.

Above: A Legba Voodoo Shrine Where Only Vegetable Sacrifices Are Offered. *Below:* A Legba Altar with Fruit, Vegetable, and Flower Offerings.

Left: The Author Under Protection of Machete and Flag. *Right:* Maman Célie at the Baptism of the Drums.

Above: Egg Used Symbolically in the Voodoo Mysteries. Note the Two Protective *Ouanga* Packets at Its Right and Left. *Below:* Corn Meal Traceries Used in the Voodoo Mysteries.

"Papa Nebo," Hermaphroditic Oracle of the Dead, Garbed as Half Man, Half Woman.

"Papa Nebo," Flanked by Gouedé Mazacca the Midwife and Gouedé Oussou the Drunken One. These Are Sorceresses Who Use Corpses for Magical Purposes.

Above: New Grave with Offerings of Food and Water for the Dead. *Below:* Tomb in the Mountains, with Water Jug and Legba Tree-of-Life Painted Above Niche.

Left: Garments of a Sorceress' Son, Hung Above Her New-Made Grave. *Right:* Girl Wearing a Ouanga Charm—a Small Bag Hung Around Her Neck.

Soulouque, Crowned King of Haiti and Emperor of the Isles in 1848 Under the Name of Faustin I: The Queen Adelina, Empress Consort of Faustin I.

Faustin E. Wirkus Crowned King of the Haitian Island of La Gonave in 1924: A Crown of Modified Tribal African Design Was Constructed of Ribbons, Feathers and Mirrors for the Coronation of King Wirkus.

Left: A Typical Haitian of Pure African Blood. *Right:* A Man of La Gonave. Observe that the African Mode of Cutting the Hair Has Survived Through the Centuries.

The Queen Ti Meminne, Whom Wirkus Found on La Gonave and Confirmed in Power Subject to His Authority.

The incessant booming of the drums, the sight and taste of blood, and the great amount of rum drunk cause a religious form of hysteria to sway over the audience. At the close of this sacrificial ceremony the worshipers begin a dance called the "loiloichi," a stomach dance which is well known in West Africa. The dance gets wilder and wilder and more degraded until it ends in the orgy of the worst description which lasts until daylight.

The worship of the snake in Haiti is by no means so literal as commentators have supposed. It is true that on every Petro altar in Haiti there is a serpent symbol, sometimes painted on the wall, sometimes carved of wood and elevated on a staff. It is true also that living snakes are regarded as sacred objects, not to be injured or molested. One of the commonest and handsomest is a harmless green tree snake which grows to three or four feet in length, but all snakes are held sacred. But the serpent is worshiped symbolically, and not because they believe he has any power of his own; he represents the great god Damballa. 'Ti Cousin, at Léogane, said to me that the serpent was the symbol of Damballa in the same way that the lamb is the symbol of Christ. Papa Théodore, with whom I often discussed this same question, was of the opinion that this symbolism was identified with the jagged lightning flash which zigzags through the sky like a serpent; the lightning is also connected with Damballa, and Damballa's heavenly consort Ayida Oueddo. It is interesting in this connection that the Yezidee devil-worshipers, whose temple I visited at Sheikh Adi in 1925, in the Kurdish Mountains east of Mosul, and who have a sacred serpent carved in stone beside the doorway of their temple (although the symbol of their principal god, Satan, is a peacock), are also worshipers of fire and lightning.

So far as I am aware no living serpent is kept "in a box" or otherwise on any Voodoo altar today in Haiti. A negro friend has told me, however, of an Obeah ceremony which he had seen in Cuba in which a living snake was the central object. He said that a large non-poisonous snake was kept in a big earthen jar on an altar, that some ten or fifteen negroes made a sort of circular endless chain beginning and ending at the rim of the jar by locking their arms around each other's shoulders; that the snake was then drawn from the jar and induced to crawl over their shoulders, making the circuit and returning to the jar.

With reference to the belief that meetings of the cult "are held at night about bonfires at secret places in the forest," Maman Célie and others told me that ceremonies were held on rare occasions in that way, usually at times when criminal prosecution was particularly active, but the normal place for holding these ceremonials is the Voodoo temple and the compound adjacent to it, always in the neighborhood of human habitation. Miot of Kenscoff told me also of a special ceremony which he had seen in his youth in which in time of epidemic or local famine the worshipers repaired by tortuous zigzagging routes to some very remote place in a gorge or forest to perform ceremonies placating certain of the elder demons, who were so dangerous and dreadful that they did not dare to invite them to the temple or to the neighborhood of human habitation.

Hatred of the whites has no normal part in the Voodoo ceremony or creed. The majority of Haitian peasants are normally either friendly or utterly indifferent to whites. From the earliest times, however, at periods when there was war and hatred between the blacks and whites for other causes, the Voodoo gatherings have naturally played a part. The first great insurrection and massacre of white French colonials by the slaves was planned on the night of August 14, 1791, at a Voodoo gathering arranged by a slave named Boukman. Dr. J. C. Dorsainvil in his *Manuel d'Histoire d'Haiti*, Port-au-Prince, 1925, says:

Né à la Jamaique, Boukman était un N'Gan [Hougan] ou prêtre du Vaudou, religion principale des Dahoméens. . . . Pour faire tomber toutes les hésitations et obtenir un dévouement absolu, il réunit, dans la nuit du 14 aout 1791, un grand nombre d'esclaves, dans une clairière du Bois-Caiman, près du Morne-Rouge. Tous étaient assemblés quand un orage se déchaîna.

Au milieu de ce décor impressionnant, les assistants, immobiles, saisis d'une horreur sacrée, voient une vieille négresse se dresser. Son corps est secoué de longs frissons; elle chante, pirouette sur elle-même et fait tournoyer un grand coutelas au-dessus de sa tête. Une immobilité plus grande encore, une respiration courte, silencieuse, des yeux ardents, fixés sur la négresse, prouvent bientôt que l'assistance est fascinée. On introduit alors un cochon noir dont les grognements se perdent dans le rugissement de la tempête. D'un geste vif, la prêtresse, inspirée, plonge son coutelas dans la gorge de l'animal. Le sang coule, il est recueilli fumant et distribué, à la ronde, aux esclaves; tous en boivent, tous jurent d'exécuter les ordres de Boukman.

Similarly during the caco uprising in 1918-20 against the American Marines, Voodoo priests were active in aiding the revolutionists. In normal times, however, hatred of whites and fulmination against them has no more place in Voodoo ceremonial than hatred and fulmination against the Germans has normally in the Christian temples of England and America.

2. Dr. Arthur C. Holly of Port-au-Prince, though he leans strongly toward the esoteric, has written an extraordinary moral and philosophic defense of Voodoo in the preface to his book *Les Daimons du Culte Vodu* published by Edmond Chenet, Port-au-Prince, 1918.

He says, in part:

We are Latin-Africans. But our Latin civilization is all on the surface; the old African heritage prolongs itself in us and dominates us to such an extent that in many circumstances we feel ourselves moved by mysterious forces. Thus, our sensibility and our will undergo strange emotions when the unequal rhythms of the sacred dances of Voodoo, now melancholy, now passionate, always full of magic effects, are heard in the silent night.

By a sort of dilettantism, the cultured Haitian possesses the elegant art of deceiving himself. By constantly counterfeiting his ideas and sentiments, and feigning to adapt himself with facility to a borrowed estheticism, the Haitian has lost his personality as a human type. Unconsciously he joins his voice to the doctrinal error erected against the traditions of his race; he humiliates himself and discredits himself by becoming a witness in the serious accusation formulated by the white against the moral spirit and the manifestation of mystical ideas of his Negro ancestors whose group constituted in times gone by a luminous landmark and the most living and fecund center of religious humanity.

Today, a new world, after the great cataclysm, is under construction. Now more than ever is the moment to try to cleanse our ancestral cult of the stain which has been put upon it. In this, much of the honor of the African race in general is involved, and much of the dignity of our posterity, of us Haitians.

Our salvation will not be secure until the day when, ridding ourselves of vain scruples and putting aside all fears of criticism, we shall resolve to perpetuate the purified cult of Voodoo and shall raise to Legba and the powerful Damballa hymns of prayer coming from the bottom of our hearts.

I have written these pages, on which I call for the meditations of the present and future generations, without hesitating before the responsibility I assume in battering down certain inveterate ideas and beliefs—considering that, from these meditations, there may result a little more faith in ourselves and in our interrupted destinies, which it is not impossible to resume if we know how to act.

The formation of religious ideas implies deep contemplation on the nature of the world, the universe, the soul, life, death, etc.

The patient study of these matters gave birth to our animistic cult, according to which personified supernatural beings or spiritual forces control and direct the material forces of nature and of life. The entire hieroglyphic system of Egypt is based on the symbolic relations which exist between such beings and the cosmic forces, between such beings and the laws of creation. The Greeks likewise had their daimons and gods; the Romans their deities, their Lares and Penates.

All these manifestations of the religious sentiment carry with them certain rites, ceremonies, appropriate symbols, pageantry calculated to captivate the imagination and necessary for the recruiting of the greatest number of neophytes.

Why then refuse to apply to Voodoo this esoteric principle according to which the visible is the analogy of the invisible, and according to which everything in the physical world has its counterpart in the world of ideas?

One recalls with what heroic vigor the Occupation assaulted the peaceful sanctuaries of the African temples (*houmforts*), with what energy it sacked them.

The booty, which consisted of sacred objects and ritual accessories (drums, gourd rattles, banners, collections of thunder-stones, etc.) was packed up and shipped to the United States of America, in order to serve as proof and illustration of the state of mental inferiority in which the people of Haiti live. People saw in these material objects only the external character, the physical qualities. They could have acted the same way toward the Catholic churches, taking as a pretext that the Roman faith includes the adoration of figures of stone and wood. . . .

If Christianity is, after all, only a neo-Judaism, can the pure, primitive source from which both these religions originated, lose anything of its preëminent dignity?

This book has not been conceived, as may be thought, in a spirit of undignified controversy—still less with the intention of undermining the teachings of the Church. Its principal aim and even its only aim has been to analyze the fundamental nature of the moral and religious beliefs of black humanity and their relation with the ideas propagated by later religions.

I see some retorting angrily and others smiling.

"What an aberration!" the pious and the Tartuffes will exclaim. "What audacious impiety to compare the divine religion of Christ with a superstition as gross as it is repellent!"

Chained to his feet like the ball of the convict, the African pulls after him the criminal and implacable accusation of offering sacrifices to the "DEVIL."

The African, that is to say the Voodooist, offers sacrifices to devils, they say. . . .

It is proper to note here that, according to the historical periods and temperaments of various races, according to accepted religious conceptions, according to the degree of civilization, the forms and the means by which man manifests his veneration of the Divinity which he loves or fears, vary infinitely. They range, in a rather swift evolution, from the human sacrifice practiced by the pagans to that of the ram, the bull, the *cabrit*, or white cock. No! No! The Voodoo cult hides no shameful or diabolic practice.

I hasten to add—for it cannot be denied—that alongside of every dominant religion there stand dissident groups, sects which by a perversion of religious sense believe that it is possible, while honoring the Divinity, to conciliate the favor of the inferior and malevolent spirits—of Satan, in a word. Vices, practices not only immoral but abominable, may soil the purest religion.

But I have strong reasons to assert that the Negro initiated into the real Voodoo cult, in conformity to the pure traditions, entertains no relations with Satan.

The devils to whom he is accused of sacrificing are not the spirits of darkness, that is to say the malevolent. They are Daimons similar to the Greek conception, "luminous spirits." Criminal sorcery, black magic, are incompatible with the spirit of Voodoo as a ritual religion.

May my feeble efforts contribute to disengage from the dross that soils it the pure essence of the Voodoo beliefs!

And then, from the depth of our valleys, from the gorges of our mountains, from the forests whose century-old trees have shielded the sacred meetings of our ancestors in epic times, will rise in the air, mingled with mysterious effluvia, the songs of joy of the legions of Invisibles who watch over us—as in the past they inspired and protected the invincible founders of our independence—happy to see us reëstablish the chain of union and fraternity between blacks and mulattoes in an unalterable sentiment of piety, of love toward the Old Divinities, the Ancestors, the immortal and revivified Mother-country.

Eugène Aubin, a French writer who lived in Haiti for a number of years prior to 1898, interested himself in the study of Voodoo without ever apparently having wished to witness or participate in its sacrificial ceremonies. It is possible that he was restrained by moral scruples. He wrote, however, an excellent book called *En Haïti*, published in Paris in 1910, which shows he was on the friendliest terms with the leading *papalois* and *hougans* of that period. He discussed sympathetically and at length with the more intelligent ones the nature of their creed and was admitted to a number of their temples.

He says:

> However crude may seem some of the beliefs and rites of Voodoo, the fault does not lie with the underlying principles of Voodoo belief, which is a sort of nature worship, finding divinities in the various forces of nature. Voodoo is a form of pantheism. . . .
>
> From the medley of purely African Voodoo tradition brought over by slaves from all parts of Africa, two principal rites became predominant, the Guinea rite and the Congo rite. The Guinea rite is predominant in the matter of beliefs and superstitions—the Congo, perhaps in practice.
>
> The Guinea rite has several subdivisions, Arada, Nago, Ibo, corresponding to the different tribes of North and Middle Africa. The Guinea rite believes more in good spirits than evil ones, and consequently had less need of bloody sacrifice than the Congo rite.
>
> The *lois*, spirits, saints and mystery-powers which personify forces of nature, take their original name from old kings and gods of Africa, and also from the geographical names of African localities. The qualifying titles of Papa, Maître, Maman, and sometimes Monsieur are prefixed to the old names. Legba, Damballa, Agoué, Guédé, are from the Guinea rite but generally worshiped by all. Other Guinea divinities are Ogoun, Loco, Saugo, Badère.
>
> Damballa Oueddo and his wife, Ayida Oueddo, are considered the ancestors of the human race. Agoué is the navigator, Legba the legislator in the Haitian Voodoo mythology. Many of these are now confounded with or identified with Christian saints. Their special celebration days fall on the same days as the Catholic saints' days.
>
> The Haitians say of a *papaloi* who serves only Legba and the benevolent gods that he is one who is accustomed to *servir d'une main*. To *servir de deux mains* means to engage in blood sacrifices.

From my own observations I am inclined to believe that this is generally accurate, but perhaps not quite so sharply defined as M. Aubin believed. The Petro (Congo) ceremonials, which I witnessed, were always accompanied by blood sacrifice. Most of the purely Legba (Guinea) ceremonials I saw were without blood sacrifice, but twice during Guinea rites I saw doves and cocks sacrificed to Legba.

Again quoting Aubin:

The true *papaloi* is a man thoroughly instructed in the rites, and the priestly function is frequently handed down from father to son. The *papaloi* is reared in the Voodoo hierarchy and frequents the renowned *houmforts* [temples] of the Cul-de-Sac plain, Léogane, and l'Arcahaye where he finally is given secret initiations and ordained. When these last ceremonies are accomplished he presents himself before the faithful and intones his first prayers to the gods.

However, every head of a family, if important, enjoys also priestly powers and renders service occasionally to the household gods. A small room in the family *caille* [house] may have in it a small altar of earth or masonry on which a light is kept burning.

3. It was a local variation of the following chant:

It means: "Ybo, the hour has come! This is the hour of blood, Ybo! What are you bringing me, Ybo? It is I whom you see."

4. Here are two Voodoo invocations made up almost entirely of old African words. The first I have heard, with slight variations, in several Voodoo temples. The second, which was given me by Dr. Price Mars, of Pétionville, I have never heard in actual use. I do not know the meaning of either:

Eh! Eh! Bomba, Hen! Hen!
Canga bafio té,
Canga moune de lé,
Canga do ki la,
Canga li.

Aia bombaia bombé!
Lama Samana quana!
Evan vanta, a
Vana docki!

5. It is not my intention to gloss over the fact that actual human sacrifice is also an occasional integral part of the Voodoo ritual in Haiti. Blood sacrifice which includes even that of human beings, and sometimes of gods, is and has always been an integral part of nearly all strong primitive religions, of no matter what race or color, including the Egyptian, Greek, Roman, Druid, Hebrew, and Christian. That human sacrifice occurs in Voodoo today may seem strange and to many persons horrible, but only, I think, because they consider it in terms of "time." With the "time" element removed and considered in terms of "space," religious human sacrifice becomes, in a technical sense, both normal and moral. I have described no human sacrifice in the pages of this book solely for the reason that I never saw one. If I had lived for many years instead of months with Maman Célie in the mountains, it is probable that I should have seen one. Such sacrifices, however, Maman Célie tells me, are rare and performed only under stress of seeming dire necessity. That they never reach the courts or public notice is due to the fact that when they are pure authentic Voodoo, the sacrificial victim is never kidnaped, stolen, or procured by other criminal means, but always voluntarily offered from within the religious group. Occasionally also, however, occurs some extraordinary criminal abuse of this practice, followed by denunciation and prosecution. In this category was the case of Cadeus Belle-

garde which occurred in 1920. He was a *papaloi* turned criminal, a pathological monster comparable religiously to Gilles de Rais, criminally to Landru and the "Hamburg Butcher." He was feared, bitterly hated, and finally denounced by the fervent Voodoo peasants themselves. The case was investigated at a U. S. Marine Corps provost court hearing at Mirebalais, and the evidence subsequently turned over to the Haitian courts on a ruling, I am informed, of the Judge Advocate General that it was outside military jurisdiction.

In the course of the hearing, twenty-seven peasants testified that at various times between 1916 and 1918 they had been present at human sacrifices made by Cadeus Bellegarde in which the blood of the victims was drunk and their flesh eaten. The witnesses included a woman who lived with Bellegarde, another who had been his mistress, and a young niece. They testified also, however, that Cadeus had debased the religious ritual, that he had procured victims by trickery, had robbed and terrorized the peasants of the neighborhood, had committed a number of murders, plain criminal acts which had no connection with even debased ritual, had burned the houses of persons who threatened to denounce him, and forced people unwillingly, under threats of death, to participate with him in his criminal practices. I repeat that even the peasants who believed with utmost sincerity in the Voodoo blood sacrificial cult, even old *hougans* who had themselves participated in human sacrifice and perhaps would do so again, considered this Cadeus Bellegarde not to be a true priest, but rather a criminal and murderer.

NOTES ON PART TWO

CHAPTER I

1. With Lieutenant F. E. Wirkus, I saw and photographed a grave to which similar offerings had been brought, in the bush near Anse-à-Galet on La Gonave. At the head of the grave, which had been dug beneath a tree, a candle fixed on a stone was burning. From a branch overhanging the grave dangled an armband of black crêpe, a pair of trousers, a woman's black dress, and two mourning veils. Two more candles were burning on the grave, and an upright stick was stuck in the mound.

2. So far as I was able to learn, this *culte des morts* practices neither human sacrifice nor murder, but molests only the dead. There is a misleading tale current among the white Americans in Haiti that three members of the Marine Corps, the late Sergeant Lawrence Muth of Los Bonas, California, Pilot Clarence E. Morris of Buffalo, and Private Henry Lawrence of Mound Valley, Kansas, who were killed during the caco uprising, were victims of this cult, murdered by its members. I found Marine Corps officers in general, however, fair in their attitude toward such matters, and I have the Marine Corps to thank for the true facts concerning that particular tragic story.

I was motoring one day with two friends, a major and lieutenant, from Port-au-Prince to Hinch, when we passed, in the mountains beyond Mirabelais, a military post with a big signboard on which was written "Camp Muth."

"Named," said the lieutenant, "after Lawrence Muth, who was murdered—"

"Where do you get that stuff, murdered?" interrupted

the major. "That was war. He was killed in the fighting."

"Well, I guess that's right, sir," said the lieutenant. "But the 'apes' did chop him up after he was dead. They mutilated the body." The major said this was true.

Muth was killed in a skirmish near Las Cahobas. The surviving Marines, vastly outnumbered, retired fighting, killing ten of the cacos, but unable to take Muth's body with them.

It was recovered later, mutilated, with the head, heart, and liver missing.

On my return to Port-au-Prince I was given access to an unofficial report in the Marine Corps files at Gendarmerie Headquarters, from which I quote:

> Followers of Voodooism and kindred faiths believe that certain qualities dwell in the bodies of the dead and that when eaten these qualities are also absorbed.
>
> In the heart lives courage, they believe; hence, eating the heart gives the eater the courage that infused it. By eating the liver, they acquire sagacity and cunning, as well as immunity to edged weapons. The Voodoo worshipers also believe that if a white man's brain be rubbed on the sights of a rifle it will impart to the gun a power to see with accuracy; make it indeed an unfailing weapon.
>
> With all this in mind it is not hard to understand the fate that overtook Sergeant Lawrence Muth, of Los Bonas, California.
>
> Sergeant Muth with three Marines was reconnoitering in the vicinity of St. Michel. This is a mountain base; on the west Las Cahobas, a typical Haitian village. There is a road from Las Cahobas leading over the top of St. Michel; it is little more than a narrow trail between the dense masses of tropical jungle.
>
> It had been reported that a number of bandits were in the vicinity, and Sergeant Muth and his little patrol were sent out scouting. They passed Las Cahobas while night still lay black in the valley. At daybreak they were at the top of the rise. Suddenly out of the tangle before them a few men darted. The four Marines opened fire and pursued. They had not gone far when a withering volley raked them from both sides and the rear. The fleeing men had only been a decoy to lure them into the ambush. Had the aim of the Haitians been

anywhere equal to their opportunity, the four Americans must have been riddled immediately; as it was, Muth fell, shot through the head and stomach. Stone, the next in command, tried to lift the body of Muth to his horse. A bullet grazed his neck and struck the stock of his rifle. Stone, though stunned, landed on his feet, raised his damaged rifle, and fired; the weapon exploded, blinding him. The two remaining Marines swung him across his horse and retreated down the trail. They fought steadily until close to Las Cahobas; how effectively, the bodies of ten of the bandits, found later, were evidence.

At the village they managed to get word of the fight to Lieutenant Colonel Little, who was at the Marine Camp in Mirebalais, some twenty miles away. Twenty-four patrols were sent out to recover Muth's body and punish the blacks. It took them four hours to reach the top of the mountain. They fought a guerilla warfare all the way up.

At the very peak they found what was left of the Sergeant.

"It was all right to kill Muth," said the Marines. "That was war. But why did they mutilate his body?"

Some days later a prisoner was taken and he told them why. Their leader, he said, had been a black named Benoit. While the three Marines were retreating under fire, Benoit examined Muth. The Sergeant was not dead.

Benoit, having assured himself of that, swung his war machete and chopped Muth's head nearly off. Then he called his Lieutenant, one Francingue. Benoit then had ordered his men to rub their sights with parts of the head to assure the accuracy of their fire when they shot at Muth's comrades.

"Then," this prisoner said, "the white man's heart and liver were cooked and passed around. Benoit said that whoever swallowed them could not be hit by white man's bullets or cut with white man's bayonets."

3. On May 9, 1920, General Benoit Batraville, then commander of the caco revolutionary forces, was killed by Sergeant Passmore, U.S.M.C., in an engagement between cacos and American Marines which took place near Bois Pin in the Mirabelais district.

This caco leader had never been a *papaloi* or Voodoo

priest, but was generally believed among his followers to be a *bocor* or sorcerer and was apparently a member of the *culte des morts.* He was also a devout Catholic. A booklet of secret formulas written by himself in creole was found upon the body. The following excerpts are translated literally:

To call up spirits. Arriving at a crossroads at midnight on a Friday, get a candle made of honey wax, ox tallow and swallow's liver, which you will light on that corner in the name of Belzebuth, saying: "Belzebuth, I am calling you to me in order that you may acquaint me with (such and such a thing) this very moment." You will then fire one shot, the gun to be loaded with incense and dirt, putting the dirt on top of the counter load. Fire to the east, saying: "Upon the thunder's rumbling, may all Kings of the earth kneel down. May Puer, Agrippa Berke, Astaroth, spare me. Amen."

To put a woman to sleep that you may know all her guiles. Kill a toad on a Friday, take out the heart and liver and put the heart of the toad over the woman's left breast, so as to have her tell all her secrets, and say: "Biristo, Faculta, Sialevanto. Amen."

To call up the dead. Go to a cemetery on a Friday night at midnight, one where shootings have taken place. Go to a man's grave, taking along with you a white candle, one leaf of wild acacia, and a fully loaded gun. On arrival you will make this appeal: "*Exurgent mortui et acmo venuient.* I require of you dead that you come to me." After saying these words you will hear a stormy noise; do not take fright, and then fire one shot. The dead will appear to you; you must not run away, but walk backward three steps, saying these words: "I besprinkle you with incense and myrrh such as perfumed Astaroth's tomb," three times.

Sending back a dead spirit after you have called it. Pick up a handful of dirt, which you will throw to the four corners of the earth, saying: "Go back from where you came, from dirt you were created, to dirt you may return. Amen."

How to create an invisible human face. Take a fresh egg and in the inside of the egg put a human gland [male semen]; then go to a corner on a Friday night where you will bury the egg, which must remain underground for twenty-one days; be careful in writing your request, which is to be put underground also. After twenty-one days dig up the egg and it will look like a human face and it should be fed with ground charcoal and verbena. Put to it your request, and having done so, when it is fulfilled, you must kill it or else put it underground alive in a cemetery on either a Monday or a Friday night.

How to bathe a fighting horse. Before going to the battlefield and in order to make the animal more warlike, make a bath with incense, dirt from a cemetery, and a small crucifix, which is to be fastened to the animal's tail with these words: "Jemuel, Jaccil, Vamiel, Jurimiel, Virimiel. Amen."

To prevent your enemies from poisoning your saddle. Take seven pins and a white candle and go on a Friday to a crossroads. Upon arrival, say this prayer: "I require of you, King Buer, Gusogu, Agrippa, for the sake of that august greeting's fragrancy, that you show yourself to me, or that you let me understand that you are present." At that very moment, after saying those words, lay the seven pins on the ground in the form of a cross in the middle of the crossroads and light the candle. Then take dirt from the crossroads and the pins and go home. Fix up an ointment with three handfuls of ground penguin flowers, which you will mix up with incense and white vinegar. Perfume the saddle and wash the saddle also in cross movement, saying: "King Gaspard, King Melchior, King Balthazar, be my guide, my support and my strength, keep me and defend me from all my enemies, may they be confounded. Amen." These words should also be written on a piece of paper and placed inside the saddle where no one can see it.

Prayer against bullets. Have a shirt made of rough rag which you will wear and also be careful in securing a belt of Aaron's Crown [cat-eye] having three rows with the following words: "God of the Heaven and of the earth, immortal and invisible King, everything trembles at your name. May I, by myself, be not vanquished, but victor. Amen." Every Friday, as a charity, give the poor four centimes.

To avoid persecution. Carry with you carefully an orison and a relic made of a small *mapou* cross, cemetery dirt, a small piece of sheeting, with which people have been buried. Carry them along when you go to church and see that they are blessed at the very moment of the besprinkling. The following orison must also be included: "Acuerdate, piadossi suma del virgin de Maria de Higuen par los dolores de filios Dios, Jesu Christi que me corpo, este protection de tos Sanctos, para quel divisauno. Amen esu."

When confronted with torture. When one finds himself tied up, it is very necessary to make this prayer: "For the sake of the great pains which Jesus Christ suffered from Judas, the traitor, in walking along Golgotha's hilly road, may I be relieved from the rope which is piercing through my (mention the part) to the heart, just as the left side of Christ's body did abundantly spill blood by Herod, the infamous executioner. Amen." Order a mass in the name of all the saints.

In order to be released from prison. At midnight rehearse this prayer: "Sesame, Sesame, allow and open yourself," and the fetters shall be opened. As you come out say these words: "Sesame, shut again," and on your arrival at the prison gate, if you find it locked, say these words: "Pastoo, Vidoo, Agrimento. Agrippa, deliver me from this lion which is trying by any means to take my life. Everything yields at your name, all knees bow before you. Mane, Thecel of the three Marys, Agrippine, Mariannie and Farres, be my guides and conductors. Amen."

To combat insincerity. When you know that a person is not sincere, on seeing him coming to your house without his being able to see you, take some ashes, make a cross underneath the chair upon which he will sit, and threaten him with a pin, saying: "I am conjuring you in the name of the evil spirits who are commanding you, whether Buer, Agrippa or Belzebuth, that you may be recognized this very moment. Amen."

In order to chase away some one who is persecuting you. Take along with you a picture of St. Antoine, a candle, and a white plate, and go at noon to a far-distant large field and there put the candle in the plate, light it, and say the following prayer: "Great Saint Antoine, prince and true charitable conductor, deliver me from . . . who is persecuting me; make him get out of that place, my strength and my support rest within you and I promise you, Great Saint ——

(such and such a thing)." After saying this prayer, be careful in throwing a few grains of salt and pepper about the four parts of the world, N. S. E. W., in repeating the same prayer. On arriving home, put the saint in question face to the ground for nine consecutive days and repeat the same prayer each and every day.

To remove a curse from a child against whom some one has made and hidden an evil, ouanga, *bag charm, subsequently found.* After seven days remove the words and compounds which have been found, burn them up, and make a bath out of them, in which you will bathe the child in the name of Belzebuth, asking him to be patron and guardian of this angel. This you will do after blessing the child. Amen.

Relic made by the Queen of Evil Spirits against other spirits and which will be used as a child's safeguard. Take a piece of charcoal, some incense, and one leaf of three paroles. Write out the baptismal name of the child and his birthday and these words: "Buer Boyon, guardian of the orphans, take this child under your care, that he may never yield to temptation. Amen." Make up this relic on a Thursday and put it around the child's neck the next day in the name of Sancta Ritadel. Amen.

In order to destroy a father's fondness. Fix up a bath with a great amount of catkins, seven leaves of Palma-Christi, three leaves of God the Father, three leaves of God the Son, and three leaves of God the Holy Ghost. Also be careful to put in indigo and burnt incense. Dig three holes, one for the mother, one for the father, and one for the godmother and godfather, over which pass the child three times, saying the following prayer: "Prayer Maledicto, Vade Sataneh, may you leave this child as Judas left and betrayed Christ. Amen." [*Note.* A sinister and obscurely motivated formula, apparently employed to remove family protection from a child against whom evil intentions are entertained.]

To relieve a woman in pains of childbirth. Make a tea of the following mixture: dirt from the four corners of the house and the following leaves: Pains Cutter, called Verbena; Abra Homo, called Elm Wood. Write the woman's baptismal name and her usual name on a parchment, or ordinary paper, the ashes of which must be mixed with the tea. This being done, before giving her the tea, go to the rear of the house, and facing the east, call her three times; there will be no reply to the first and second calls, but there must be a reply to the third. Soon afterward give her the mixture. She will certainly be relieved. If the child is a boy name him Emanuel; if a girl, name her Anna.

For sprained ankle. Say these words about the bruised part: "Ante, Anetete, Saparlants," three times, and Jesus Christ will do the rest. Then bind up the bruised part with ash-colored water and seven Spanish Cachimenta leaves, thus during three days.

To heal an injured eye. Kill a black chicken with a spot on it; take the liver from the chicken and put it in a small quantity of water, which you will expose to the sun for three days; the bottle must always be placed toward the east and the following words must be added to it: "In the name of Toby, traveler, I beg you to enlighten me through your powerful guide, as Toby brought back salutary medicines to his father. Toby. Toby. Annot. Toby. Amen." [*Note.* Presumably, the eye is afterward to be bathed or poulticed with this concoction.]

When a woman is losing blood [from excessive menstruation]. Take seven petals of cotton flowers, not open, and boil with seven roots of verbena, seven roots of cotton, seven handfuls of carobonicos, or ladies' collar, leaves in the shape of a heart. The whole will be made into a cooling drink, which must be used for three days by the patient. After three days she will thank the Great Physician, Agrippa, by saying: "Sange, Sangeno, Sangenone, Vade Agua, Corpo, Amen." ("May Saint Agrippa, the physician, preserve me from that sickness and may it stop from torturing me. Amen.")

In order to get rid of worms. Mix up a potion with a handful of semencontra (worm seed), one ounce of ground garlic, one ounce of leek, which must all be put in alcohol. Mix the whole thing in a pot and have the child drink it. The worms will surely be ejected from the child's entrails. Amen.

For toothache. Get hold of a new nail and threaten the tooth three times with a stone, saying, "Abracadabra" three times. Go to a mango tree and make a cross on it, saying, "Abracadabra" twice. Cut off the cross and boil the bark and wet the sick tooth. The ache will certainly be relieved.

For rheumatism. Apply the following ointment over the sick part: Ground Carobornico (leaf in the shape of a heart), catkins, male verbena, three handfuls of boxwood, which you will mix with oil; then carefully rub the sick part with tepid water mixed with ashes. Before applying the ointment, say: "I conjure you by the great pains Jesus Christ endured over the sacred tree of the cross. Amen."—Cured after three days. [*Note.* It is characteristic that many of these formulas, though not all, involve not only conjurations but the employment of herbs and simples which may frequently have an actual medicinal value.]

To preserve yourself from yellow fever. Ere the fever comes to your house, plant a lemon tree at the gate of your property, bearing on it three nails in the form of a cross, and another cross made of twenty-one leaves of the grand mapou. Place at your front door a citron with seven pins set in the form of a cross about the citron. Place on each of your children one small citron, a piece of indigo, some incense, and these words, placed in a shroud: "Malo. Presto. Pasto. Effacio. Amen."

Regarding a beast in a conception way. Make up a purgative with twenty-one leaves, or three handfuls of verbena, some bark of Milan Wood (elm wood), and ground incense, and put the whole in tepid water. Before giving the purgative to the animal, take a piece of indigo and mark a cross on its left side, saying: "Nerestros, Jose et Petro, onuma de la virgin del Maria que señorita modo. Amen."

When an animal has bellyache. When the animal is bitterly suffering, take seven roots of stinking peas, seven handfuls of verbena, and ground incense soaked into human bathing water; mix up the whole thing together and make a purgative pot, which shall be bottled up and given to the animal. If he is standing up make a cross over his forehead, saying this prayer: "Magnus, Anima, Dolor, Dolori, Passa. For the sake of the sufferings which Christ endured on the Cross. Amen." Say this prayer before giving him the potion.

To revive a strangling beast. Make the sign of the cross and also make the sign of the cross on the animal's forehead, saying these words: "God who is born. God who died. God who came to life again. God who was crucified. God who was hanged." Pull the animal's tail three times in the name of Atogu Gaspard. Amen.

Turning a bad horse into a good horse. As soon as you buy the horse, take the rope which is around his neck, cut off his tail and also some of his mane. Then dig a hole in the yard of the one who sold you the animal and bury the whole thing. When you get to your house, bathe him with seven handfuls of buso, seven handfuls of avo, seven handfuls of garlic, and seven handfuls of verbena soaked in human urine for three days.

To protect a field from evil influences. On the day you are planting in your garden, get up without saying a word to anybody. Go to a cemetery and take dirt and a cross from a man's grave. Turn your back and go to the garden, and plant underground in the middle of the field the said cross. The dirt will be used as a perfume and thrown toward all parts of the garden, at the same time asking the dead man to become the said garden's faithful watchman. You are recommended to light a candle before making the appeal.

How to take care of a fighting cock. Put together a piece of ox-tongue, seven verbena leaves, a handful of earth, verbena root, a few catkin roots and ginger or pimiento. This must be ground together and put into red alcohol together with a small quantity of gunpowder and incense. Amen. [*Note.* This is commonly rubbed thoroughly into the cock's body, between the parted feathers.]

Prayer to aid fighting cocks. Before the fight, say these words: "Great Saint, King Gaspard, in the company of all other chiefs of ghosts, allow that by means of the great Belzebuth's weapon, my adversary be defeated. Amen." Before going to the fight it is necessary to light a candle in the name of Agrippa.

Another way to fight cocks. Go to a cemetery on a Friday night and on arrival there take the length and width of a dead person's grave by means of a piece of twine, which you will use to tie up the cock. You will light a candle first. The next day you will go to that grave and take what remains of the candle and a handful of dirt from that grave, which you will mix up with indigo, three paroles leaves and incense, and rub the cock with it.

To insure the success of a new undertaking. On the day of taking up the business, go to a cemetery and at the grand cross light a candle made from cow tallow kneaded into a black donkey's milk. At the bottom of the grand cross you will place a brand-new earthen pot, which will contain twenty-one centimes, some wine and some bread, which you will throw to the four parts of the earth—N. S. E. W. The twenty-one centimes will be like alms-giving, after which you will make this prayer: "Baptiso, Crucius"—then mention your own name three times—"may I come out victorious (in such and such a business). I promise, great saint, to serve you faithfully and am offering Christ's blood and body in holocaust. Amen."

4. On trails and roadsides in Haiti one frequently sees animal bodies, that of a chicken, sometimes of a pig or goat, suspended from the limb of a tree, but these objects, though sometimes also connected with sorcery, are not always necessarily so. The Haitian Code Rural contains a curious provision which reads as follows:

Pourrant neanmoins être abattus les cochons et les cabrits qui auront été trouvés dans les jardins et les champs cultivés; dans ce cas les trois pieds et la tête de l'animal seulement appartiendront à celui qui l'aura abattu.

It is interpreted to mean that trespassing pigs and goats caught in cultivated gardens or fields may be killed. The carcass, however, which is valuable, may not be confiscated. The farmer trespassed against may cut off three of the animal's feet and its head. He is not required to return the carcass of the trespassing animal to its owner, but hangs it up by its remaining foot on the roadside, where the owner may come and get it if he likes. In the central plain where corn is grown, one frequently sees also rows of whitened skulls of horses, donkeys, goats, stuck up on poles, but these, so far as I have been able to learn, have no connection either with Voodoo or with sorcery. They are erected to scare off the crows. I have seen human skulls and bones used in various ceremonies, but never those of an animal, with the exception of snake vertebrae.

5. Two men carry the coffin on their heads, balancing it with their hands. They dance zigzagging as they go to the grave, even on the steep trails. The procession goes behind, not singing or mourning, but howling and making wild noises. The dancing and zigzagging with the coffin, as well as the howling, are to prevent evil spirits from entering the corpse. The theory of dancing and zigzagging is just as when a live man dodges and runs at angles when he is being shot at.

CHAPTER II

1. Descending the trail beside the Rivière Froide with Dr. Robert Parsons, we came one day to a group of women washing clothes in the stream. They knew him and we stopped to talk. As we were taking leave, some of the older women drew us aside and said, "You'd better go round over the hill because the *Loup Garou* is just below." Parsons smiled and said, "She can't hurt whites." An old woman said, "Just the same, you'd better go round." In Haiti the *Loup Garou* is a creature, human or demoniac, which sucks human blood. It is akin to the medieval vampire. Further downstream we found the *Loup Garou*, a middle-aged negress squatting in the water with a pile of clothes beside her, sullenly engaged in her lonely task. She was a *griffone*, the color midway between mulatto and black, but by some accident of pigmentation, her hair was a rusty, unpleasant, decided red. We tried to talk with her, but she refused to look up or speak. There was something definitely repellent about her. The story of this woman as recounted circumstantially by the peasants of the Rivière Froide section was this: She went by the name of Mina Rouge. Her sister had died in childbirth, and her sister's children, a little boy and girl, also the newborn baby, had been taken to Mina's *caille*. The baby died, which was natural enough. But Mina already bore an evil reputation because of the color of her hair. A little while

later, the boy wasted away and died. The community muttered and let it pass, for infant mortality is high in Haiti. But when the little girl began to waste away, a sorceress was called in by the indignant neighbors. Meanwhile the child had been taken from Mina's *caille.* The sorceress stripped the little girl naked, had her emaciated body scrubbed, and made a minute inspection of every inch of the skin. Finally, on the inner sides of the big toes, she found a number of tiny scars, and a small sharply defined recent cut as if made with the point of a knife or razor blade. To the sorceress and peasants it was clear that Mina had killed the newborn baby and the boy by sucking their blood, and that she was in process of killing the girl in the same way. There are herbs in Haiti which produce stupor. They believed that Mina had been putting them in the girl's food. She was driven from the village with exorcisms, her *caille* burned, and she now lived ostracized like a leper. I asked why they hadn't killed the woman or delivered her to justice. They replied that they wouldn't dare to kill her because she would have more power dead than living and could come back from the grave to drain the life-blood of others. And the whole affair, they said, was one which "did not concern the courts." Such things never came out satisfactorily in the courts, and often caused trouble for the witnesses. It was best to let the courts alone. So she lived on, suffered ostracism, but was in a way protected by their fear of her.

I was told of a similar case by Madame Charles Moravia, wife of the famous Haitian poet. She had no personal knowledge of the matter, but had heard of it from her father. A child was wasting away at Jeremie. Neighbors intervened, and a woman confessed that she had been sucking its blood through needle holes made in its arm-pits; she averred that a demon entered her body and forced her to do it.

Cases of this sort do occasionally reach the criminal

courts, as may be seen from the following item in the daily newspaper, *Le Matin*, of January 27, 1927:

Aux Assises

Audience du mardi 25 Janvier

Azéma Daou originaire de Boucan-Carré, Commune de Mirebalais, est assise au banc des criminels. Elle ignore son âge. Il n'importe. N'ont-elles pas, les femmes, que l'âge qu'elles paraissent avoir? En tout cas, celle qui comparait aujourd'hui est « majeure », aux yeux de la justice, puisqu'elle est grand'mère. Mais le contour de sa forme, son nez droit, ses yeux expressifs d'une jeunesse non encore éteinte, qui s'ouvrirent largement quand elle aura à nier le fait qui lui est reproché, feraient encore le charme de plus d'un. Et, l'on ne s'étonne pas que le Substitut Benjamin ait dit dans son acte d'accusation qu'elle s'était fait un « visage de sœur de charité» au cabinet d'Instruction, alors qu'elle aurait précédemment avoué, et à la police et à la Justice de paix, avoir réellement exercé le 13 août 1925, des actes de sorcellérie sur un enfant qui en est mort.

Quatre témoins comparaissent, déposent d'abondance, mais hésitent à répondre aux questions qui leur sont respectivement posées par le Ministère Public, Mes Ed. Cassagnol, P. D. Plaisir et M. Charlemers. Mais Azéma Daou, elle-même, nie avoir tué l'enfant de son petit neveu qui n'aurait vécu que 7 jours.

A la fermeture des débats particuliers, on pouvait encore se demander si l'accusée était véritablement coupable du crime qu'on lui reprochait.

Apparently this woman confessed that she was a sorceress, but denied having caused the death of the child. She was subsequently acquitted.

2. Stephen Bonsal, in *The American Mediterranean* (Moffat, Yard and Company, 1912), gives the following account of a case which occurred in 1908 during the presidency of Nord Alexis:

A man of the working-class in Port-au-Prince fell ill. He had at intervals a high fever which physicians could not reduce. He had joined a foreign mission church and the head of this mission visited him. On his second visit this clergyman saw the patient die and at the invitation of the dead man's wife and his physician, he helped dress the dead man in his grave-clothes. The next day he assisted at the funeral, closed the coffin lid, and saw the dead man buried.

The mail rider to Jacmel found some days later a man dressed in grave-clothes, tied to a tree, moaning. He freed the poor wretch, who soon recovered his voice but not his mind. He was subsequently identified by his wife, by the physician who had pronounced him dead, and by the clergyman. The recognition was not mutual, however. The victim recognized no one, and his days and nights were spent moaning inarticulate words no one could understand. President Nord Alexis placed him on a government farm, near Gonaives, where he was cared for.

3. Here is the French text from the Code Pénal:

Article 249. Est aussi qualifié attentat à la vie d'une personne, l'emploi qui sera fait contre elle de substances qui, sans donner la mort, produisent un effet léthargique plus ou moins prolongé, de quelque manière que ces substances aiént administrés, quelles qu'en aiént été les suites. Si par suite de cet état léthargique la personne a été inhumeé, l'attentat sera qualifié assassinat.

CHAPTER IV

1. In Hayti for almost two hundred years the bulk of the people have been faithful in their allegiance to the snake god, worshiped not merely by the dregs of the colored populace, but also by many, if not by most, who are leaders of their race. In one of the Voodoo Temples hangs a banner of red silk presented to the serpent deity by the consort of Emperor Soulouque.—MARVIN DANA.

That Soulouque, who ruled as the Emperor Faustin I in 1848-1859, as well as his consort Empress Adelina, were adherents of the Voodoo faith, is a known fact in Haitian history. Among the original manuscript documents in the collection of H. P. Davis is a letter written in ink which is faded yellow and almost illegible, addressed to the Emperor Faustin I, dated St. Suzanne, September 12, 1849, and bearing the signature "Romain fils, Adjutant Général Etat Majeur." This General Romain was Faustin's confidant and chief of his General Staff. He discusses military-political affairs which have been going badly, says that enemies are plotting against Faustin, and recommends that a sacrifice be made in the palace to the Voodoo gods. The concluding phrase is:

> En conséquence, vous aurez, Empereur, à faire une cérémonie au nom de Oguegui et Obachoron et Foom. Tous trois ont le pouvoir de vous défendre dans le malheur.

2. Stephen Bonsal, from whose book, *The American Mediterranean* I have quoted in a previous note, says:

> Within the last fifteen years human victims have been sacrificed to the gods of Voodoo in the national palace. . . . During the life of Madame Nord [wife of President Nord Alexis] not a week passed but what a meeting of the Voodoo priests was held in the executive mansion. There is in the capital a committee of Voodoo priests who have a central meeting place. Until quite recently [1912] it was the Chamber of Deputies or the Executive Mansion.

ERRATA

Ernest Chauvet of Port-au-Prince, editor of the *Nouvelliste*, visited New York in October, kindly read Chapter III of Part Three, which concerns him, and pointed out two errors. Henri Chauvet, his distinguished father, is still alive. The book *Sena*, which I attributed to L'Herrison, was written by Hibbert. This note is to thank Mr. Chauvet and acknowledge the corrections.

W. B. S.

Nov. 1, 1928.

I wish to thank Dr. Arthur C. Holly for several photographs never heretofore published.

W. B. S.

AFTERWORD

William Seabrook and the Haitian Zombie

On the morning of 24 October, 1936, in the village of Ennery in north-central Haiti, the entire population was aroused by the appearance of an old, naked woman whose eyelashes had fallen out and whose face was bound in a ragged cloth. Hysteria swept the village, and in time a member of the Mentor family who lived outside of Ennery noticed that the woman bore a resemblance to a sister, Felicia Felix, who had died and was buried in 1907. Moreover, the mysterious woman was lame; the sister had also been lame as a result of a fracture of her left leg.

The case drew national and, to some extent, international attention. The woman was taken to a government hospital, and one by one a number of relatives were called upon to verify her identity. Many did, and for a while the case was heralded as the first legitimate instance of zombification. However, arguments in favor of this conclusion soon fell apart. X-ray examination showed that her leg had never been broken. When placed on a proper diet, she soon gained weight and began to menstruate. Felicia Felix had been twenty-seven at the time of her death, almost thirty years before. The age of this unknown woman, once she had partially regained her health, was estimated to be about forty. In the end, the attendant physician's diagnosis was schizophrenia.

The case of Felicia Felix Mentor was highly significant, for it had been critical to the argument of a young American anthropologist and folklorist, Zora Neale Hurston, a student of Franz Boas and arguably the most vocal proponent of the idea that zombies actually existed. Hurston became the object of scathing remarks. Alfred Métraux dismissed her as being "very superstitious." Louis Mars noted: "This American writer came to Haiti with no doubt in regard to the popular belief in the zombie pseudo-science. Miss Hurston did not go beyond the mass hysteria to verify her information." These scholars were correct in exposing the Mentor case as fraudulent.

At the same time, they were guilty of ignoring the central tenet of Hurston's argument.

Zora Neale Hurston did believe that zombies were created, but not by magic. "It is not a case of awakening the dead," she wrote, "but rather a matter of a semblance of death brought on by some drug known to a few. Some secret probably brought from Africa and handed down generation to generation. It is evident that it destroys that part of the brain which governs speech and will-power. The victim can move and act but cannot formulate thought."

Although Hurston alone gave credence to this hypothesis, previous and subsequent investigators certainly knew of the reputed poison. The historian James Leyburn refers to "those who believe that certain bocors (sic) know how to administer a subtle poison to intended victims which will cause suspended animation and give the appearance of death. Men in the prime of life suddenly sicken and die for no apparent reason. Once these pseudo-corpses are safely buried, the sinister person who arranged the death will hasten to the graveyard and dig up the body; giving the proper antidote to the poison, he restores the body to activity but the mind only to semi-consciousness." According to French ethnographer Alfred Métraux, "it is generally believed that hungan (sic) know the secret of certain drugs which can produce a profound state of lethargy as to be indistinguishable from death." Anthropologist Harold Courlander adds: "The victim is not really dead but has succumbed to a virulent poison which numbs all senses and stops bodily function but does not really kill. Upon disinterment, the victim is given an antidote which restores most physical processes but leaves the mind in an inert state, without will or the power to resist."

References to a reputed zombie poison appear not only in the academic literature but also in newspapers and popular books, missionary reports and private journals. Indeed the Haitian government accepted the existence of this poison with such assurance that it was specifically mentioned in the Code Pénal, Article 249, of which reads: "Also to be considered as attempted murder the use that may be made against any person of substances which, without causing actual death, produce a more or less prolonged lethargic coma. If after the administering of such substances the person has been buried the act shall be considered murder no matter what result follows."

Although it now seems remarkable that reports of the poison were not investigated, there are in fact good historical reasons for the oversight. The rumors first appeared during a period when both foreign and Haitian social scientists trained in the tradition of cultural relativism and objective analysis were most anxious to promote the legitimacy of peasant institutions. These intellectuals were repelled by the sensational publications of an earlier decade that, in their minds, had both unjustly misrepresented the Haitian peasantry and in effect rationalized the American military occupation of the country between 1915 and 1934.

The most popular of these books was William Seabrook's *The Magic Island.* In it the author, an American adventurer, presented as fact the reputed use of nine zombies in the fields of the Haitian-American Sugar Company. The story, distilled from ten pages of Seabrook's text, is as follows:

> *One morning a certain Ti Joseph of Colombier appeared with a ragged band of docile men and women. It was a good year for sugar and the company needed cane cutters, and so the zombies went to work immediately with Ti Joseph pocketing their wages.*
>
> *One day while Ti Joseph was away on business, his wife impulsively decided to take the zombies to see the procession at Croix de Bouquet. She fed them their breakfast of unsalted plaintains and led them into town.*
>
> *The zombies paid little attention to the procession and the wife taking pity on them offered a small handful of sweets to each one. Little did she know that the confections contained salted peanuts. The zombies woke with a dreadful cry and turned immediately back to the mountains. They reached their old settlement at Morne au Diable where they were recognized by their grieving families. The zombies ignored their families and instead walked directly to the village cemetery, where in turn each dug up his grave, struggling to reenter the earth. The dismayed family members made a collection and bought a wanga to place a curse on Ti Joseph. Lest the spell be ineffective, they also hired a man to cut off his head.*

On the surface this account was not unlike many zombie tales commonly heard in the Haitian countryside, but what made it potent was the context in which it was presented. Seabrook was a well-known author, who had by the time he went to Haiti, published several highly regarded books based on his journeys in Arabia and Africa. For its time, *The Magic Island* was not a bad travel account, and in many ways the author was remarkably sympathetic to the peasant society and the Vodoun religion. This sympathy, of course, only made it that much more controversial when he presented the story of Ti Joseph not as folklore but as fact. Seabrook went on to describe his own encounter with three reputed zombies, for which there was no serious evidence. *The Magic Island* created a furor among the Haitian intellectual elite, but it was not the only such publication.

Indeed, for some time American and other foreign correspondents had indulged their readers' odd infatuation with what was known as the Black Republic, serving it up garnished with every conceivable figment of their imaginations. To Americans in particular, Haiti was like having a little bit of Africa next door—something dark and foreboding, sensual and terribly lurid. These other popular books of the day, with titles such as *Cannibal Cousins, Black Baghdad, The White King of La Gonave, Voodoo Fire in Haiti,* and *A Puritan in Voodooland,* cast the entire nation as a caricature, an impoverished land of throbbing drums, ruled by pretentious buffoons and populated by swamp doctors, licentious women, and children bred for the cauldron. Most of these travelogues—which gave rise to the RKO films of the 1940s, *Night of the Living Dead, Zombies of the Stratosphere, The White Zombie Slave* and many others—would have been soon forgotten had it not been for the peculiar and by no means coincidental timing of the publications.

Until the first of this genre appeared in 1884—Spenser St. John's *The Black Republic,* with its infamous account of a cannibalistic "Congo Bean Stew"—most books that dealt with Vodoun had simply emphasized its role in the uprising of 1791, the only successful slave revolt in history. But these new and sensational publications, packed with references to cult objects such as voodoo dolls that didn't even exist, effectively served a specific political purpose. It was no coincidence that many of them appeared during the years of American occupation (1915–34), or that every marine above the rank of sergeant seemed to land a book contract. There were many of these books, and each one conveyed an important message to the American people during the era of Jim Crow: any country where such abominations took place could find its salvation only through military occupation.

Haitian intellectuals and foreign scholars alike were repelled by these sensationalized publications. So much so that the subject of the zombie, which had figured so prominently in the books became virtually off-limits for serious academic inquiry. Individual researchers would respond to purported appearances of zombies on a case-by-case basis, but no sustained, calm and systematic study was undertaken that might resolve once and for all the troubling and embarrassing notion that zombies might be real. Report after report in the ethnographic literature heralded the remarkable ability of traditional healers to manipulate natural products as both medicines and poisons. Yet remarkably, no scholar made any attempt to seek out and identify the ingredients of the powders that had been widely reported as being implicated in the zombie phenomenon. Zora Neale Hurston, who in fact came close to solving the mystery in the 1930s, was at the time dismissed and indeed ridiculed for her claims.

*****

My interest in the Haitian zombie came half a century later, prompted by the discovery by a team of researchers of the first actual case that was scientifically verifiable. The putative victim, Clairvius Narcisse, had been pronounced dead in 1962 at an American-directed hospital in Haiti that kept excellent records. His death had been witnessed by two physicians, both American trained, one an American, and observed by his sister. In 1980 Narcisse returned to his family's village, where he presented a chilling tale of having been victimized by a *bokor,* a negative priest or sorcerer.

Lamarque Douyon, then Haiti's leading psychiatrist, conducted a thorough investigation and, in collaboration with the late Nathan Kline, winner of two Lasker Awards and a pioneer in the field of psychopharmacology, concluded that Narcisse had indeed been misdiagnosed dead. Their attention then focused on reports of the folk preparation, mentioned as we have seen frequently in the popular and ethnographic literature. Intrigued by the medical potential of such a substance, Kline in 1982 contacted Harvard's Botanical Museum and I was dispatched to Haiti to seek the formula and collect raw samples. The assignment, initially but a fortnight, would in the end consume four years.

Although each bokor had a unique formula, the consistent ingredients, aside from human remains, were species of marine fish belonging to the order Tetraodontiformes. The viscera and skin of these fish contain tetrodotoxin, a nerve poison roughly a thousand times stronger than cyanide: a lethal dose of the pure toxin would balance on the head of a pin. Exposure to the poison causes metabolic rates to fall dramatically. The pulse becomes imperceptible and peripheral paralysis is total. Though unable to move, the victim remains fully conscious until the moment of actual death.

In Japan tetrodotoxin containing fish are a culinary delicacy, and the biomedical and popular literature contains numerous accounts of individuals being misdiagnosed dead, nailed into coffins alive or by folk tradition laid out by their graves for several days until known to be dead. These accounts confirmed without doubt that the sorcerers in Haiti had indeed found in their environment a natural product that not only could induce a state of apparent death but evidently had done so many times in the past in a quite different cultural context. That Narcisse's symptoms were consistent with the known effects of tetrodotoxication suggested at least the possibility that he had been exposed to the poison.

While the formula of the preparation took the zombie phenomenon from the phantasmagoric into the realm of the plausible, it by no means solved the essential mystery. For the Vodounist the *poudre zombi,* the zombie powder, is seen as but a support for the magical force of the sorcerer, and it is this power, not a poison, that creates the zombie.

In Vodoun there are two kinds of death: those that are natural, acts of God beyond the reach of sorcery; and those that are unnatural, mediated by the bokor. Only those who die an unnatural death may be claimed as a zombie. The poison is an effective way to induce such a death, but the performance of a magical rite is what actually creates a zombie.

The bokor gains power over the victim by capturing the *ti bon ange,* the little good angel, which is the component of the soul that creates character, personality, and willpower. A zombie appears cataleptic precisely because it has no ti bon ange. Trapped in purgatory, the body is but an empty vessel. The notion of external forces taking control of the individual, and thus breaking the sacred cycle of life, death, and rebirth that allows human beings to give rise to the *lwa,* the spirits of the pantheon, terrifies the Vodounist. The fear in Haiti is not of zombies, but rather of becoming one.

Understanding zombification from the perspective of the believer led to yet another revelation. Though there is no doubt that tetrodotoxin can induce apparent death, levels of the poison in the fish vary greatly, and at certain times of the year, as much as half the populations may contain none of the drug at all. Any particular batch of the folk preparation may range from being truly lethal to being completely inert. So what happens if the poison does not work? What insulates the sorcerer from being exposed as a fraud?

The answer is the belief system itself. The bokor does not have to account for his failures. If he administers a powder that has no effect, he can claim that his magic was deflected by the intervention of a benevolent priest. If, on the other hand, the victim actually dies, the bokor can suggest that the death was a call from God and beyond the reach of his sorcery. A bokor's failed attempts do not count, only his successes. Even if the poison was effective but once in dozens of attempts, the outcome would support the reputation earned by the zombie phenomenon. Its power as a concept depends not on how often it occurs but rather on the fact that it can and apparently has occurred.

But how and why is someone chosen to become the victim of a bokor's sorcery? From testimony of family and villagers it was clear that Narcisse had been a pariah at the time of his demise. Some claimed he had been brought before a tribunal to be judged.

In my time in Haiti I had often crossed paths with the Bizango, a notorious secret society much feared by the Haitian elite. The Bizango were said to dominate the rural peasant society, constituting a force parallel to the Vodoun temples headed by the priests. Several contacts maintained that the Bizango controlled the zombie powders. The origins of the Bizango, as in the case of so many Haitian institutions, could be traced in direct lineage to West Africa, where to this day secret societies remain the most powerful arbiter of social and political life. They function as judicial tribunals, apply sanctions, and to punish those who violate the codes of their communities, they administer poisons.

Intrigued by the possibility that the Bizango might play a similar role in Haiti, I focused the last months of my research exclusively on the secret societies, and with the help of key contacts, was able to undergo preliminary training as an initiate. What emerged after several months of study was a clear sense that beyond the ritual activities, the secret societies constitute in Haiti a true and effective political force that protects community resources, particularly land, even as they define the power boundaries of the villages. Sorcery and poisons are their traditional weapons, and within the Bizango, there is a complex judicial process by which those who violate the codes of the society may be punished. Zombification is the ultimate sanction. Clairvius Narcisse, it seems, was no innocent victim. His condition had been deserved, and his fate sealed, by his own misdeeds.

Looking back at this research after nearly three decades, I am reminded of something that Nathan Kline told me soon after I agreed to take on the assignment. "The purpose of science," he said, "is not to discern absolute truth but, rather, to generate better ways of thinking about phenomenon."

Although sent to Haiti to seek the chemical basis of a social phenomenon, my work in the end would explore the psychological, spiritual, political, and cultural dimensions of a chemical possibility. Ultimately it was impossible to prove for certain that Clairvius Narcisse had received a dose of the poison, or for that matter that he had been buried alive. But his case, provocative as it was, obliged the scientific world to take seriously a folk tradition that had historically been invoked, often in an explicitly racist manner, to denigrate an entire culture and their remarkable religious worldview. Thirty years on, the link between the toxic powder and zombification remains compelling, and the hypothesis still stands, even as Vodoun has finally become recognized as one of the more remarkable religious traditions ever brought into being by the human spirit and imagination.

Read within this context, *The Magic Island* takes on a new significance. It was in all likelihood the book that first drew Zora Neale Hurston to Haiti. Decades before I set foot in the country, Hurston essentially solved the mystery of the Haitian zombie. She noted accurately that a poison was involved that induced a state of apparent death, and she wrote that zombification was a form of punishment, a sanction invoked by the secret societies. Unfortunately she was unable to secure a sample of the folk preparation, and her descriptions of the secret societies, based on peasant accounts that she accepted at face value, had a fanciful quality that did not advance her argument. That she was an Afro-American woman in the era of Jim Crow also worked against her. This said, her achievements in Haiti were truly remarkable, and the fact that she was so inspired by *The Magic Island* surely leaves all of us in William Seabrook's debt.

WADE DAVIS

A CATALOG OF SELECTED

DOVER BOOKS

IN ALL FIELDS OF INTEREST

A CATALOG OF SELECTED DOVER BOOKS IN ALL FIELDS OF INTEREST

THE CHERRY ORCHARD, Anton Chekhov. Classic of world drama concerns passing of semifeudal order in turn-of-the-century Russia, symbolized in the sale of the cherry orchard owned by Madame Ranevskaya. Showcases Chekhov's rich sensitivities as an observer of human nature. 64pp. 0-486-26682-6

A CHRISTMAS CAROL, Charles Dickens. This engrossing tale relates Ebenezer Scrooge's ghostly journeys through Christmases past, present, and future and his ultimate transformation from a harsh and grasping old miser to a charitable and compassionate human being. 80pp. 0-486-26865-9

CRIME AND PUNISHMENT, Fyodor Dostoyevsky. Translated by Constance Garnett. Supreme masterpiece tells the story of Raskolnikov, a student tormented by his own thoughts after he murders an old woman. Overwhelmed by guilt and terror, he confesses and goes to prison. A selection of the Common Core State Standards Initiative. 448pp. 0-486-41587-2

CYRANO DE BERGERAC, Edmond Rostand. A quarrelsome, hot-tempered, and unattractive swordsman falls hopelessly in love with a beautiful woman and woos her for a handsome but slow-witted suitor. A witty and eloquent drama. 144pp. 0-486-41119-2

A DOLL'S HOUSE, Henrik Ibsen. Ibsen's best-known play displays his genius for realistic prose drama. An expression of women's rights, the play climaxes when the central character, Nora, rejects a smothering marriage and life in "a doll's house." A selection of the Common Core State Standards Initiative. 80pp. 0-486-27062-9

DOOMED SHIPS: Great Ocean Liner Disasters, William H. Miller, Jr. Nearly 200 photographs, many from private collections, highlight tales of some of the vessels whose pleasure cruises ended in catastrophe: the *Morro Castle, Normandie, Andrea Doria, Europa,* and many others. 128pp. 0-486-45366-9

DUBLINERS, James Joyce. A fine and accessible introduction to the work of one of the 20th century's most influential writers, this collection features 15 tales, including a masterpiece of the short-story genre, "The Dead." 160pp. 0-486-26870-5

THE EARLY SCIENCE FICTION OF PHILIP K. DICK, Philip K. Dick. This anthology presents short stories and novellas that originally appeared in pulp magazines of the early 1950s, including "The Variable Man," "Second Variety," "Beyond the Door," "The Defenders," and more. 272pp. 0-486-49733-X

THE EARLY SHORT STORIES OF F. SCOTT FITZGERALD, F. Scott Fitzgerald. These tales offer insights into many themes, characters, and techniques that emerged in Fitzgerald's later works. Selections include "The Curious Case of Benjamin Button," "Babes in the Woods," and a dozen others. 256pp. 0-486-79465-2

ETHAN FROME, Edith Wharton. Classic story of wasted lives, set against a bleak New England background. Superbly delineated characters in a hauntingly grim tale of thwarted love. Considered by many to be Wharton's masterpiece. 96pp. 0-486-26690-7

FLATLAND: A Romance of Many Dimensions, Edwin A. Abbott. Classic of science (and mathematical) fiction — charmingly illustrated by the author — describes the adventures of A. Square, a resident of Flatland, in Spaceland (three dimensions), Lineland (one dimension), and Pointland (no dimensions). 96pp. 0-486-27263-X

FRANKENSTEIN, Mary Shelley. The story of Victor Frankenstein's monstrous creation and the havoc it caused has enthralled generations of readers and inspired countless writers of horror and suspense. With the author's own 1831 introduction. 176pp. 0-486-28211-2

THE GARGOYLE BOOK: 572 Examples from Gothic Architecture, Lester Burbank Bridaham. Dispelling the conventional wisdom that French Gothic architectural flourishes were born of despair or gloom, Bridaham reveals the whimsical nature of these creations and the ingenious artisans who made them. 572 illustrations. 224pp. 0-486-44754-5

THE GIFT OF THE MAGI AND OTHER SHORT STORIES, O. Henry. Sixteen captivating stories by one of America's most popular storytellers. Included are such classics as "The Gift of the Magi," "The Last Leaf," and "The Ransom of Red Chief." Publisher's Note. A selection of the Common Core State Standards Initiative. 96pp. 0-486-27061-0

THE GOETHE TREASURY: Selected Prose and Poetry, Johann Wolfgang von Goethe. Edited, Selected, and with an Introduction by Thomas Mann. In addition to his lyric poetry, Goethe wrote travel sketches, autobiographical studies, essays, letters, and proverbs in rhyme and prose. This collection presents outstanding examples from each genre. 368pp. 0-486-44780-4

GREAT ILLUSTRATIONS BY N. C. WYETH, N. C. Wyeth. Edited and with an Introduction by Jeff A. Menges. This full-color collection focuses on the artist's early and most popular illustrations, featuring more than 100 images from *The Mysterious Stranger, Robin Hood, Robinson Crusoe, The Boy's King Arthur,* and other classics. 128pp. 0-486-47295-7

HAMLET, William Shakespeare. The quintessential Shakespearean tragedy, whose highly charged confrontations and anguished soliloquies probe depths of human feeling rarely sounded in any art. Reprinted from an authoritative British edition complete with illuminating footnotes. A selection of the Common Core State Standards Initiative. 128pp. 0-486-27278-8

THE HAUNTED HOUSE, Charles Dickens. A Yuletide gathering in an eerie country retreat provides the backdrop for Dickens and his friends — including Elizabeth Gaskell and Wilkie Collins — who take turns spinning supernatural yarns. 144pp. 0-486-46309-5

HEART OF DARKNESS, Joseph Conrad. Dark allegory of a journey up the Congo River and the narrator's encounter with the mysterious Mr. Kurtz. Masterly blend of adventure, character study, psychological penetration. For many, Conrad's finest, most enigmatic story. 80pp. 0-486-26464-5

THE HOUND OF THE BASKERVILLES, Sir Arthur Conan Doyle. A deadly curse in the form of a legendary ferocious beast continues to claim its victims from the Baskerville family until Holmes and Watson intervene. Often called the best detective story ever written. 128pp. 0-486-28214-7

THE HOUSE BEHIND THE CEDARS, Charles W. Chesnutt. Originally published in 1900, this groundbreaking novel by a distinguished African-American author recounts the drama of a brother and sister who "pass for white" during the dangerous days of Reconstruction. 208pp. 0-486-46144-0

HOW TO DRAW NEARLY EVERYTHING, Victor Perard. Beginners of all ages can learn to draw figures, faces, landscapes, trees, flowers, and animals of all kinds. Well-illustrated guide offers suggestions for pencil, pen, and brush techniques plus composition, shading, and perspective. 160pp. 0-486-49848-4

HOW TO MAKE SUPER POP-UPS, Joan Irvine. Illustrated by Linda Hendry. Super pop-ups extend the element of surprise with three-dimensional designs that slide, turn, spring, and snap. More than 30 patterns and 475 illustrations include cards, stage props, and school projects. 96pp. 0-486-46589-6

THE IMITATION OF CHRIST, Thomas à Kempis. Translated by Aloysius Croft and Harold Bolton. This religious classic has brought understanding and comfort to millions for centuries. Written in a candid and conversational style, the topics include liberation from worldly inclinations, preparation and consolations of prayer, and eucharistic communion. 160pp. 0-486-43185-1

THE IMPORTANCE OF BEING EARNEST, Oscar Wilde. Wilde's witty and buoyant comedy of manners, filled with some of literature's most famous epigrams, reprinted from an authoritative British edition. Considered Wilde's most perfect work. A selection of the Common Core State Standards Initiative. 64pp. 0-486-26478-5

JANE EYRE, Charlotte Brontë. Written in 1847, *Jane Eyre* tells the tale of an orphan girl's progress from the custody of cruel relatives to an oppressive boarding school and its culmination in a troubled career as a governess. A selection of the Common Core State Standards Initiative. 448pp. 0-486-42449-9

JUST WHAT THE DOCTOR DISORDERED: Early Writings and Cartoons of Dr. Seuss, Dr. Seuss. Edited and with an Introduction by Rick Marschall. The Doctor's visual hilarity, nonsense language, and offbeat sense of humor illuminate this compilation of items from his early career, created for periodicals such as *Judge, Life, College Humor,* and *Liberty.* 144pp. 0-486-49846-8

KING LEAR, William Shakespeare. Powerful tragedy of an aging king, betrayed by his daughters, robbed of his kingdom, descending into madness. Perhaps the bleakest of Shakespeare's tragic dramas, complete with explanatory footnotes. 144pp. 0-486-28058-6

THE LADY OR THE TIGER?: and Other Logic Puzzles, Raymond M. Smullyan. Created by a renowned puzzle master, these whimsically themed challenges involve paradoxes about probability, time, and change; metapuzzles; and self-referentiality. Nineteen chapters advance in difficulty from relatively simple to highly complex. 1982 edition. 240pp. 0-486-47027-X

LEAVES OF GRASS: The Original 1855 Edition, Walt Whitman. Whitman's immortal collection includes some of the greatest poems of modern times, including his masterpiece, "Song of Myself." Shattering standard conventions, it stands as an unabashed celebration of body and nature. 128pp. 0-486-45676-5

LES MISÉRABLES, Victor Hugo. Translated by Charles E. Wilbour. Abridged by James K. Robinson. A convict's heroic struggle for justice and redemption plays out against a fiery backdrop of the Napoleonic wars. This edition features the excellent original translation and a sensitive abridgment. 304pp. 0-486-45789-3

LIGHT FOR THE ARTIST, Ted Seth Jacobs. Intermediate and advanced art students receive a broad vocabulary of effects with this in-depth study of light. Diagrams and paintings illustrate applications of principles to figure, still life, and landscape paintings. 144pp. 0-486-49304-0

LILITH: A Romance, George MacDonald. In this novel by the father of fantasy literature, a man travels through time to meet Adam and Eve and to explore humanity's fall from grace and ultimate redemption. 240pp. 0-486-46818-6

LINE: An Art Study, Edmund J. Sullivan. Written by a noted artist and teacher, this well-illustrated guide introduces the basics of line drawing. Topics include third and fourth dimensions, formal perspective, shade and shadow, figure drawing, and other essentials. 208pp. 0-486-79484-9

THE LODGER, Marie Belloc Lowndes. Acclaimed by *The New York Times* as "one of the best suspense novels ever written," this novel recounts an English couple's doubts about their boarder, whom they suspect of being a serial killer. 240pp. 0-486-78809-1

MACBETH, William Shakespeare. A Scottish nobleman murders the king in order to succeed to the throne. Tortured by his conscience and fearful of discovery, he becomes tangled in a web of treachery and deceit that ultimately spells his doom. A selection of the Common Core State Standards Initiative. 96pp. 0-486-27802-6

THE RED BADGE OF COURAGE, Stephen Crane. Amid the nightmarish chaos of a Civil War battle, a young soldier discovers courage, humility, and, perhaps, wisdom. Uncanny re-creation of actual combat. Enduring landmark of American fiction. 112pp. 0-486-26465-3

RELATIVITY SIMPLY EXPLAINED, Martin Gardner. One of the subject's clearest, most entertaining introductions offers lucid explanations of special and general theories of relativity, gravity, and spacetime, models of the universe, and more. 100 illustrations. 224pp. 0-486-29315-7

THE ROAD NOT TAKEN AND OTHER POEMS, Robert Frost. A treasury of Frost's most expressive verse. In addition to the title poem: "An Old Man's Winter Night," "In the Home Stretch," "Meeting and Passing," "Putting in the Seed," many more. All complete and unabridged. Includes a selection from the Common Core State Standards Initiative. 64pp. 0-486-27550-7

ROMEO AND JULIET, William Shakespeare. Tragic tale of star-crossed lovers, feuding families and timeless passion contains some of Shakespeare's most beautiful and lyrical love poetry. Complete, unabridged text with explanatory footnotes. 96pp. 0-486-27557-4

SANDITON AND THE WATSONS: Austen's Unfinished Novels, Jane Austen. Two tantalizing incomplete stories revisit Austen's customary milieu of courtship and venture into new territory, amid guests at a seaside resort. Both are worth reading for pleasure and study. 112pp. 0-486-45793-1

THE SCARLET LETTER, Nathaniel Hawthorne. With stark power and emotional depth, Hawthorne's masterpiece explores sin, guilt, and redemption in a story of adultery in the early days of the Massachusetts Colony. A selection of the Common Core State Standards Initiative. 192pp. 0-486-28048-9

SELECTED POEMS, Emily Dickinson. Over 100 best-known, best-loved poems by one of America's foremost poets, reprinted from authoritative early editions. No comparable edition at this price. Includes 3 selections from the Common Core State Standards Initiative. 64pp. 0-486-26466-1

SIDDHARTHA, Hermann Hesse. Classic novel that has inspired generations of seekers. Blending Eastern mysticism and psychoanalysis, Hesse presents a strikingly original view of man and culture and the arduous process of self-discovery, reconciliation, harmony, and peace. 112pp. 0-486-40653-9

SKETCHING OUTDOORS, Leonard Richmond. This guide offers beginners step-by-step demonstrations of how to depict clouds, trees, buildings, and other outdoor sights. Explanations of a variety of techniques include shading and constructional drawing. 48pp. 0-486-46922-0

STAR LORE: Myths, Legends, and Facts, William Tyler Olcott. Captivating retellings of the origins and histories of ancient star groups include Pegasus, Ursa Major, Pleiades, signs of the zodiac, and other constellations. "Classic." — *Sky & Telescope.* 58 illustrations. 544pp. 0-486-43581-4

STRIP FOR MURDER, Max Allan Collins. Illustrated by Terry Beatty. Colorful characters with murderous motives populate this illustrated mystery, in which the heated rivalry between a pair of cartoonists ends in homicide and a stripper-turned-detective and her stepson-partner seek the killer. "Great fun." — *Mystery Scene.* 288pp. 0-486-79811-9

SURVIVAL HANDBOOK: The Official U.S. Army Guide, Department of the Army. This special edition of the Army field manual is geared toward civilians. An essential companion for campers and all lovers of the outdoors, it constitutes the most authoritative wilderness guide. 288pp. 0-486-46184-X